# SportsCAR
## Chronicle

By the Auto Editors of
Consumer Guide®

Publications International, Ltd.

Louis Weber, CEO
Publications International, Ltd.
7373 North Cicero Avenue
Lincolnwood, Illinois 60712

Permission is never granted for commercial purposes.

Manufactured in China.

8 7 6 5 4 3 2 1

ISBN: 0-7853-7989-4

Library of Congress Control Number:   2003111434

*The editors would like to extend their thanks to the following photographers for supplying the images to make this book possible. They are listed below, along with the page(s) featuring their photography.*

**Derek Bell:** 140; **Jan Borgfelt:** 119; **Chan Bush:** 134; **Thom Cannell:** 171; **Bob Cavallo:** 99; **Fred Chamberlain:** 132; **John Conde:** 83; **Mirco Decet:** 43, 100, 143, 169, 195, 265, 279, 288, 289; **Steen Fleron:** 122; **Roland Flessner:** 226, 249; **Chuck Giametta:** 307; **David Gooley:** 32, 42, 75, 130, 140, 141, 148, 149, 152, 156, 159, 160, 162, 171, 184, 190, 192, 193, 234, 254, 255, 258; **Thomas Glatch:** 64, 90, 101, 116, 232; **W. Goodfellow:** 182; **Sam Griffith:** 28, 44, 79, 86, 88, 139, 144, 149, 162, 174, 192, 201, 243, 257, 260, 261, 272, 277, 283; **R. Harrington:** 204; **Jerry Heasley:** 205; **Don Heiny:** 83; **Greg Jaren:** 98; **David Jensen:** 60; **Bud Juneau:** 17, 57, 93, 121, 131, 154, 215; **Bill Kantz:** 109; **Harry Kapsalis:** Table of Contents, 123; **Milt Kieft:** 14, 47, 123; **Bill Kilborn:** 97; **Dan Lyons:** 85, 153, 156, 191; **Vince Manocchi:** 15, 41, 42, 43, 53, 56, 58, 64, 65, 66, 70, 71, 72, 73, 77, 80, 84, 86, 91, 110, 111, 114, 115, 117, 120, 123, 124, 125, 128, 129, 133, 138, 139, 158, 159, 161, 163, 164, 165, 166, 168, 175, 178, 179, 186, 188, 189, 193, 198, 199, 208, 211, 217, 220, 229, 231, 242, 264, 275; **Doug Mitchel:** 9, 12, 27, 45, 52, 54, 62, 63, 69, 71, 103, 106, 132, 142, 155, 157, 167, 188, 190, 202, 205, 217, 226, 248, 265, 281, 284, 286, 317; **Mike Mueller:** 8; **David Newhardt:** 36, 255; **Nina Padgett:** 56, 82, 99, 137, 285, 291; **Albert Porter:** 145; **Scott Rosenberg:** 170; **Paul Sable:** 77; **Ron Sessions:** 180, 181; **Gary Smith:** 59; **Richard Spiegelmen:** 37; **Bob Tenney:** 76; **Phil Toy:** 10, 14, 60, 61, 68, 80, 95, 96, 147, 197; **Gary Versteege:** 150; **W.C. Waymack:** 65, 67, 74, 83, 89, 104, 127, 194; **Joseph Wherry:** 11, 13, 26, 90, 92, 100, 131, 163, 228; **Nicky Wright:** 9, 19, 24, 30, 48, 50, 78, 81, 92, 124, 148, 151, 152, 154, 168, 183, 196, 200, 210.

*Special thanks to the following collectors, curators, dealers, and manufacturers who supplied us with additional imagery and resources that made this title a reality.*

Acura; Alfa Romeo; The Appel/Kapustka Archive; Aston Martin; Audi; Automotive Hall of Fame; BMW; Bugatti; Tom Burnside Motorsport Archive; Caterham Cars; Chevrolet; Tom Clifford; Continental Auto Sports; Daimler-Chrysler; Dodge; Fiat; Sam Fiorani; Ford Motor Comany; Fox Valley Motorcars; General Motors; Ken Gross; Jaguar; The Klemantaski Collection; The Collection of Tim Kuser; Lamborghini; Lotus; Maserati; Mazda; McLaren; Mercedes-Benz; Nissan; Panoz; Pebble Beach Concours D'Elegance; Porsche; Cheryl Barnes, Road America; Saab; Saleen; The Society of Automotive Historians; Toyota; Volkswagen.

*Additional thanks to the owners of the beautiful automobiles featured within these pages.*

Eugene & Geri Andersen, Jake Anderson, John Angwert, Skip Barber, Jack Bart, Bell & Collville Lotus, Edward Berstein, T.W. Berstein, Les Bieri, Blackhawk Collection, Mike Brady, Ray Bragassa, Bob Briggs, The Brumos Collection, Norm Canfield, John Carlsen, Cars of San Francisco, Inc., CC Classic Cars, Int., Paul Chandeysson, Bernie Chase, Bill Ciembroniewicz, Classic Cars of LaJolla, Classic Showcase, Mike Cleary, Edward Cline, Thomas R. Coady Jr., Ralph W. Coldewe, Collier Auto Museum, Patrick & Kay Collins, Dennis & Erin Conley, Bob Constable, Ron & Penny Cooper, Harry Cornelius, Bob Cortese, David Couling, Tim & Sue Coulson, Alan Cummings, Briggs S. Cunningham, Peter Davison, Nigel Dawes, Domino's Rearview Museum, Don W. Drabik, Jeff Dranson, Pete Dunkel, Richard A. Emery, Rob Fair, Nick Fasola, Richard Fedigan, Michael Feldman, Femhurst Motor Co., David L. Ferguson, Alfred Ferrara, Peter L. Fino, Jr., Dennis Gatson, Jack Gersh, Mark D. Gessler, Gillamanders, David & Mary Glass, Ellen Goodman, William Goodsell, Irwin H. Gordon, Jerry Gordon, Philip Guiral, Marvin Gunchick, Craig & Pat Hanna, David Hans, Torben Stiig Hansen, Duane Hedke, Jack & Helen Heist, Steve & Laura Hendricks, D. Herning, David Hill, David & Mary-Hoe Love, Holly Hollenbeck, Thomas Hollfelder, Bob & Joan Houillon, Robert Howlett, Neil Huffman, The Hunter Collection, Mark Hyman, J. Bruce Jacobs, Tim John, Marvin L. Johnson, Bill Jones, David Jones, T. Donald Kamm, Donald W. Katz, Jack Kellam, James Keller, W. Michael King, Gordon & Dorothy Klemmer, Lauritz K. Knudsen & Suzanne, Gary Lapman, Lynn Larson, Ralph Lauren, Dennis Levine, John Ling, Klaus Lischer, Philip & Sandy LoPiccolo, Dennis Machul, Dr. Vijay Mallya, Mr. Mandarano, S.W. Mann, Gene Marburger, Joe Marchetti, Ken Marcoski, James A. Matthews, Larry & Betty Mayer, Michael W. McBroom, Gordon McGregor, Jack McGregor, Ray McLaughlin, W.A. McNight, Robert Metzler, Bruce Meyer, Mini-Motors Classic Coachworks, Brian Minton, Abel Miramon, Harvey Moyses, Rebecca Munk, Gerald Nell, Wayne Nelson, David C. Newkirk, Larry Nicklin, Steve Ooley, Edward E. Oritz, Ann Page, Daniel M. Pankratz, The Parker Family, Al & Lois Parodi, Rear Admiral Thomas J. Patterson, A.J. Pegno, Bill Peter, Edsel H. Pfabe, The Robert J. Pond Collection, Hilary Raab, Jr., Ragtops Motorcars, Norm Reeves, Reinhold, Randy Ressler, Daniel & Pat Rideout, Conrad W. Roellchen, James L. Roman, Albert Romvari, Marty Rooney, Ben Rose, Jack Rosenzweig, Rudinsky, Paul Sable, Glen Sager, Carroll Shelby, Howard Shimon, Jeffrey A. Silva, John Slowiak, Douglas D. Smith, Danny L. Steine, Jeff Steptian, Brooks Stevens Museum, Jack Stewart, C.A. Stoddard, Judd Stone, A.J. Sutton, Martin Swig, Steven Tillack, Steven & Joyce Toms, Bob Trawick, Ronald J. Varley, Alan Vejo, Tony Voiture, Alan Wagner, John Weinberger, Peter Welch, Rosalie & Jim Wente, Len Wilby, Dean Wilke, Evelyn & John Willburn, Jay Williams, David W. Witt, Gary Wutke, Mike & Laurie Yager.

# Contents

# Foreword

Books about sports cars often seem compelled to introduce themselves by explaining what sports cars are. It's as if the authors feel the breed needs defending somehow. Well, many people do think of sports cars as frivolous, dangerous, a waste of money, or half a dozen other disreputable things, but that's not why this book begins with definitions. We just want you to be clear on what it deals with, now that "sport" is used to describe all kinds of vehicles that aren't all that sporty.

Sports cars began as racing cars that were modified so they could be driven legally on public thoroughfares. Auto racing, like the much older sport of kings, is all about reaching the finish line first, with winning speed related directly to power and weight. That's why even the earliest racing cars were stripped-down machines with the biggest, most potent engines available. Anything that wasn't absolutely necessary was left off, so no doors, no top, no windshield in many cases. Seating was provided for only a driver—preferably of horse-jockey heft, if not stature—and sometimes a "riding mechanic" to fix things that broke en route to hoped-for victory.

Fairly soon, though, someone got the idea of selling a race car fitted with headlights, windshield, a skimpy fabric top, and maybe doors and side curtains so the beast could be driven with some comfort and safety away from the track, hillclimb, or trials course. Experts disagree on who did this first and when, but "sports cars" were certainly plentiful by the Roaring Twenties. Many were purchased by wealthy swells who might gad about like Mr. Toad, terrorizing other "automobilists" in town and country. More serious owners liked that they could remove the road equipment for entering their sports car in some competition on a convenient weekend, then—if fate were kind—drive the same machine home.

This "race-and-ride" ideal still prevailed in the late 1940s, when Americans began discovering sports cars in significant numbers. By that time, however, competition cars were becoming too specialized for ready adaptation to road use, and sports-car buyers in both Europe and America were demanding un-racy amenities like roll-up windows, a proper heater, even a metal roof. Purists moaned, but the public would not be denied. The result was the GT or grand tourer, which might be as fast and agile as a "real" sports car, but was also sufficiently comfortable, reliable, and practical for long drives and even daily commuting. Of course, GTs can and do go racing, as can most any road car (or truck) if it's altered enough. There are even GTs designed primarily for certain types of competition, with a roadgoing version built for public sale to qualify the model as "production" where rules require.

But let's not get ahead ourselves. Suffice it to say that this book chronicles America's love affair with sports cars new and old, simple and high-tech, popular and obscure, fast and not so fast. It's not meant to be an encyclopedia, but it does cover traditional sports cars and a good many GTs spanning three continents and more than 100 years. If a significant model could be sold in these United States, no matter where it was built, we've tried to include it. Federal safety and emissions regulations narrowed the choices some after 1967, and an ever-changing market has always loomed large in U.S. sports-car history. But though models still come and go, America's sports-car love affair burns as brightly as ever—maybe more so in this 21st century of dull "transportation modules" and clumsy sport-utility vehicles.

More than just hardware, however, this book is about sports-car people—the builders, sellers, and, yes, racers who are such a colorful part of the story. You'll find brief profiles of significant figures here, as well as recollections from original owners about their experiences with various models and what might be called the "sports-car lifestyle."

Since you're purusing these pages, you probably have at least a passing interest in sports cars yourself. Certain ones may even stir some fond memories or dreams. The sleek Corvette you saw in traffic yesterday. The sexy Ferrari that "Magnum P.I." drove on TV. The burly Aston Martin from the latest James Bond flick. The lithe Alfa Romeo Spider your lucky best friend drove in high school. The mighty Porsche Turbo or posh Mercedes-Benz SL you've promised yourself—someday, when you win the lottery. Or maybe you already have, say, a faithful Mazda Miata or a shiny Nissan Z-car waiting patiently in the garage for another romp on your favorite twisty road.

Whatever "sports car" means to you, this book is dedicated to everyone who loves automobiles that make driving fun. Cars that encourage driving well, and not merely in a straight line. Cars created for romancing the road, not just traveling it. Cars that embody passion and exuberance, inspiration and dedication. Cars that stir one's soul and fire one's heart. In short, cars built by driving enthusiasts, for driving enthusiasts. If that's your kind of car, welcome to our club!

The Auto Editors of Consumer Guide®
Lincolnwood, Illinois; and Glendale, California
October 2003

The automobile sputtered to life in the late 1880s. Sports cars weren't far behind. Briggs Cunningham, the storied American sports-car builder of the 1950s, once declared that "in the beginning every car was a sports car, because they weren't practical or particularly useful on a day-to-day basis." Echoed writer David E. Davis: "Every trip in an [early] automobile was an adventure, and you bought one with that in mind—to have fun. When you needed fast, reliable transportation, you took a train."

The "horseless carriage" was smoky, noisy, and frightening, but it was also a dream come true. Inventors in both Europe and the United States had been groping toward a "mechanical horse" for at least 120 years before Gottlieb Daimler and Karl Benz built the first true automobiles—self-propelled vehicles with internal-combustion gasoline engines instead of steam power.

Others were quick to seize on what those Germans started. The automobile, after all, promised to revolutionize personal mobility in the way personal computers would alter everday life almost 100 years later. Though only a wealthy few could afford motorcars at first, there was obvious money to be made by those with luck, pluck, and some good ideas. As a result, technical progress was swift. As historian Ralph Stein observed circa 1960: "By 1914 the automobile was, in almost every respect, as good as the car standing in your driveway right now. In those few years since the [1890s] the automobile advanced more than anytime before or since."

Indeed, a good many "modern" features were then already widespread or had at least been tried: overhead-camshaft engines, shaft drive instead of simple chain, geared transmissions, electric starting. Even acetylene-gas headlamps had given way to safer, brighter electric lights. The horseless-carriage look changed quickly too. As early as 1902, French engineer Emile Levassor decided a car's engine should be ahead of the driver, not underneath or behind—and enclosed in a metal box, something no horse-drawn wagon ever possessed. A transmission sat behind the engine for delivering power to the rear wheels. This Systeme Panhard, named for Levassor's patron, Rene Panhard, soon became almost universal.

Then, starting in 1913, one Henry Ford made the motorcar itself universal by using a moving assembly line to crank out his simple Model T with unheard-of speed in unheard-of numbers. Competition and free enterprise did the rest. Soon, most anyone who wanted a car could afford one. The motor industry boomed, sparking huge growth in related businesses like petroleum refining, rubber- and glass-making, road-building, and a host of others. By 1920, America was a rolling consumer society and the richest nation on earth.

It was in this heady, fast-paced era of technical innovation and industrial growth that the sports car began to emerge as something beyond mere transportation. As pioneer American auto journalist Ken Purdy explained it: "The automobile had tremendous appeal for the sportsman of the [early 1900s]: It was the fastest vehicle at man's bidding, it was new, much about it was unknown. It offered a great challenge. And since the motorcar was designed to transport people over ordinary roads, it was logical to test it for speed in that fashion. To the manufacturers, turning out perhaps a few score automobiles a year, racing was the best kind of advertising. Because it was a brand-new sport, the newspapers gave it extensive news coverage, and the manufacturer whose car won an important race on Saturday could be sure of a full order book the following Monday evening." In short, the first racing cars were also the first sports cars. They've been close cousins ever since.

It was but a short step to the idea of a car that looked racy and might even compete on occasion but that was designed mainly for driving on public roads as a personal pastime—for driving as "sport." Historian Karl Ludvigsen cites 1910 as the pivotal year: "Racing machines [by then] had engines so large that they were approaching impracticability for road use [while road cars] were getting heavier as bodywork and equipment became more elaborate. Between them there was space for an automobile fit for touring use but lighter than a normal road car, with a power-to-weight ratio closer to that of the racer. Arguments have raged ever since over which is better as a sports car: the detuned racer or the stripped, lightened touring model. There have been excellent cars of both types—and terrible ones."

Good or bad, the sports car evolved up to World War II as a creature mainly of Europe and England, not the U.S. Though motorsports remained very popular on both sides of the Atlantic, the topography and economic conditions "over there" tended to breed sportier cars with the defining attributes of quick acceleration, agile handling, and strong brakes. Public interest in such cars was relatively higher too. Though that didn't translate into many sales by American standards, it did encourage more entrepreneurs to cast their lot with sports cars. The Twenties and Thirties thus produced a legion of models from now-legendary companies including Alfa Romeo in Italy; Aston Martin, Bentley, and MG in Britain; Bugatti and Talbot in France; and Mercedes-Benz and BMW in Germany.

By contrast, America was a land of wide-open spaces that favored big, strong cars able to go the distance. Speeding around corners wasn't a big priority. Also, most Americans didn't think of driving as fun. They just wanted to get someplace, hence the cheap, simple, comfort-oriented cars that fast became Detroit's stock-in-trade. In a nation of hard-working farmers and city dwellers, the sports car came to be viewed as another frivolous toy for the monied elite, just like the first horseless carriages. And even the Astors, Vanderbilts, and other high-society folk often chose a racy "foreigner" because it was rarer, more exotic, and thus more appropriate to their social station than even the sportiest domestic cars, which weren't that numerous anyway.

Still, America produced a few notable sports cars in the early years, two of them historic. The Mercer Type 35 Raceabout lasted only four years (1911-1915) and was just a sporty variation of an upper-class road car. Yet with its uniquely dashing appearance, exhilarating performance, high dynamic ability, and obvious stamina (it ran with distinction in the Indianapolis 500 and other contests), the Raceabout was the very model of the "race-and-ride" sports car evolving overseas. The Mercer soon had a keen rival in the Stutz Bearcat, which was just as much the competition hero and soon came to symbolize America's Jazz Age exuberance. Its much-improved successor, the Black Hawk, won world acclaim with a second-place finish in the grueling LeMans 24-Hour race of 1928. Then the Depression hit, killing smaller companies like Stutz and prompting drastic survival measures among major U.S. automakers, none of which included sports cars. With the start of a terrible new world war, some thought the sports car as good as dead.

But the pundits were wrong again. Liberated by unprecented prosperity in the early postwar years, some Americans began rejecting homegrown automotive values for cars that looked good and were actually fun to drive. Though no one knew it at the time, a revolution was underway. The sports car was about to captivate America as never before.

**1885** Carl Benz in Germany builds world's first gasoline-engine "car," a three-wheeler **1886** Germany's Gottlieb Daimler builds first four-wheel gas-engine car **1895** Charles and Frank Duryea win first U.S. auto race, averaging 5 mph over 52.4 miles from Chicago to Evanston, IL **1900** First U.S. auto show staged in New York City **1902** American Automobile Assn. (AAA) founded • Locomobile offers first U.S. car with 4-cyl, water-cooled, front-mounted engine **1903** Buick, Cadillac, and Ford companies established • First coast-to-coast trip by a gasoline car (Winton) takes 2 months, 3 days **1904** Henry Ford drives "999" racer to world one-mile speed record of 91.37 mph • First Vanderbilt Cup Race staged **1906** A modified Stanley Steamer runs one mile at 127.66 mph, a new record **1908** William C. Durant incorporates General Motors • Ford Model T introduced **1909** Hudson Motor Car Co. established **1910** Austro-Daimler sports cars finish 1-2-3 in "Prince Heinrich" race; engineer Ferdinand Porsche drives winning car • Italian-born engineer Ettore Bugatti sets up in Molsheim, France, to produce his first car, the sporting Type 13 **1911** Mercer debuts Type 35 Raceabout speedster, arguably "America's first sports car" • Ray Harroun wins first Indianapolis 500 race **1914** Stutz introduces sporting Bearcat models to rival Mercer • Cadillacs boast America's first V8 engine **1916** Ex-GM president Charles W. Nash forms Nash Motors **1919** British motoring magazines coin the term "sports car"

Mercer of Trenton, New Jersey, was just two years old when it introduced the Type 35 Raceabout in 1911. A lightweight body, robust chassis, and a 58-horsepower 300-cubic-inch T-head four-cylinder engine provided excellent performance for the day, on and off the track. Though built only into 1915, the $2150 Raceabout won many races and captured the public imagination like few other Brass Age cars. Only about 30 Raceabouts still exist, and they rarely change hands. Mercer struggled until 1923, when it was forced out of business.

Harry C. Stutz built his first cars in 1911. One finished a creditable 11th in that year's Indianapolis 500. Further successes prompted Stutz to create the racy Bearcat roadster in 1914. It outperformed and outlasted the Mercer Raceabout, its main domestic rival. An improved Bearcat bowed in 1917 with a modernized body, more amenities, and a new 80-bhp, 360-cid four-cylinder engine good for 85 mph flat out. This ad touts the new edition and its racing heritage. Later Bearcats were the "bee's knees" in the Roaring Twenties but never had the same impact. Stutz enjoyed moderate racing success into the late twenties, but didn't survive the depression.

**Above:** Mercedes-Benz built winning race cars and sporty touring models in the early 1900s, but its first true roadgoing sports car was the Model S of 1928. Relatively large and heavy in the German manner, the S packed a supercharged 7.0-liter inline six-cylinder engine evolved from an earlier design by the talented Ferdinand Porsche. Horsepower was 120 normal, 180 with the "blower" engaged, enough to make this one of the world's fastest cars at the time. Lighter SS, SSK, and SSKL models followed with even higher performance. Many S chassis got custom coachwork. This two-seat touring cabriolet is typical of factory-bodied models. Note the triple exhaust pipes exiting the hood.

**Below:** Morris Garages began as a sideline at Britain's Morris Motors in the early 1920s. One of its specialties was making sports cars out of mundane "saloons." This business prospered, and was spun off in 1928 to become the MG Motor Co. under hard-driving manager Cecil Kimber. In 1929, MG introduced the petite M-Type Midget as Britain's first low-priced sports car. The jaunty roadster shown dates from 1930. There was also a "Sportsman's Coupe" with the same 20-bhp, 847-cc overhead-cam four-cylinder. Though little known in the U.S., the M-Type helped put MG on the motor enthusiast's map. It was the grand-daddy of the MGs that Americans would take to after World War II.

Special 16-cyl Duesenberg sets Land Speed Record of 158 mph at Daytona Beach **1921** New roadgoing Duesenberg Model A introduces four-wheel brakes **1923** June: France stages first 24-Hour endurance race at LeMans **1924** Britain's Morris Garages advertises first MG sports cars **1925** Chrysler Corporation formed from remains of Maxwell-Chalmers company **1926** Germany's Daimler and Benz merge, begin building Mercedes-Benz cars **1927** Racing-bred Bugatti Type 43A debuts as one of the world's fastest road cars • Potent Mercedes-Benz Type S debuts with Porsche-designed supercharged six **1928** Cecil Kimber forms MG Car Co. separate from Morris Garages • Mercedes-Benz S replaced by more-potent SS; shorter, lighter new SSK roadsters are faster still **1929** New Alfa Romeo 6C-1750 series boasts hemihead dohc sixes • MG M-Type Midget bows as Britain's first mass-market sports car **1931** Supercharged Alfa Romeo 8C-2300 introduced **1932** Bugatti replaces Type 43 with powerful new Type 55 roadster • Ford offers America's first low-priced V8 cars • MG launches stark J2 Midget and "blown" 6-cyl K3 Magnette roadsters **1933** Railton formed in Britain, offers Hudson Terraplane-based sports tourer **1934** BMW gets into sports cars with 6-cyl 315/1 and 319/1 roadsters • Big new 8-cyl Mercedes-Benz 500K series includes sleek "special roadster" **1935** Alfa Romeo bows racing-powered 8C-2900 two-seaters • The ultimate Bugattis debut with fast, roadable Type 57S/SC • More-powerful MG PB replaces interim PA

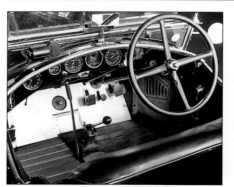

Italy's ALFA (Anomina Lombardo Fabbrica Automobili) was five years old when industrialist Nicolo Romeo took control in 1915. Within a few years, Alfa Romeo was a dominant power in major-league European racing and a respected builder of fast, roadable touring and sports cars brimming with competition-proven technology. Among the most impressive roadgoing Alfas of this era was the 6C-1750 Gran Sport, the fastest and most rakish member of a new Alfa line introduced in 1929. The GS and a companion Super Sport roadster used the basic 6C-1750 chassis, but with wheelbase trimmed to 108 inches. The engine, designed by Vittorio Jano (later of Ferrari fame), was an advanced 1754-cc supercharged straight six with dual overhead camshafts. Maximum horsepower was 85 and combined with a four-speed gearbox to give the lightweight two-seaters a top speed of 95 mph. Most Gran Sports wore handsome bodywork by Zagato, but styles by Touring and Brianza were also available. Alfa Romeo wasn't yet a volume producer as it would be after World War II, and only 369 GS/SS were built through the series' finale in 1933. Today, the 6C-1750 GS is a rare, bona fide classic commanding high-six-figure prices.

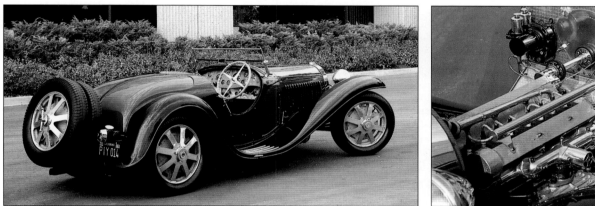

**Above:** Italian Ettore Bugatti settled in France to build *pur sang* (pure-blood) cars starting in 1910. Bugattis were models of meticulous, weight-efficient engineering, as his roadgoing sports cars were often based on his winning race-car designs. Among Bugatti's best road cars was the Type 55, a dashing roadster designed by Ettore's talented son Jean. Its chassis was lifted from Bugatti's contempoary Type 51 single-seat racing car, as was the supercharged 2.3-liter twincam straight-eight, detuned to 135 bhp but capable of up to 112 mph. Only 33 T55s were built, all in 1932. **Right:** MGs evolved despite the Depression. Arriving in 1932 was the Type PA Midget with a new 36-bhp 847-cc overhead cam four-cylinder engine. Beside two- and four-seat roadsters, the PA was also available in this snazzy Airline coupe model, all on a trim 87.7-inch wheelbase. Top speed was 75 mph, up 10 mph from the predecessor J-Type Midget.

Britain's H.F.S. Morgan launches his first four-wheel sports car, the 4/4 • William Lyons' SS Cars Ltd. launches its first sports car, the SS90 roadster **1936** BMW offers first "ultimate driving machine" in racy new 328 roadster • Duesenberg SSJ "sports car" specials built for film stars Gary Cooper, Clark Gable • Mercedes-Benz replaces 500K with mightier 540K • MG regroups with larger, all-new TA models with ohv 4-cyl • Jaguar name bows on new SS100 roadster **1938** GM's Harley Earl creates futuristic 2-seat Buick Y-Job, a hint of U.S. sports cars to come • SS Jaguar 100 updated with sleeker lines, more power, true 100-mph speed **1939** Oldsmobile offers world's first fully automatic transmission

**Above and left:** A rarity among Thirties MGs, the Q-Type racing model was built for sale to non-factory teams so as to improve MG's chances for victory—and publicity. The body and chassis were similar to those of the earlier competition model K3, while the engine was a supercharged version of the roadgoing P-Type's four-cylinder, sized at 746-cc. The blower, a higher-pressure Zoeller unit, sat ahead of the radiator, not under the hood, and was operated from the front of the crankshaft. With 113 hp available at 7200 rpm (rather high for the time), a Q-Type could reach 122 mph. Alas, drivers found it a handful on the track and the car scored no major wins. In 1937, however, a Q-Type with special single-seat body and tuned engine set a class speed record at the Brooklands circuit of 122.4 mph. Only eight Q-Types were built, all between May and October 1934. MG then turned to an improved racer, the single-seat R-Type.

**Below:** Founded in 1899, Fiat grew to dominate the Italian industry with affordable family cars but occasionally offered more sporting fare. This slick little Balilla 508S coupe was sold in 1934-37 along with more-traditional-looking two- and four-seat roadsters. All shared a rugged chassis, 36-bhp 995-cc four-cylinder engine, and four-speed gearbox. The coupe's streamlined styling reflected a popular automotive trend of the early Thirties, inspired by aircraft design.

Small "cottage industry" sports-car builders flowered in England almost from the dawn of motoring. Typical was Archie Frazer-Nash, who started with chain-drive cars in 1922. After changing hands several times, his firm turned to shaft-drive machines with a variety of "bought-in" engines and bodies. Here, a six-cylinder Shelsey roadster from 1935.

# CECIL KIMBER
## English Hot Rodder

"I have the satisfaction of having created a car that has given lots of fun and pleasure to thousands." Spoken by MG founder Cecil Kimber, these words at once sum up his design philosophy and the outcome of his efforts.

Kimber was fun-loving—even in adversity. Early interests included bicycling, sailing, and motorcycling. Cecil was an enthusiastic motorcycle racer, though an accident on a routine errand nearly cost Kimber his right leg. Left with a limp the rest of his life, Kimber had to give up cycles for cars.

An argument with his stern father forced Kimber to leave the family printing supply business. A position as assistant to a chief engineer in a car company provided some engineering training and led to other jobs in the auto industry.

In 1921 William Morris, whose Morris Cowley is sometimes called the Model T of England, hired Kimber to manage his Morris Garages in Oxford. Selling and servicing Morris and other cars, Morris Garages soon started selling Kimber's customized Morris. Kimber took a Morris chassis, modified the engine and suspension, then added a special body. Had he been in post war California he would have been labeled a hot rodder. A former employee said Kimber had "the magical ability to make an ordinary exercise into a magical expedition." That ability was needed to get Morris Garages employees to work after hours creating the specials that would eventually become MGs. While some question Kimber's engineering ability, all agree that his styling, organization, and motivational abilities were excellent.

Demand for his specials grew, and the cars became a unique make rather than a modified Morris. The name gradually changed from Morris Garages to MG. In '28 William Morris built a factory for MG, and the low-priced Midget introduced sports car ownership to a new class of buyers.

The early Thirties were good times for MG. Kimber believed racing was the best way for a small firm to get international publicity and to grow technologically. MG replaced Bentley as the most successful British racing team. That changed in '35 when William Morris reorganized his holdings and MG became part of Morris Motors. The factory-racing program was killed and Kimber no longer had complete control over MG design. In 1941 Kimber obtained a contract to build a section for a bomber—without getting approval from the Morris organization. He was forced to resign. Although shattered by the loss of the company he had created, Kimber remained loyal and upbeat. The workforce threatened to strike, but Kimber insisted they had war work to do. When urged to sue William Morris for wrongful dismissal, he refused on the grounds he couldn't do that to the man who had given him his chance. Cecil Kimber was killed in a train accident in 1943.

Kimber attracted talented personnel and created a style that would stay with MG long after his death. His concept of a small, fun, affordable sports car would spread throughout the post war world.

France's Delahaye built solid but dull upper-class cars from its 1894 founding to 1935, when it suddenly turned to fast, roadable touring and sports cars that could—and did—win races. Among the best of the late-prewar Delahayes was the Type 135, here in short-chassis "Competition" guise with streamlined coupe coachwork by Figoni et Falaschi. A 3.6-liter overhead-valve inline-six based on a Delahaye truck engine sent 120/130 bhp through a four-speed gearbox; an electric "pre-selector" transmission was available. Independent front suspension, still a novelty in the mid-Thirties, made all 135s fine handlers. Large Bendix drum brakes delivered ample stopping power. Competition models were lighter and more agile. They're also among the rarest and most desired of the breed, which returned postwar and was built through 1954.

After achieving fame for their winning race-car engines, brothers Fred and August Duesenberg teamed with tycoon E.L. Cord to create "the world's finest motorcar." Bowing in late 1928, the Duesenberg Model J was big, heavy, opulent, and ultra costly, but also America's fastest, most technically advanced car. A supercharged SJ soon followed with at least 320 bhp and up to 140 mph flat-out. Shown here is one of two short-chassis SSJ roadsters built for movie stars Gary Cooper and Clark Gable. It was as close to a sports car as a Deusey ever got.

The first sports car named Jaguar appeared in 1936 from William Lyons' SS Cars, Ltd., an outgrowth of Swallow Sidecars, the motorcycle-sidecar business he started in the 1920s. A follow-up to the previous year's SS90, the SS-Jaguar 100 came with either a 2.7-liter straight-six or a new, more potent 3.5-liter unit. The latter could deliver 0-60 mph in under 11 seconds and over 100 mph flat out, sensational for a non-supercharged car in those days. Handling and roadholding were first rate, too. The styling—classically correct but sleek and slow slung—was largely Lyons' own work. Alas, only 314 of these cars could be built before war came to Britain in 1939.

## FINLEY ROBERTSON PORTER
### Got the Ball Rolling

Finley Robertson Porter has been called one of America's greatest auto engineers, but his productive years in the auto industry were too brief to secure him the historic accolades of a Ford or Duesenberg. Porter was born in Lowell, Ohio, in 1872. He left school when he was 14 but took a mechanical-engineering correspondence course. A test car driver remembered Porter as "...a dapper fellow, and sort of quiet." Porter was an engineer for the Worthington Pump Company, where, with Charles Worthington, he experimented with building steam cars. Frequent boiler explosions ended the project. Porter was more successful at this next job.

The Mercer Automobile Company was started by members of the Roebling family—of Brooklyn Bridge fame. Washington Roebling II was young and socialized with Astors and Vanderbilts. He wanted to build sporting machines. The combination of Roebling's vision and Porter's engineering talent proved dynamic. The 1911 Mercer Raceabout was Porter's masterpiece. Just before World War I, many makes such as Stutz, Simplex, and National offered stripped-down versions of their touring cars—really America's first sports cars. The Mercer was a purpose-built sportster: lower, lighter, and somewhat smaller than

its competitors. The steering was precise, and the gearbox made downshifts a pleasure. As late as the Fifties and Sixties, writers were comparing the Mercer's handling to contemporary sports cars.

Porter, who believed racing improves the breed, was competition manager as well as chief engineer. Mercer was one of the most successful race cars of the time not only because of the factory program but also because the cars could be taken from showroom to race track—and many owners did.

Porter was designing an overhead camshaft engine for the Mercer line when the company decided to go with a simpler engine designed by another engineer. Washington Roebling had died on the *Titanic* and wasn't there to support Porter.

Undeterred, Porter set out to build his own car, the F.R.P. The car was to sport a high-performance engine that featured an overhead cam, hemispherical combustion chambers, and, on later versions, four-valve heads. Though promising, money was a problem and the project never really got off the ground before the factory was taken over for World War I munitions work.

During the war Porter found work testing Liberty airplane engines. Aviation was Porter's new passion. He was chief engineer for Curtiss Airplane Company before becoming a consulting engineer in New York. During World War II he was a consulting engineer for Bendix Corporation—maker of aircraft components.

Porter, who died in 1964 at the age of 92, lived to see his Raceabouts become some of the most cherished collector cars of the brass era.

Founded in 1914, Aston Martin, like British compatriot MG, specialized in sports cars from the first but gave little thought to roadgoing models until the mid-Thirties. Aston also built far fewer of its prewar models, no more than 100 each. This 2-Litre Speed roadster, for instance, was one of only 13 crafted in 1936-38. Despite its small four-cylinder engine, it could do up to 110 mph.

# ETTORE BUGATTI
## Cars Were His Medium

Artists ran in the family, and Ettore Bugatti wanted to be one as well.

Bugatti's father designed furniture, and his brother, Rembrandt, was a renowned sculptor famous for his lifelike animal sculptures. But gifted with a natural mechanical aptitude, Bugatti was taken on as an apprentice to a firm making motorized tricycles in 1896. This led to other engineering jobs and in 1910 Bugatti obtained an abandoned dye works in Molsheim, Alsace, to set up his own company. Alsace was French or German territory, depending on which way the wars went. During most of Bugatti's years there it was French. That suited Bugatti, who considered himself as much French as Italian. Though born in Milan, Bugatti had spent much of his childhood in France.

Bugatti, by now the frustrated artist, applied his artistic self to his cars. Not only were the cars as a whole beautiful, but the components were works of art. Front axles were polished and gracefully curved. Every surface of the engine was either polished or engine-turned. Bugatti made up for his lack of formal education with instinct and improvisation. Similar to Henry Ford, Bugatti was a brilliant man with some blind spots. Both resisted hydraulic brakes and independent front suspension. Critics tend to write off Bugatti as a great artist but a poor engineer. Though biased toward design, Bugatti's cars enjoyed some of the most successful racing efforts of the era.

Bugatti's factory was more feudal estate than industrial plant. Le Patron was lord of all he surveyed. He was paternalistic but had no tolerance for shoddy workmanship or misuse of tools. A hotel was kept near the factory for customers taking delivery or servicing cars. This allowed Bugatti to scrutinize his clients. King Zog of Albania was not allowed to buy a $20,000 Royale chassis because of his poor table manners. Also near the factory was the Bugatti chateau. Bugatti lived like a country squire with a taste for the best horses, dogs, and food. He had a renaissance man's mind and the craftsmen to make his ideas reality. Furniture, cloths, saddles, and boats were turned out for his own use. Bugatti was a devoted family man, and Molsheim must have been a happy place for both the Bugatti family and employees.

However, a wave of communist-provoked strikes swept through France in '36 and the splendid isolation of Bugatti's fiefdom was broken. Bugatti moved to Paris. His talented son Jean took care of running the works until he was killed while testing a car just a month before the outbreak of World War II.

The Germans took over the factory during the war. Bugatti died not long after the ordeal of regaining his property in 1947. A few cars were produced in the Fifties, but without Le Patron it was over.

The Bavarian maker of aircraft engines and motorcycles expanded in the late 1920s to building small British Austins under license. Just a decade on, BMW was producing quality touring cars of its own design, plus very capable dual-purpose sports cars. The last and the greatest of the sporting prewar BMWs was the long-legendary 328 roadster. Appearing in 1936, it carried an efficient 2.0-liter inline six-cylinder engine with hemispherical combustion chambers, BMW's first and a rarity at the time. At a svelte 1830 pounds, the 328 could exceed 90 mph in stock trim despite a modest 80 bhp. Competition versions won many trophies in the 1936-40 seasons, cementing a performance image for BMW that persists to this day.

Car accessories have been around nearly as long as the automobile itself. Vehicle makers found them an easy way to earn extra money, and other companies quickly sprang up to provide what manufacturers didn't. Because sports cars usually came with just the bare essentials, accessory sellers found sports-car owners a ready market for all sorts of goodies. These ads from Britain's weekly *Motor* magazine are typical of the appeals.

# W.O. BENTLEY
## Outlasted the Fast

Born to wealth, Walter Owen Bentley was a rail-obsessed Brit with the means to follow his passion. Accepting a position with the railroad instead of seeking more lucrative work, Bentley had realized a childhood dream.

Bentley (as well as Henry Royce) assimilated his engineering knowledge at the Great Northern Railway locomotive shops. Frustrated by slow career advancement, Bentley took his talents to the emerging auto industry, where he was one of the first to develop aluminum alloy pistons. While visiting the French DFP automobile factory, which he had begun importing to England, he noticed an aluminum piston used as a paperweight. The supplier made it as a novelty—thought too delicate for use in an engine. Bentley tested the design in racing cars and consistently won. World War I broke out soon afterward. Bentley knew his secret weapon in racing could help the British air force. He sold the air industry on aluminum pistons and also designed aircraft engines. Bentley knew failures in his engines could cost lives and won the respect of pilots by going up in the planes near the front to diagnose problems. After the war, aluminum pistons gradually became common in automobile engines.

Bentley was honest and methodical, qualities that were reflected in his work. Other sports cars were smaller and lighter, but Bentleys were meant to be rugged and absolutely reliable. Because W.O. appreciated a fast, good handling car, Bentleys were a pleasure to drive in spite of their heft. Materials and workmanship had to be first rate to live up to the five-year warranty. The integrity of

Bentley's cars proved itself on the track. The British had few successes in international racing until Bentley's five victories at LeMans. The 24-hour endurance race was the perfect showcase for Bentley's reliability. Bentley was quick to realize that races could be won in the pits. Tools and tasks were organized with military precision. The result was that cars weren't stressed to make up time lost in the pits. Drivers were told in what order to race and what speed to lap. While some faster rivals broke down early, Bentleys maintained a steady pace to victory. The drivers, known as the "Bentley Boys," tended to be rich sportsmen whose lifestyle provided good fodder for the papers. The "Boys" were also extraordinary drivers. On the track, Bentley's authority was not questioned. Off the track he played the role of a favorite uncle.

Bentley lost control of his company in '31. The racing successes, the glamour of the "Bentley Boy" drivers, and splendid road cars had created an enduring legend in a little over a decade. The cars became a British national symbol and inspired a fanatical following.

W.O. didn't stop with the original Bentleys but developed a V12 for Lagonda in '38 and a dual-overhead-cam six for post-war models. The six later powered the Aston Martin DB2. In retirement, W.O. was a much-loved member of the Bentley Owners Club.

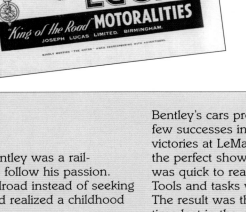

*W.O. Bentley, center*

**Above:** Bugatti reached the sports-car peak in 1935 with its Type 57S and supercharged 57SC. The chassis came from the two-year-old Type 57 but was modified with a shorter wheelbase and lower ride height. The 57's 3.3-liter twincam straight eight was retained, with 175 hp for the S, a hearty 200 for the SC. With one of the sleeker closed bodies, like the Jean Bugatti-design Atlantic coupe shown here, an SC could reach 135 mph, making it one of the fastest things on four wheels other than an all-out racing car. A comparable 57S wasn't much slower. Only some 40 S/SC models were built before World War II, after which the Bugatti company began a long slide into oblivion. Today these cars are virtually priceless. **Left and below:** The same can be said for this 1938 Talbot-Lago, a late-prewar great from France. Just three years before, Major Anthony Lago had taken the helm at the old-line Sunbeam-Talbot-Darracq company. He immediately staked its future on high-performance cars that could double as competitive racers. Though not that successful on the track, Talbot-Lagos were wonderful on the road, thanks to a new 140-bhp 4.0-liter straight-six and a well-sorted chassis. This is one of a handful of "teardrop" coupes bodied by Figoni et Falaschi. Original price was $17,500, a towering sum for the day.

# 2

## 1940-1949: Coming to America

It started innocently enough. just a few score GIs return-ing from World War II Europe with a foreign sports car in tow. The cars were mostly British and mostly ended up in the ritzier enclaves of the East Coast and California. Even here they were curiosities and quite fascinating with it. Not much as invasions go but enough. The sports car had landed, and America would never be the same.

For most Americans in 1945, sports cars seemed as foreign as the people who drove them. Though Detroit had long offered jaunty rumble-seat models and even some snazzy two-seaters, only a small group of Yanks knew much—or cared—about the genuine sports cars available from England and Europe. Not surprisingly, the cognoscenti tended to be well off, well educated, well traveled. They also tended to affect manners that made them "a race apart," as Ken Purdy described them. Purdy first met other U.S. sports-car devo-tees in the mid-1930s. To him they were a strange, secret society. "They spoke only to each other and in their native tongue," he wrote. " 'I shouldn't turn that much over five-thou, old boy; the big ends simply won't stand up to it.' They treated their mounts like newborn children."

Purdy relates being dumbfounded when he saw one worried owner heat "a gallon and a half of pure castor oil on a portable electric burner. He had a candy thermometer in the reeking stuff and he peered steadily at it. Just as it rose to the tem-perature he wanted...he snatched the instrument out, grabbed the kettle, and turned to me to say, 'Do stand aside, please; the oil mustn't cool before I get it into the engine.' "

A few years later, Purdy witnessed a small but telling inci-dent involving an MG parked on a busy street in the Big Apple: "The dashing pilot, pulling on a pair of pierced-back chamois driving gloves, was about to board, when one of the staring yokels (an MG would draw a crowd in New York in those days) asked him what the letters MG stood for (Morris Garages of Oxford). 'MG?' he drawled, affecting surprise. Why, "Mighty Good," of course.' 'Where can you buy one?' the fellow asked. 'You can't buy one,' he was told. 'They're available only as gifts.' "

Long enshrined as "the sports car America loved first," the MG seemed an unlikely object of desire in the land of Buck Rogers. Even MG's new TC roadster, introduced in late 1945, was just a mild evolution of the TA/TB design, which dated from 1936 but was conceptually rooted in the Twenties. As British auto journalist Graham Robson observed in Consumer Guide®'s Great Book of Sports Cars, the TC "was a slow, hard-riding, crude little traditional British roadster, and [was] never sold with left-hand drive. But America took to it because...it had oodles of character and looked right: classically pure and very different from any-thing Detroit had to offer... It wasn't big, powerful, flashy, or even particularly comfortable. But a relatively small yet vocal group of buyers...found it well-nigh perfect: compact, responsive, and 'urgent' somehow despite its [small four-cylinder engine and] leisurely acceleration. The TC also offered good fuel economy, plus cheap and easy mainte-nance—a good thing, the latter, as it was needed often. Like the [Ford Model T], you either put up with the TC's idio-syncrasies or your didn't. It was the sort of car that demand-ed involvement. And isn't that the way love affairs begin?"

Love is one thing, commitment quite another. Although the TC and its cohorts won many American hearts, they did-n't attract many U.S. sales. And they never would. Most

primed for futuristic new models, which had been breath-lessly forecast during wartime. Why, they wondered, would any sane person waste money on an old-fashioned thing like an MG?

Why, to make a statement, of course. As David E. Davis opined in 1970, sports-car enthusiasm in late-Forties America was an "easily defined protest movement...[P]eople were sufficiently fed up with the dumb cars coming out of Detroit to express their disgust by buying dumb imported cars...They were a hopelessly outgunned minority in the beginning, but they were a tough breed...driving cars that flew in the face of everything that Detroit, and thus America, stood for." No wonder sports-car drivers would toot horns and wave when they encountered each other on some back-road less traveled, or that they were very often "tweedy, English-looking, tanned, and healthy," as Davis wrote. Being dedicated birds of a peculiar feather, it wasn't surprising that a few eager Northeasterners flocked together to form the Sports Car Club of America even before V-E Day.

Little by little, sports cars became more common on U.S. roads and public interest grew. Of course, most any new car was of interest right after World War II, because Americans hadn't had any to buy for nearly four years. Domestic automakers mostly satisfied the huge pent-up demand with warmed-over versions of prewar fare, which was enough until about 1950. But most foreign automakers had been ravaged by war and desperately needed to export for dollars. They too, resumed production as quickly as possible, but began to realize that sports cars were making an impression in affluent America. Britain's Jaguar was among the first to capitalize on America's burgeoning sports-car "fad." It happened with the 1948 introduction of the all-new XK120, rightly hailed as the state of the sports-car art with its advanced twincam six-cylinder engine and sleek, modern styling.

Meantime, more and more U.S. dealers were starting to take up the sports-car cause. One was Max Hoffman, who bravely opened a toney New York showroom in 1946 to sell pricey French Delahayes, though he soon added more afford-able cars, including Jaguars and MGs. Over the next 25 years, Hoffman introduced the U.S. to dozens of other foreign marques and models, notably the VW Beetle and the first Porsches. In fact, Hoffman did more to grow the U.S. for-eign-car market than anyone else except Kjell Qvale, who served the West Coast market from his San Francisco-based British Motor Car Distributors starting in 1947. That same year saw the first issue of a national magazine called Road & Track. Born of the "protest movement" Davis described, R&T also stimulated U.S. interest in foreign cars generally and sports cars in particular.

By the end of the Forties, sports cars were definitely on the American scene, if not in many Americans' garages. Even Detroit could see something new and maybe important was going on. Motown might easily dismiss sports-car owners as a "lunatic fringe," but it could also see that the vast mainstream market was being captivated by the racy, romantic two-seaters from overseas. One can almost hear the boardroom debate: "Hey, maybe we ought to build our own sports car." "Heck, we can't make money with one of those." "Yeah, but it would sure bring in the customers, and that will make money."

The beachhead had been secured for a full-scale assault. Come the Fifties, a battalion of new models would charge into a booming U.S. economy and spread sports-car excitement

1940 Axis powers stage Brescia Grand Prix; BMW wins Europe's last "prewar" race • Chrysler shows 2-seat Thunderbolt "dream" sports car 1941 December 7 U.S. enters WWII with Japanese bombing of Pearl Harbor • Automobile Racing Club of America (ARCA) disbands 1942 U.S. civilian vehicle production suspended by government order 1943 Death claims Edsel Ford, German electrics-company founder Robert Bosch 1944 Sports Car Club of America formed by ex-ARCA members • D-Day brings historic Allied invasion of Nazi-held Europe • Standard Motor Co., Ltd. buys British compatriot Triumph Co., Ltd. 1945 Britain's S.S. Cars, Ltd. changes name to Jaguar Cars, Ltd. • U.S. War Production Board approves restart of civilian production • Ferdinand Porsche jailed in Dijon, France as wartime collaborator 1946 War-ravaged Mercedes-Benz resumes regular car production • Britain's Sydney Allard and Donald Healey build their first sports cars for general sale • Ace Italian racing driver Luigi Chinetti receives U.S. citizenship • U.S. upstart Kaiser-Frazer builds its first cars • MG TC starts U.S. sale, attracts much public notice • Triumph adds semi-sporting 1800 (later 2000) Roadster, drops it four years later • Austrian expatriate Max Hoffman opens New York City dealership, sells only French Delahayes at first 1947 Norwegian Kjell Qvale opens British Motor Car Distributors in San Francisco to sell MGs, other British marques • Ferrari marque debuts with V12 Tipo 125 road racer winning at Piacenza • First issue of *Road & Track* magazine

Like America's pioneer hot rodders of the 1930s, Englishman Sydney Allard created performance machines using low-cost Ford hardware. After building a few "backyard" sports cars for himself, Allard decided to try selling copies in 1946. His first "consumer" model, the K1, stemmed from a late-prewar effort and retained a 221-cubic-inch flathead Ford V8 with 85/95 horsepower. Allard designed the frame (advertised above) around stock Ford parts but managed a clever, effective independent rear suspension, then a rarity among British cars, sporting or not. The Allard-built body draped steel panels over traditional wood framing. Though not super-quick, the K1 paved the way for faster, more exciting Allards in the 1950s. Just 151 were built through 1949.

**Above and left:** Maserati was founded in 1926 by five brothers in Bologna who won fame designing competition engines and cars, which they sometimes drove on the track. The Orsi industrial group took over in 1938, but kept the surviving brothers on the payroll. Seeking a more prosperous future, Maserati branched into roadgoing sports cars with the A6/1500, the last "Maser" with direct family ties. Ernesto Maserati based the 1.5-liter twincam six-cylinder engine on an earlier racing unit, but horsepower was just 65, a concession to Italy's low-grade postwar gasoline. Even so, top speed was a creditable 95 mph. The only transmission was a four-speed manual supplied by another Orsi-owned company. Suspension was fairly modern for the day, with coil springs all around, independent via twin wishbones in front, and a solid rear axle. Only 61 A6/1500s were built, all essentially by hand, in 1946-50. Most carried simple, elegant coupe bodies designed and supplied by Pinin Farina of Turin, but a few were crafted as "spider" roadsters. **Below:** The race-and-ride nature of many prewar sports cars remained a potent force in the design and marketing of postwar models. This 1947 ad from Britain's weekly magazine *The Motor* used a vintage Bugatti to tout the expertise of a Hertsfordshire engineering firm catering to would-be racers—presumably those with more than a bit of money to spend.

• Ferdinand Porsche released from prison, returns home to Austria • Death claims Ettore Bugatti, Henry Ford, GM founder W.C. Durant • Industrialist David Brown buys Aston Martin of Newport Pagnell, England • British aero-engine maker Bristol launches first car, uses prewar BMW designs • Piero Dusio bows roadgoing Cisitalia with styling soon hailed as modern art • Luigi Chinetti orders five Ferrari "passenger cars," becomes U.S. Ferrari distributor • Maserati launches sporting A6/1500 as first production model **1948** Porsche company regroups, builds first cars under its own name • Jaguar unveils sleek XK120 at Earl's Court Motor Show • New Tipo 166 is Ferrari's first road car, wins grueling Targa Florio and Mille Miglia road races • Luigi Chinetti and Lord Selsdon win 12 Hours of Paris race for Ferrari • Honda Motor Company formed in Japan to build motorized bicycles • Famed race-car designer Frank Kurtis launches Kurtis Sport roadster • Goodyear introduces the tubeless tire • Hoffman and Kvale dealerships sell their first Jaguars **1949** Stock Jaguar XK120 reaches 126 mph on Belgium's Jabbeke Highway • Cadillac, Oldsmobile offer world's first high-compression V8s • Crosley unveils tiny, spartan Hot Shot roadster • Ferrari wins 24-hour races at Spa in Belgium and LeMans in France • Ferrari builds 30 cars for the year • Jaguar XK120 begins regular production • Michelin in France introduces the radial tire • *Motor Trend* magazine debuts • John R. Bond takes over as *Road & Track* owner/publisher • Volkswagen Beetle arrives in U.S., sells two copies

**Above:** The MG-TC was the sports car most often brought home by World War II GIs, and it almost singlehandedly fired the sports-car enthusiasm that began sweeping America in the late 1940s. Ironically, the TC was but a mild update of the prewar MG-TB, with the same 1250-cc four-cylinder engine, four-speed gearbox, flexible ladder-type frame, hard ox-cart suspension, and "trad" roadster styling. But with its long hood, sweeping fenders, cutaway doors, and 19-inch wire wheels, the TC cut a dash that many Yanks found irresistible. A trim 94-inch wheelbase and 144.5-inch overall length meant a cramped cockpit, but also maneuverability and handling that simply amazed drivers accustomed to period Detroit cars. With only 54 hp, the TC was anything but fast despite weighing just 1735 pounds, but it was jolly good fun and that was news. It was also quite affordable at under $1900. MG built some 10,000 in 1945-49. Most were sold in the U.S. **Below:** Introduced in 1947, the Cisitalia 202 Gran Sport clothed humble Fiat mechanicals in artful styling by Pinin Farina. In fact, New York City's Museum of Modern Art displayed one as part of its permanent collection starting in 1951.

Beside an award-winning coupe, the Cisitalia 202 Gran Sport was also available in this cabriolet style. "Available" is misleading, though, as only 17 were built along with 153 coupes during the model's 1947-52 run. Piero Dusio formed Cisitalia ("CHEES-ee-TAHL-ee-ah") as a sporting-goods maker, but his passion for racing led him to bankroll 50 single-seat competition machines before attempting a production sports car. Like the racers, the 202 GS was built around low-cost Fiat components. It had a modern chassis but just a 66-hp 1100-cc four-cylinder engine, so it was slow off the mark, though it could approach 100 mph. It was also wildly expensive for the time at $5000 for the coupe, $7000 for the cabrio. No wonder sales were so few and far between.

## SIR WILLIAM LYONS
### Launched the Leaping Cat

To many, Sir William Lyons was Jaguar. An autocrat, Lyons exercised final say on all aspects of the business. Fortunately, he had a range of talents appropriate to the task. Lyons had the marketing savvy to know what the public wanted. He was famously thrifty and held tight control of expenses, helping him deliver cars at a fraction of the price customers expected to pay. His dealings with labor were tough but fair. Although he was distant and never tried to be "one of the lads," he could be generous with his staff when times were good. Lyons was an enthusiastic driver "able to assess what my engineers were doing." Finally he had unfailing good taste and sense of line. He not only designed some of the most beautiful cars of his era but maintained a continuity of design that endures today. Lyon's influence is still seen in current Jaguars. The basic lines of his last design, the XJ6 of 1968, are carried on in the new XJ8 of 2004.

William Lyons, the son of an Irish musician turned music store owner, was from the English seaside resort of Blackpool. Born in 1901, the last year of Queen Victoria's reign, Lyons always retained a Victorian sense of honor and formality. After school, he apprenticed with the Crossley car company and took engineering courses at night.

Staunchly indepen-dent, Lyons wanted to be his own boss and left Crossley. A neighbor's son, William Walmsley, was building motorcycle sidecars in a shed behind his home. Lyons realized there was a future in the stylish sidecars and convinced Walmsley to form a partnership and expand the business. The firm branched out, building special bodies for Austin Sevens and other cars.

Easy going, Walmsley began dragging his feet as the ambitious Lyons pushed for expansion. In '34 Walmsley was bought out and a dedicated engineering staff was soon brought in. Lyons now had complete control, and the company began the transition into a full automaker. The first use of Jaguar as a model name came in 1936. After World War II the company name was formally changed to Jaguar. William Lyons was knighted in 1956 in recognition of the export dollars Jaguar brought to Great Britain.

Happily married for over 60 years, Lyons had two daughters and one son. In the Fifties, daughter Pat was married to rallyist Ian Appleyard.

Son John Lyons was expected to succeed his father but was killed in a car accident, contributing to the senior Lyon's decision to merge Jaguar with British Motors Corporation in '66. Retirement in '72 allowed Lyons more time for his interests in golf and farming. His interest in Jaguar was renewed with Jaguar's revival in the Eighties, and he visited the factory often to offer suggestions on an XJ replacement. Sir William Lyons died in 1985—one year before that XJ was launched.

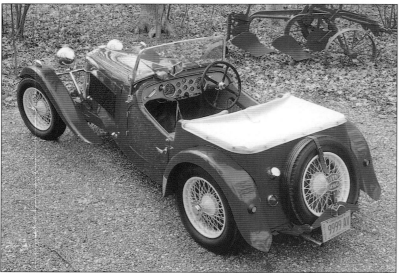

MG was just one of many British sports-car makers in the years bracketing World War II, though few of the other marques were then widely known in the U.S. HRG, for example, was founded in 1935 by E.A. Halford, Guy Robins, and H.R. Godfrey as one of The Sceptred Isle's many "cottage industry" concerns in the small-scale mold of Morgan and Frazer Nash. All typically purchased engines and transmissions from larger companies but designed and built most everything else. HRG favored engines from Singer of Coventry, gearboxes by Moss, an orthodox frame with leaf springs and solid axles at each end, and old-fashioned wood-framed roadster bodies with a skimpy folding top and few comforts or conveniences. In fact, the basic design of this 1948 model "1500," named for its 65-bhp 1496-cc engine, dates from HRG's founding. A similar 1100-cc version was also rated at 65 bhp. Either could reach 90 mph on a good day. HRGs did well in hillclimbs and track competition, but sales were always difficult. The company soldiered on until 1955, when it closed shop after building just 240 cars, all but 33 of them in the postwar period.

Even before it turned to roadgoing sports cars, Maserati was known to many Americans for its wins in the 1939 and 1940 Indianapolis 500 races. Veteran pilot Wilbur Shaw did the honors on both occasions. As it happened, Indy cars had switched to European Grand Prix specifications for the 1938 season, which allowed supercharged engines of up 3.0 liters displacement. Maserati devised a "blown" straight eight with 350 bhp, good for over 150 mph in a single-seat machine weighing 1540 pounds. Ironically, the resulting Tipo 8CTF looked a strong GP challenger to German juggernauts Mercedes and Auto Union but proved unreliable. Not so at Indy, where it broke the long victory string of Offenhauser-powered cars, the only years other than 1946 that the Offys would be beaten before the mid-1960s.

# MASERATI BROTHERS
## A Family Affair

Cast into the hand of the bronze Neptune watching over Piazza del Nettuno in the city of Bologna is a three-pronged staff. This was the hometown of the six Maserati brothers, and among them, only Mario had little interest in race cars. He wanted to be an artist. So, inspired by Neptune's prop, he designed for his brothers an insignia. The trident he drew would come to symbolize native genius in automotive high performance. From the road courses and Grand Prix tracks of Europe to the bricks of Indianapolis, the cars and engines built by the Maseratis were among the fastest, most technically advanced, and most beautiful sporting machines of their age.

It's a family story. To Rodolfo and Carolina Maserati in 1881, and at roughly two-year intervals, came Carlo, Bindo, Alfieri, Mario, Ettore, and Ernesto. Carlo led the charge, home-building a single-cylinder car, driving in competition as early as 1907. He went to work for Isotta-Fraschini and found jobs there for Alfieri and Ettore. They quit in 1914 to establish a garage that did performance hop-ups. Ernesto joined, and the brothers went racing in earnest, at first by putting aircraft engines in Isotta-Fraschini chassis. Their first complete car was the Tipo 26, a supercharged 1.5-liter dohc straight-8 Alfieri drove to first in class in the 1926 Targa Florio. That led to larger engines, better transmissions, and more wins. In 1929, a 280-bhp 4.0-liter 16 cylinder Maserati set the 10-kilometer world speed record at 153 mph.

Bindo came aboard, and Maserati became a force in Grand Prix racing. Their cars were typical of European GP machines of the day. Essentially low-slung road cars, they were raced with or without fenders and headlights, depending on the venue. All were distinguished by expert craftsmanship and mechanical innovation. For example, the Maserati 8C of 1933 pioneered hydraulic brakes and won Grands Prix for Tazio Nuvolari.

But the independent family concern was little match for Germany's government-backed Mercedes and Auto Union teams. In 1937, the brothers yielded financial management to the industrialist Orsi family but retained engineering control. That freed them to concentrate on racing. A focus was specialized single-seaters, and their 8CTF took Wilbur Shaw to consecutive Indianapolis 500 wins in 1939 and '40.

The Maseratis developed a few postwar production sports cars, but when Orsi pushed for more, the brothers severed the relationship to form Officine Specializate Costruzione Automobili in 1947. OSCA through the 1950s turned out mostly smaller-displacement race engines and Formula 2 cars. The trademark Maserati engineering was there but not the development money to beat Alfa Romeo and Ferrari. After a final whiff of success with the 1960 Italian Formula Junior title, the surviving Maserati brothers sold out to the MV Agusta motorcycle company in 1962.

Under a succession of corporate owners, their name remained associated with racing glory on such luminaries as the F1-champ 250F and the Birdcage sports racer. It also became a byword for roadgoing glamour in a series of hot-blooded exotics leading in the late 1990s to cars engineered by old rival Ferrari itself. Road or race, each carried the Maserati trident, symbol of a proud tradition and a brother's bond.

Ferdinand Porsche made history with a humble "people's car" but also created magnificent sports and racing cars for Austro-Daimler, Daimler-Benz, and Auto Union beginning in the 1920s. After being jailed two years in France as a World War II "collaborator," the brilliant engineer returned home to Austria with his son Ferry to revive their prewar idea of a sports car based on the Nazi-mandated *Volkswagen*. They first built a midengine roadster, strictly for experience, but quickly decided on a slick beetle-shaped coupe with a modified VW chassis and rear-mounted air-cooled engine. Though it had just 1100 cc and 40 bhp, this "356/2" could reach almost 90 mph, thanks to an aerodynamic shape and lean 1300-pound build. The Porsches built only four such cars in 1948, 25 the next year, and 18 in 1950. All were essentially hand-crafted, the company premises in Gmund being too small for anything like serious production. Ferry would remedy that problem in mid-1950 by relocating the company to a proper factory in Stuttgart, West Germany. It was the start of a sports-car dynasty. A few cabriolets were also built to this initial design, which was soon improved and renamed simply 356. Sadly, papa Ferdinand barely lived to see the first cars bearing his name, succumbing in January 1951 to complications from a stroke.

Cincinnati appliance tycoon Powel Crosley, Jr. began stocking his stores with tiny two-cylinder economy cars in 1939. He then moved to somewhat larger four-cylinder models that sold well until a waning postwar seller's market exposed overwhelming buyer preference for "standard" cars. Hoping to recover with something unique, Crosley added the Hot Shot for 1949, a jaunty, spartan two-seat roadster priced at just $849. It wasn't quick—0-60 mph took 20 seconds, top speed was just 77 mph—but was easily souped-up and could even go racing. But demand was weak and remained so despite the 1950 addition of the Super Sport, a Hot Shot with doors. Crosley built just 2498 two-seaters in all before quitting the car business in 1952.

# FERDINAND PORSCHE
## The Passionate Pioneer

In 1919, a young, enthusiastic Austro-Daimler engineer built for an Austrian count a modern, lightweight, race car that got 90 mph from a 1.0-liter engine. Dubbed "Sascha," for its royal patron, Ferdinand Porsche's creation combined low mass, prudent dimensions, and ample power in a package that proved greater than the sum of its parts. Porsche's enthusiasm turned to disgust when, at a meeting, company directors declined to put the Sascha into production. Furious, Porsche hurled his cigarette lighter at directors and stormed away.

The incident was one of countless episodes that laced Porsche's career, demonstrating his dedication to the automotive ethic that "less is more." And though it was son "Ferry" who ultimately built the first car bearing the family name, Ferdinand Porsche laid the groundwork, demonstrating that technical innovation and restrained design could triumph over shear mass and brute force.

Born the second of three sons to a Czech metal fabricator in 1875, Ferdinand Porsche became the heir-apparent to the family business when his older brother died suddenly in 1890. Ironically, the mechanically gifted Porsche showed little aptitude for metalwork, desiring instead to attend technical school. Though disappointed, his father acquiesced.

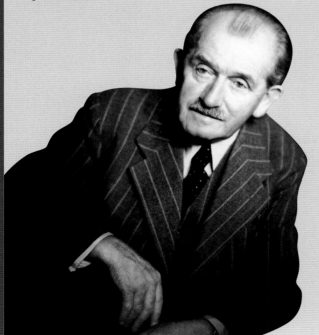

At school Porsche was immediately distracted by the mysteries of electricity. Putting his newfound interest to use, Porsche equipped his parent's house with a generator and incandescent light—a decade before the town was wired for power.

Following his new interest, Porsche left school and worked briefly for an electrical equipment maker before joining Viennese coachbuilder Jakob Lohner in 1898. There Porsche set to work on a horseless carriage better suited to the firm's royal clientele than the crude, smoky vehicles then available.

Porsche's background served him well, as his first design featured electric drive. Considered the first front-wheel-drive car, the sprightly "Electric Chaise" clocked a best-ever time at the Semmerling Hillclimb in 1910. Archduke Franz Ferdinand, who later awarded Porsche a knighthood, purchased a Chaise for personal use.

While at Lohner, Porsche experimented with a number of drivetrain variations including "hybrid" systems that combined gas and electric power.

After leaving Lohner, Porsche's career wove, tumultuously, through the various arms of German autobuilder Daimler. On September 6, 1909, while with Austro-Daimler, the company's Austrian branch, Porsche piloted a Maya, the company's smallest offering, to a class victory at Semmerling. Son Ferry was born the same day.

As Porsche continued to tinker, Austro-Daimler continued to win. Incorporating such advancements as overhead cams and tuned aerodynamics, A-D scored a 1-2-3 victory at the 1910 Prince Henry Trials.

Hoping to continue working with high-performance cars, Porsche left Austro-Daimler for Germany and parent company Daimler. There he worked on such legendary vehicles as the K, S, SS, and SSK. Porsche's open criticism of the sheer mass of these vehicles led to bad blood between him and the company, however, and led to his eventual resignation.

In 1930, after a brief stint with Austrian autobuilder Steyr, Porsche founded Porsche G.m.b.H.; the design firm that would, in his son's care, build the cars that bear the family name. Ferdinand Porsche died on January 30, 1951.

Ferdinand Porsche has been criticized for his indifference to the politics of his era. Indeed, his work for the Nazi regime is well documented. It is perhaps ironic then that the most enduring example of his Reichstag work was not war related, but his "people's car," a car now affectionately known as the Beetle.

Donald Healey won renown as a rally driver in the 1920s and as technical chief for several British factory racing teams in the Thirties. Like Sydney Allard, he longed to put his name on road cars and did so starting in 1946 from a small workshop in Warwick. His first offerings were mostly touring models with coach-built bodies, British Riley engines, and a Healey-designed chassis, but he also offered a true sports car named Silverstone after Britain's then-new racing circuit. "Streamlined" in late-1930s style, the Silverstone weighed just over a ton on a trim 96-inch wheelbase and could reach 110 mph with the 104-bhp 2.5-liter four-cylinder engine typically fitted. Only 105 would be built over eight years. A good many came to America, as Healey intended, where they competed at venues like Connecticut's Thompson Raceway (*below*) into the late Fifties. Note the small racing windscreens and lack of headlights on the main example pictured.

Amateur "club racing" was popular from the automobile's earliest days. It became even more so in the late 1940s, spurred by rising postwar prosperity and a growing array of sports-car models. As ever, owners met to swap stories and tips about their favorite and to participate in tours or friendly off-road competition. This period ad from Britain's weekly magazine *The Motor* announces a Sunday hillclimb organized by the country's Bugatti Owners' Club. The single-seat open-wheel car pictured was typical of hillclimb contestants at the time.

# ENZO FERRARI
## Il Commendatore

His life had the color and sweep of an Italian opera. In fact, his first ambition was to be an opera singer. Even the title of his 1962 autobiography was worthy of Puccini. He called it *Le Mie Gioie Terribili* (*My Terrible Joys*).

The world's most-desired sports cars bear the name of a metalsmith's son who used charm and manipulation, temper and pride, inspiration and intelligence to forge their legend and his. Enzo Ferrari wasn't an engineer or designer. He disdained formal education and had little of it. He wasn't widely traveled and preferred that people come to him—where he'd let them cool their heels as he worked at his desk, head down, pretending not to notice them. It was an imperious gesture, fitting for a man who signed documents in royal purple ink.

Of course there was more to Ferrari than stagecraft. He was urbane enough to navigate the most influential circles and won admirers among the world's wealthy and celebrated. He spoke cultured Italian, more than adequate French, and a dip of English. He was surprisingly tall, his posture dignified. He could be bright and mischievous and was a renowned womanizer. He was brave enough to wriggle out of a takeover agreement with Ford and cagey enough wrangle

concessions from international racing authorities.

But nothing matched his genius for collecting the cream of motoring's talent—driver Tazio Nuvolari, engine designer Vittorio Jano, stylist "Pinin" Farina, among scores of giants—and stimulating them to sate his most intense obsession. He called it "an overpowering passion for cars."

Enzo Anselmo Ferrari was born in 1898 in Modena, Italy, to a family that owned a small metalworking company. He traced his life's guiding light to the thrill of a boyhood excursion to an open-road race in Bologna. As a young adult, he landed seat time in a variety of competition cars, and by 1920, was at Alfa Romeo, where his duties ran from sales to race driving. At the latter he enjoyed some success, including second place in the Targa Florio. Impressed, the family of a fallen World War I fighter ace bestowed upon Enzo their son's squadron insignia, and a black stallion on a field of yellow became Ferrari's coat of arms. In the '30s, Enzo formed Scuderia Ferrari to race Alfas, then founded a contract design and manufacturing firm. Chased from Modena to Maranello by World War II bombing, it went on to produce, in wide variety but low numbers, an array of racing and road cars that made the word "Ferrari" synonymous with speed, prestige, and beauty.

In Enzo's eyes, the purpose of roadgoing Ferraris was to fund the racing program, and his stubborn racing mantra "engine above all else" meant Ferrari sports cars were late to such advances as independent rear suspension and disc brakes. He famously dismissed midengine designs with, "The horse does not push the cart, it pulls."

Underlying such pique were years of profound despair over the 1956 death of his son, Dino, who succumbed to muscular dystrophy in his mid-20s. Bemused by those who venerated his "classic" sports cars, Enzo's fire for racing never abated. He lived to see his cars cross finish lines first more than 4000 times, winning 13 world championships, nine of them in Formula 1. Enzo Ferrari died in 1988, of kidney failure. Today, cars from the company he founded represent the pinnacle of the sports car art.

*Enzo Ferrari, left*

**Opposite page, this page above, and left:** After some 20 years spent racing Alfa Romeos, Enzo Ferrari set up after World War II to build his own competition sports cars. To fund the business, he reluctantly sold roadgoing versions with nearly identical track-oriented engineering. The first of these was based on the Tipo (Type) 166 chassis, introduced in 1948. Compared with the initial handful of racing Ferraris built in 1947-48, the 166 boasted a larger, 2.0-liter version of Gioacchino Columbo's recently designed overhead-cam V12 with 110-150 bhp. Also setting a pattern for future street Ferraris was a sturdy tubular-steel ladder-type chassis with coil-spring independent front suspension and a live rear axle on leaf springs. Some 166s were designated "MM" after Clemente Biondi drove one to win the 1948 Mille Miglia road race. Early Ferraris were all handcrafted customs, so few 166s were built: just 70 or so through 1953. Among the most famous and desirable of the breed is this roadster with lightweight *barchetta* ("little boat") bodywork by Touring, a design that would later influence the British A.C. Ace and its Shelby Cobra descendants. **Below:** Factory-installed heaters were still uncommon among foreign cars in the early postwar era, leaving accessory makers to plug the gap. This September 1949 ad from *The Motor* extols the virtues of one unit available for a variety of British saloons, but doesn't mention sports cars.

William Lyons' newly renamed Jaguar Cars, Ltd. rocked the sports-car world in late 1948 with the XK120. Originally, the sleek, sexy roadster was intended as a limited-time showcase for Jaguar's new twincam XK-series six-cylinder engine, but demand proved so strong that Lyons put the car into full production. That got underway in fall 1949 and, for the first few years, was earmarked mostly for the lucrative U.S. market. The first 240 cars had aluminum body panels over wood framing, hence the license plate on this example; later cars used all-steel bodies. All rode a new-design Jaguar sedan chassis with wheelbase trimmed to 102 inches. Prototypes recorded 120 mph all-out, hence the name. Comfortable as well as quick—0-60 mph took just 10 seconds—the XK120 firmly established Jaguar's sports-car credentials in the U.S. and thus helped assure the company's long-term future.

Noted race-car designer Frank Kurtis was one of many Americans who dreamed of making postwar millions with a sports car. His Kurtis Sport was far more professional than most such efforts, but only 36 were built, all in 1948. Engine was to customer choice, but most Sports had flathead Ford V8s. All featured a stout chassis with Kurtis-tuned suspension and sleek, handsomely furnished roadster bodies made mostly of aluminum.

# FRANK KURTIS
## Quick and Quiet

Frank Kurtis's significant contributions to the sports car world are just chapters in his incredible, long-running career as a consummate metalsmith and builder. Over the years his astounding output encompassed custom auto bodies, travel trailers, champ cars, midget racers, go-karts, pedal cars, children's scooters, toy cars, dragsters, racing boats, Bonneville streamliners, experimental all-terrain and amphibious vehicles, rocket sleds for parachute and ejection seat testing, and SR-71 jet aircraft starter carts. Kurtis-built Indy cars and midgets dominated circle track racing in the late Forties and Fifties, and Kurtis 500-S sports cars upstaged foreign-built rivals on the early Fifties West Coast sports car scene.

Born in Crested Butte, Colorado, on January 25, 1908 to Croatian immigrants, Frank learned metal-shaping skills at a very young age by working in his father's blacksmith shops. His family shifted around Colorado and Utah, even moving back to Croatia briefly, before settling in Southern California in 1921. By 1923, both Frank and his father were working for Don Lee Coach and Body Works in downtown L.A. Frank was barely 15 but was already over six feet tall and could easily pass for an 18-year-old. During his time at Don Lee, Frank worked under legendary automotive designer Harley Earl, who helped polish Frank's draw-

ing skills and taught him the art of body design.

A lifelong passion for race cars was born when he and a friend took the streetcar to an auto race at the board track in Culver City, Cal. Young Frank was entranced by a bright red Fiat driven by Ralph DePalma and vowed to himself that he would build a car like it someday. He would get his chance soon enough. The onset of the Depression spelled the end of Frank's days at Don Lee, and Frank ended up working out of his garage, where he began building and repairing race car bodies. Eventually, he was constructing entire race cars in his own bustling shop. By the early Fifties, Kurtis's race cars ruled Indianapolis. In a field dominated by outsized egos and aggressive personalities, Kurtis was a shy, unassuming man. He often found it difficult to work with the wealthy race car owners, who often vetoed his ideas and put his innovations on hold.

Producing sports cars was a welcome diversion from the pressures of racing and a way to keep the shop busy in the off-season. Though none of his sports cars were resounding market successes, they boasted an impressive track record and, like all his products, impeccable craftsmanship. Artisan first and businessman second, Kurtis entered into an ill-fated partnership with supercharger and chainsaw magnate Robert McCulloch that bankrupted his company, effectively ending his forays into sports cars. Kurtis was forced to move out of his shop and on to other ventures.

Frank moved to Arizona in 1968 and was diagnosed with a heart condition in 1980. He passed away on January 17, 1987. His son Arlen still builds and restores Kurtis sports cars and midgets today.

Everyone needs money, and Americans had plenty to spend after World War II. That in a nutshell explains the parade of new sports cars that charmed Americans in the 1950s. Jaguar, MG, and other British makes had begun the procession. Now European companies and even some U.S. automakers fell in step.

Despite problems at home and abroad, America in the 1950s was generally prosperous, upbeat, and eager to meet the future. A booming economy and relatively high employment and wages created a burgeoning, more affluent middle class that began fleeing crowded cities for spacious new suburban communities, where a family might own two cars instead of one. Consumer spending soared, spurred by all manner of new products that industry worked feverishly to provide. Styles and fads came and went, but rock 'n' roll was here to stay and nothing seemed impossible.

With all this, Americans could afford to indulge themselves for the first time since the Roaring Twenties, and they indulged in sports cars to the tune of $30,000-$60,000 a year. Though small-potatoes by Detroit standards, that volume was well worth going after for a tiny outfit like Morgan or Aston Martin, where the added income from U.S. sales could spell the difference between life and death, especially when home-market sales flagged. For larger companies, having a sporty model in the line could be a valuable, even necessary, showroom lure.

The sports cars available to Americans in this decade spanned a dazzling array of types and prices. At the high end were the thoroughbred likes of Ferrari, Jaguar, and Porsche, offering well-heeled aficionados a combination of sophisticated engineering, superb performance, and a competition-proved aura. Mercedes-Benz joined the ranks in 1954 with the fabulous 300SL Gullwing coupe, a racer-turned-road car costing more than a Cadillac limousine—a towering $7000. Two years later, BMW launched the 507, its first sporting car since the prewar 328, priced at an astronomical $9000. Testifying to the importance of the U.S. market, both German uberwagens might not have been built without the lobbying efforts—and firm orders—of New York import-car impresario Max Hoffman.

Moderately priced sports cars also blossomed, mirroring the growth of America's middle class. Among the most popular were 1953 British newcomers, the Austin-Healey 100 and Triumph TR2. Though both were designed around existing components from mass-market models, each had a character all its own, and they fast won devoted U.S. followings.

Nineteen fifty-three also introduced the one showroom sports car ventured by Detroit's Big Three. A mix of traditional British roadster and period American "dream car," the Chevrolet Corvette cost as much as a Jaguar XK but lacked its performance and handling. Purists scoffed, and limited availability greatly hampered initial sales. Had Ford not introduced the Thunderbird, the Corvette would have died after 1955. Happily, General Motors answered its crosstown rival by transforming the 'Vette into a genuine sports car.

The Thunderbird was of one of the more successful semi-sportsters on the Fifties scene. Though it resembled a true sports car and had more power than most, the rakish two-seat convertible was slanted toward comfortable cruising, not slicing up twisty roads. It could be made to race, and did. But though this "personal car" immediately outsold the Corvette by no less than 16-1, Ford was after even bigger profits, and found them by blowing up the Bird into a luxury four-seater after just three years.

Chrysler ran up several sporty "idea cars" in the Fifties, but went no further. GM, Ford, and even Packard also conjured up snazzy two-seat dream machines each year, mainly as auto-show attention-getters for their regular wares. Attention they got, but they were not sports cars in the strictest sense. Neither was the Kaiser-Darrin, which came and went in 1954. It had style and a fiberglass body like the Corvette. But its potential went unrealized because Kaiser-Frazer, the U.S. industry's "postwar wonder," was but a year away from oblivion after making several major mistakes. Designer "Dutch" Darrin showed what could have been when he replaced the weak Willys six in some K-Ds with a potent Cadillac V8. A few even won races.

The 1951-54 Nash-Healey sold little better than the Darrin, but was a far more credible sports car, thanks to co-father Donald Healey. Like the smaller Austin-Healey that followed it, the N-H clothed a humble powertrain in cool two-seater duds, yet was surprisingly raceworthy and could go the distance. Over its short career, the Nash-Healey made impressive high finishes in several international events, including Le Mans. Until the Corvette came along, it was the one real sports car sold under a major U.S. nameplate.

But there were plenty of minor-leaguers. Indeed, the early postwar years were filled with dreamers who figured to make untold riches by putting a sporty body on a borrowed chassis. Most of these efforts were poorly financed lash-ups that died aborning and are little remembered today. Many were sold as mere kits, leaving assembly to the owner. But not all were so unprofessional. Famed Indy-car engineer Frank Kurtis built thoroughly modern sports cars, though not many, starting in 1948. A few years later, Chicago dealer S.H. "Wacky" Arnolt brokered beautiful Italian bodywork for MG and British Bristol chassis. At about the same time, sportsman Briggs Cunningham bankrolled a handful of Chrysler-powered sports cars that could match most anything from Europe. In 1957, Californian Bill Devin turned from selling bolt-on fiberglass bodies to building complete sports cars that could pace with a Ferrari (just 4.8 seconds 0-60 mph) and cost half as much ($5950).

No doubt about it: Americans were treated to a sports-car smorgasbord in the 1950s, with something for most every taste and budget. Of course, new versions of established favorites were also on the table. The Jaguar XK, for example, was updated twice during the decade. And there were some tasty surprises like 1955's new MGA, a comparatively shocking advance on the classic T-Series it replaced.

As the years passed, it became increasingly clear that import cars in general and sports cars in particular were influencing the American public out of all proportion to their sales. This undoubtedly accelerated the shift in buyer attitudes that hit home in 1958, when a sharp recession caused many consumers to reject Detroit's overstyled, outsized gas-swillers for thrifty European compacts and minicars. As it happened, a wee British roadster bowed just as the recession set in: the winsome Austin-Healey Sprite, budget-priced at around $1500. Few cars have benefited from such serendipitous timing.

But whether cheap and cheerful or exotic and expensive, sports cars were a permanent part of the American scene by decade's end, no small achievement considering their higher cost and less practical nature versus mainstream machinery. Moreover, the ranks of sports-car fans were still growing. For them, the Fifties had been a great ride. The Sixties would be something else.

**1950** First German-built Porsche 356s delivered • First *Carrera Panamericana* (Mexican Road Race) staged • Briggs Cunningham's stock Cadillac finishes 10th at LeMans, his Cad-powered special 11th • First Sebring 12-Hour race • Alfa Romeo bows new 1900 series • Allard launches sports-racing J2 and roadgoing K2 • Aston Martin DB2 bows; critics applaud • Crosley adds $925 Super Sports, a Hot Shot with doors • Briggs Cunningham builds single roadgoing C-1 • Ferrari adds bigger-bore Tipo 195/212 series and big-block 340 America • MG replaces classic TC with more civilized TD roadster • Morgan drops 4/4, concentrates on larger Plus 4 • Anglo-American Nash-Healey annnounced • Prototype Nash-Healey takes 9th in Mille Miglia 4th at LeMans • SCCA Chicago Region starts racing around Elkhart Lake, Wis. • Sports-car racing begins in Pebble Beach, Cal. **1951** Ferdinand Porsche dies • Nash-Healey starts U.S. sale at $4063 • New Cunningham C-2Rs don't impress at LeMans; Nash-Healey takes 3rd in class, 6th overall; Jaguar wins outright • Chrysler hemi-head V8 introduced • Ferrari releases 342 America, an improved 340 • Maserati opens new chapter with A6G series • Porsche adds 1300 engine as option over basic 1100 **1952** Triumph previews its future with prototype 20TS (TR1) • Allard offers updated K3 for the road, hairy J2X for the track • Mercedes 300SL prototype wins *Carrera Panamericana* and LeMans 24 Hours • Nash-Healey gets Italian style, higher price; finishes 3rd at LeMans

**Above:** Alfa Romeo got back to health starting in 1950 with the four-cylinder 1900-series of sedans and sports cars and could soon afford to go racing again. One early result was the *Disco Volante* ("flying saucer"), an aerodynamic body design used on nine competition Alfas built in 1952-53: five coupes like this, plus four topless spiders. Though the styling helped liven up Alfa's image as intended, the cars' only track triumphs were second overall in the '52 Mille Miglia and first in the 1953 *Supercortemaggiore* road races. Legendary driver Juan Manuel Fangio did the honors on both occasions. **Right and below:** Sydney Allard returned to his roots with the 1950-51 J2 and, pictured here, the J2X of 1952-54. Both were designed as racing cars that could be used on the road if need be. The X boasted an improved front suspension requiring an extended frame, hence the suffix letter, plus an outside, instead of concealed, spare tire. Allard still favored Ford/Mercury flathead V8s, but also listed potent new overhead-valve engines from Cadillac and Chrysler. Suitably powered, these Allards were popular low-buck rides for period American road racers and were always a threat, though difficult to drive. But rivals soon surpassed the low-tech J2 and J2X, so Allard gave up after turning out just 90 and 83, respectively.

" Not much space inside for a car this monstrous, but the view over that long, scooped and louvered hood makes you feel like a tank commander. Plus you have to be impressed with the engine-turned dash and the way the speedo is so far over it can't do much except terrify passengers. And they're most likely already on edge, seeing as how the Allard looks like a battering ram and sounds like heavy artillery. The weird split front axle and DeDion rear conspire to point the wheels in what appear to be four different directions, but the handling's better than you might think on smooth roads, and the brakes are gosh awful huge. They need to be. Matching the unstoppable grunt of a big-inch V8 with the car's considerable heft means slowing can be a serious problem. It isn't that Allard brakes are bad—they just have more to do than anybody else's brakes. But get that sucker hauled down, arm-wrestle it through a corner, and get it pointed approximately straight again and you could let the horsepower stampede begin again. Not especially elegant or refined, but the J2X can sure gobble up pavement in a hurry! "

– Burt Levy
Oak Park, Illinois

• Porsche builds 20 race-ready "America" roadsters at the behest of U.S. retailer Max Hoffman • Designer Brooks Stevens begins racing his Excalibur J **1953** Chevrolet Corvette unveiled at GM Motorama • Chevy begins Corvette production • Ferrari announces small-engine 250 Europa and revised 375 America • Aston Martin replaces DB2 with improved DB2/4 • Austin-Healey 100 debuts in U.S. at $2985 POE • Race-bred Cunningham C-3 bows as $9000 coupe, $10-grand convertible • Excalibur J runs 1st in class, 3rd overall in U.S. Grand Prix • Jaguar again places first at LeMans • MG introduces sleeker, modernized TF roadster • Triumph begins building 100-mph TR2 based on "TR1" prototype • Last year for original Mexican Road Race • Road America circuit opens at Elkhart Lake, Wis. **1954** Ford announces 2-seat Thunderbird for '55 • Mercedes launches production 300SL with mechanical fuel injection • Ferrari scores first LeMans win in 5 years • Facel Vega bows as plush Franco-American GT • Porsche debuts 356 Speedster, another Max Hoffman idea • Britain's tiny AC delivers first Ace roadsters • Alfa Romeo Giulietta series arrives • Anglo-Italo-American Arnolt-Bristol introduced • Chevrolet wows with three Corvette dream cars • DeSoto shows Italian-bodied Adventurer "idea car" • Ferrari begins long-lived 250 series with 250GT Europa • Jaguar XK120 morphs into faster, roomier XK140 • Fiberglass-bodied Kaiser-Darrin starts one-year run • Maserati issues A6G/2000, the

**Above and left:** Replacing the K1 as Allard's touring sports car was the 1950-52 K2, with smoother lines, a few more cockpit amenities, and twin front coil springs instead of a crosswise leaf. Four Ford-based V8s were offered, including a 239 with "Ardun" overhead-valve heads and 140 horsepower. But the engines, like the car, were British-built, and some parts didn't interchange with counterpart U.S. engines. No matter. With only 119 built, K2s were rare on both sides of the Atlantic. **Below:** The replacement K3 bowed in 1952 aimed at American tastes, with an all-new chassis, modern slab-sided styling and a choice of four engines, including Chrysler's hemi-head V8 and Jaguar's XK twincam six. But Allard was still short of money and resources, so workmanship and some detail features weren't in line with the stiff $5300 price. As a result, production was halted in October 1954 after just 61 units. A smaller follow-up, the Palm Beach, sold just 73 copies through 1959.

**Right:** Britain's tiny Aston Martin and Lagonda got a new lease on life when industrialist David Brown took control in 1947. Soon, the firm was advertising a new Lagonda sedan and cabriolet with a 2.6-liter six-cylinder engine designed earlier by the famed W.O. Bentley and a new Aston DB1 with aluminum bodywork and a 90-bhp 2.0-liter four. Most DB1s were four-seat Tourer convertibles, but only 15 were built; the lightweight two-seater Sports shown here would be one-of-a-kind. **Above:** Seeking to bolster his "bit of fun" business, Brown put the Lagonda engine in the DB1's strong multi-tube chassis to create a truly sporting two-seat Aston, the DB2. It bowed in 1950 with convertible and coupe models, 105 bhp, four-speed gearbox, and well-appointed cockpit. A 125-hp Vantage engine was added later and became standard for the improved DB2/4 of 1953, which added cramped "+2" rear seating within the same trim 99-inch wheelbase. Mark II models arrived in 1954 with a 140-bhp 3.0-liter six. By Aston standards, this line was a big success, with 410 DB2s and 765 DB2/4s built through 1957.

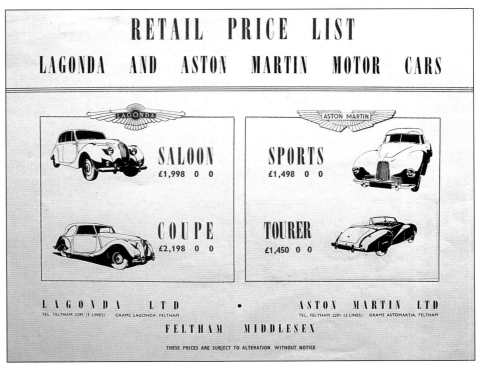

RETAIL PRICE LIST

LAGONDA AND ASTON MARTIN MOTOR CARS

| LAGONDA | ASTON MARTIN |
|---|---|
| SALOON £1,998 0 0 | SPORTS £1,498 0 0 |
| COUPE £2,198 0 0 | TOURER £1,450 0 0 |

LAGONDA LTD
TEL. FELTHAM 2291 (3 LINES)   GRAMS LAGONDA, FELTHAM

ASTON MARTIN LTD
TEL. FELTHAM 2291 (3 LINES)   GRAMS ASTOMARTIA, FELTHAM

FELTHAM MIDDLESEX

THESE PRICES ARE SUBJECT TO ALTERATION WITHOUT NOTICE

first twincam "Maser" • MG TF 1500 bows with more power for a short run • Packard shows one-off Panther, another Detroit-style "sports car" • Porsche builds 5000th car, offers six engine choices • Triumph TR2 starts U.S. sale at $2499 POE **1955** Fiery crash at LeMans kills over 80 spectators and driver Pierre Levegh • TR3 premieres as improved Triumph sports car • Britain's AC adds Aceca coupe based on Ace roadster • Chevy debuts new small-block V8, soon a performance legend • Chrysler answers T-Bird with sporty Falcon show car • Briggs Cunningham runs afoul of IRS rules, ceases building his C-3 • Hudson offers 2-seat Italia coupe, builds just 26 units • Mercedes-Benz 190SL introduced • All-new MGA marks complete break from classic T-Series • Morgan 4/4 returns as lower-power Plus 4 • U.S.-bound '55 Porsches get *Continental* nameplates **1956** New big-engine Ferrari bows as 410 Superamerica; sleek "Superfast" soon follows • Jaguar scores second straight LeMans victory • Austin-Healey 100 grows up to become new 100 Six • Chevy Corvette redesigned • Porsche offers fully redesigned 356A series, first twincam Carrera engines • Sweden's Saab builds half a dozen fiberglass-bodied Sonnet roadsters • Sweden's Volvo builds a handful of fiberglass-bodied P1900 convertibles • Last sports-car race at Pebble Beach **1957** Jaguar factory fire ends D-Type, XK-SS race cars • Aston Martin unveils DB Mark III • Jaguar claims its last LeMans win until 1988 • More powerful AC Ace-Bristol and

**Above:** Ferrari greatly expanded its touring sports car lineup starting in 1950 with the Tipo 195 featuring a newly enlarged, 2.3-liter V12 with 130-180 bhp. In 1951 came Tipo 212 models with a 2.6-liter version and 130-170 horsepower. Both model groups offered Inter engines with single twin-barrel carburetor and Sport and Export versions with two three-barrel carbs. The tube-steel chassis and five-speed gearbox from the earlier Tipo 166 was shared across the board, but Ferrari offered three wheelbases for custom convertible and berlinetta coupe bodies crafted by Italy's best *carrozzeria*. This 212 Export berlinetta from 1952 features Vignale coachwork designed by Giovanni Michelotti for the intermediate 88.6-inch chassis. **Below:** Prepping for a weekend sports-car race in the Fifties often meant little more than taping up the headlights, painting on some numbers, and maybe adding a rollover bar and seatbelts. This late-decade snapshot captures two smiling gents between a period MGA (left) and an A.C. Ace or Ace-Bristol.

**Above, right, below right:** Looking much like the TC it replaced in 1949, the MG TD roadster sat four inches lower on 15-inch steel wheels versus 19-inch wires. It was slightly wider and roomier too. Ride and handling improved via softer rear springs and first-time independent front suspension with coil springs and double wishbones. The TC's 1250-cc four and four-speed gearbox carried on unchanged, but MG soon offered tuning kits that might boost power from the stock 54 to near 60. Unlike the TC, the TD was built with left-hand drive in deference to the lucrative U.S. market, where it proved even more popular than the TC. Of the nearly 30,000 built through 1953, some 24,500 landed in U.S. driveways. **Below:** MGs were early favorites among American sports-car buffs who liked to go racing on weekends. Here, a group of MGs leads the field as the green flag falls at Elkhart Lake, Wisconsin, where the Chicago Region of the Sports Car Club of America began staging regular events on a road course in 1950.

Aceca-Bristol introduced • AC, Aston, Triumph, Jaguar's new XK150 all offer front-disc brakes • Chevrolet adds optional "Ramjet" fuel injection • Maserati issues 3500GT with big new race-bred engine • Mercedes unwraps 300SL convertible to replace Gullwing coupe • Bridgehampton and Lime Rock circuits open in Con. • Riverside and Laguna Seca road courses open in Cal. **1958** Jaguar adds more-potent XK150S • Olivier Gendebien and American Phil Hill win another LeMans for Ferrari • Porsche Speedster D replaces original spartan Speedster • Aston Martin issues all-new DB4 • Alfa Romeo 2000 replaces 1900 series • Spartan Austin-Healey "bugeye" Sprite bows at $1500 • Chevrolet Corvette becomes bigger, heavier, brighter • Ford replaces 2-seat Thunderbird with luxury 4-seater • Livelier MGA Twin Cam arrives • Triumph introduces restyled TR3A • USAC sanctions first sports-car race at Riverside, Cal. **1959** Britain's Daimler unveils V8 SP250 roadster • American Carroll Shelby, co-driver Roy Salvadori win LeMans for Aston Martin • Facellia debuts as smaller, semi-sporting Facel Vega • Short-wheelbase Ferrari 250 announced • Aston Martin powers up with new DB4GT • Improved Austin-Healey 3000 replaces 100 Six • Restyled, higher-power Facel Vega HK500 bows • Fiat bows first "real" sports cars with 1200 & 1500S Cabriolets • Lotus of England takes to the road with flawed, fascinating Elite • Britain's Sunbeam launches Alpine to challenge MGA, TR3 • Daytona International Speedway opens

Most Americans didn't think much about safety features in the Fifties, but sports-car buyers were probably among the first to recognize the value of seatbelts and to actually use them. After all, it's hard to pilot a low-slung roadster should a bad bump (or worse) bounce you out onto the road. This period ad for accessory Saf-Tee Belts seems aimed at sports-car enthusiasts. The lady in the picture is clearly in a dashing convertible with cutaway doors, and the text evokes sports-car thoughts by saying the belts fit "bucket type seats" with a design that "permits you to 'ride' with car on curves." Note, too, that Ray Brown Automotive was located in Los Angeles, the traditional hotbed of U.S. automotive trends, and that it also did business in "racing engines, parts and equipment." Call this an early attempt to make seatbelts seem sexy and "smart looking" as well as a safety plus.

**Above and right:** The Porsche 356 improved steadily after its 1950 debut. Soon, the little air-cooled rear-engine coupes and cabriolets were known worldwide as well built and very reliable. Performance also improved steadily, as the original 1100cc air-cooled flat-four was enlarged to 1300, then 1500cc; the last two came in Normal and uprated Super versions. Only the 1500 engines were sold in America, where 1955 models like this cabrio wore "Continental" fender script, the only 356s so named. By this point, the 356 shared hardly anything with its VW Beetle parent apart from mechanical layout. **Below:** A thoroughly revised 356A series bowed in 1956 with subtly revised styling, greater cockpit comfort, improved handling, and more power. A sleek Speedster convertible, introduced just before the changeover, continued as the "racer's choice" due to its lower weight. Serious competitors ordered it in new 1500 Carrera trim, with a detuned version of the engine that took Porsche to class victories in the 1953-54 Mexican Road Races. Shown in action here is a Speedster D, which replaced the original Speedster for 1959 sporting a taller, chrome-framed windshield.

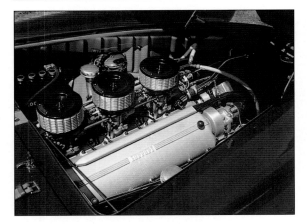

In 1950, engineer Aurelio Lampredi designed a big new 4.1-liter V12 for competition Ferraris, including four named 340 Mexico after Ferrari's 1-2 win in the 1951 Mexican Road Race. Three of these cars were berlinettas like this Vignale-bodied exercise; the fourth was a roadster. The Lampredi V12 was detuned for road use in 1952, when it was coupled with a revised chassis for Ferrari's first "deluxe" touring cars, named 342 America. The following year brought a replacement 375 America with power boosted from 200 to 300. All these early Ferraris are highly prized rarites.

" Driving a Ferrari gave you an edge that even lack of talent couldn't always overcome. And, if you were any good at all… The 340 was Ferrari's .45 magnum: a piece with the firepower to outgun anything on the road, and yet delivered with a caress instead of a kick. That's what the big V12 gave you: huge, seamless power you could dial up like a rheostat. And the driveline was stout enough to take it. The rest of the car—in typical Ferrari fashion—was just a sturdy, ordinary, but wonderfully built cart to carry it around. And that was the other part of the Ferrari magic: the toughness. There were other cars that were lighter or more nimble or handled better, but nothing else would accelerate like a cannonball down the straightaways and keep it up—hardly breaking a sweat—for 24 hours at Le Mans or the grueling 2500 miles of La Carrera Panamericana from one end of Mexico to the other. "

— **Burt Levy**
Oak Park, Illinois

Everyone needs to sell a car sooner or later, even Phil Hill, who became America's only world-championship racing driver in 1961. We're not sure of precisely when he ran this informative ad, but there's no doubting the claimed performance of his Ferrari 212 Export barchetta roadster. Like sister models and Tipo 195s, it sold new for about $9500, making the price here seem reasonable given the illustrious owner. But considering that early Ferraris like this now fetch high six-figure sums, we can't help wondering if Phil regretted letting go of his historic "little boat."

## LUIGI CHINETTI
### Are you worthy?

As Luigi Chinetti liked to tell it, Enzo Ferrari was headed for the machine-tool business until Luigi himself convinced Enzo to build automobiles. That's not exactly Enzo's account. But according to Chinetti, it was in Ferrari's threadbare office in the cold Italian winter of 1946 that he urged his friend to build cars for sale in America, where Chinetti lived. "If you order five, I will," retorted Enzo. Although he had little means to pay for the cars, Chinetti mentally surveyed his social circle in the U.S. and promptly ordered 20. That was how Ferrari came to its largest worldwide market and, by implication, got launched as a viable sports-car enterprise.

Faithful to the truth or not, the tale is revealing on two fronts. Corporate Ferrari did indeed have some lean, indecisive early days. And it shows the chutzpa of one Luigi Chinetti (ki-NET-ti), a figure of legendary self-assurance whose documented achievements make credible any number of stories about him.

Born in 1901, the Milan native raced for Alfa Romeo in the 1930s, where he became close with fellow-driver-and-later team-captain, Enzo Ferrari. Short, broad-chested, with piercing brown eyes, Chinetti was an intense driver who won LeMans for Alfa in 1932 and, after stopping a fuel leak with chewing gum, again in 1934. He fled Fascist Italy in 1940, worked as a Rolls-Royce mechanic in New York, and became a U.S. citizen in 1946. He returned to Europe, renewed contact with Enzo, and in 1948, delivered to Briggs Cunningham the first Ferrari in America. Even more important to Ferrari's fortunes, Chinetti revived his competition career at the wheel of Enzo's earliest racing cars, highlighted by a 1949 LeMans victory in which Luigi drove 23 ½ hours. It was Ferrari's first win at Sarthe.

That put the prancing horse on the map, and Chinetti, too. Soon after, he opened the first Ferrari dealership in North America. His Ferrari sales operations, first in Manhattan, later in Greenwich, Con., helped set the tone for how Americans would regard the eccentric, passionate world of costly European exotics. The New York spaces were noisy, cramped, mostly in poorly marked, out-of-the-way buildings.

Awed by the Ferrari mystique, Pilgrims would vie for Chinetti's attention as gesticulating, oil-stained mechanics revved and prodded the 12-cylinder objects of desire. The impression was that Chinetti would decide whether you were worthy of Ferrari ownership.

Who could question his right? This, afterall, was an Enzo confidant, a man who at 43, co-drove a Ferrari to victory in the 1951 *Carrera Panamericana*, then formed the North American Racing Team that took Ferrari to a succession of additional international wins, including LeMans in 1965. His judgment of character and talent was as impressive. A partial roster of racers he helped to get started includes Marquis de Portago, Dan Gurney, Richie Ginther, Phil Hill, and Pedro and Recardo Rodriguez.

Made wealthy as Ferrari's principal U.S. importer and distributor, Chinetti retired in 1977. He died at home in Greenwich in 1994. In a 1962 *Automobile Quarterly* profile, Warren Weith concluded, "In the drifting, directionless society in which we live, there is a need for more men like Luigi Chinetti—no matter how many ulcers in others they may produce."

**Above:** After a pair of near-stock XK120s finished the 1950 LeMans 24 Hours, Jaguar boss William Lyons okayed an all-out XK-based racer, the XK120C. **Below:** The C-Type fast proved its mettle by winning LeMans 1951—and setting a new speed record for the French classic.

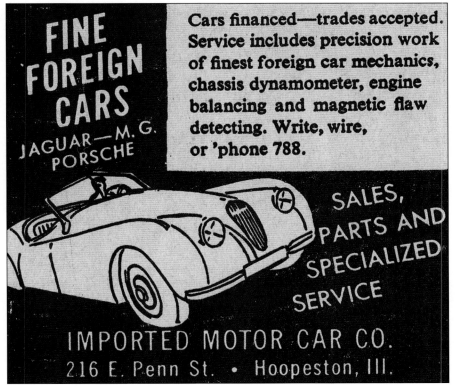

**Top:** The Jaguar C-Type used a modified XK-120 powertrain in a special multi-tube "space-frame" chassis—quite advanced for the early 1950s. So, too, the disc brakes that replaced drums for the 1952-53 campaigns. The aluminum body was shaped by aerodynamicist Malcolm Sayer and proved reasonably slippery. With a nominal 204 gross horsepower, the svelte C-Type clocked eight seconds 0-60 mph and just over 140 mph tops in a British magazine test, great going for the day. Jaguar bowed to Mercedes at LeMans '52, but triumphed again in 1953, after which the C-Type ended its factory racing career. Exactly 54 were built, some originally sold to private parties. **Above:** But those cars and various factory escapees have been racing ever since, first in late-decade amateur contests, as in this photo, more recently in vintage or "historic" events. Note the small racing windscreen here. Some C-Types got full-width screens for use on the road, where they proved surprisingly easy to drive. **Right:** Import-car demand in Fifties America was usually strongest in larger cities on the East and West Coasts, but dealers in smaller towns could make decent money by carrying several brands. The multi-franchise Illinois dealer placing this ad stressed "specialized service," then a frequent necessity with marques like Jaguar.

Lancia was all but unknown in Fifties America. No wonder. The innovative Italian automaker had been out of the U.S. market since the 1920s. But World War II devastation bred postwar determination, and Lancia returned in 1956 seeking valuable U.S. dollars with the handsome B24 Aurelia Spyder, notable for its pioneering V6 engine. But that two-seater saw only 650 copies, of which just 86 were built for U.S. sale. At the same time, however, Lancia introduced a quintet of sporty two-doors based on its mainstream Appia sedan with V4 power, a Lancia speciality since the Thirties. The Series II Appia 1089cc engine was tuned up to 53 horsepower for the clean Pinin Farina-styled coupe shown here, a Vignale cabriolet, a Viotti coupe, and two coupe styles by Zagato. All were 2+2s with modest acceleration but fine handling, though they were arguably more tourer than pure sports car. Bodies were built by the various *carrozzeria*, so workmanship was spotty. Few of these Appias were exported, and they were rare even in Italy, with just 1755 built, plus another 408 Series III models built from mid-1959 to 1963.

**Above:** The Lancia Aurelia B20 GT coupe bowed in 1951 as a sporty companion to the Italian marque's year-old senior sedan. The Aurelia line introduced Lancia's first V6, a smooth, advanced 2.0-liter with hemispherical combustion chambers. Horsepower was 75 at first, but subsequent tuning followed by substitution of a 2.5-liter engine in 1953 eventually lifted output to about 120. Also featured were unitized construction, elegant styling by the house of Pinin Farina, a costly but effective sliding-pillar front suspension, and a four-speed gearbox in unit with the rear differential (transaxle). Despite the GT tag, the B20 was a true race-and-ride sports car. Sales had barely begun when a near-stock model finished second to a Ferrari in the 1951 Mille Miglia road race, a feat noticed by enthusiasts, even in America. Full factory-prepped race cars, like the one shown here, went to LeMans in 1952 and scored 1-2 in class and 6th and 8th overall. That same year, the B20 won the long, gruelling Targa Florio and came 3rd and 5th in the Mille Miglia. This was also a stellar rally car, winning Liege-Rome-Liege in '53 and the fabled Monte Carlo in 1954. B20 production ended two years later at about 3800 units spread over six "series" variations. **Right:** After a shaky start in the late Forties, *Road and Track* established a secure niche as one of the few U.S. car magazines offering in-depth coverage of import models. Sports cars got special emphasis from the start, as suggested by this August 1951 cover featuring an MG TD and Jaguar XK120 alongside a comparatively sedate French Talbot. The tagline at the bottom wasn't just boasting. As some of this book's authors can personally attest, *R&T* was the bible for American sports-car lovers of the day, and it still serves them well more than 50 years later.

ROAD and TRACK

35c

AUGUST, 1951

MG      JAGUAR XK-120      TALBOT

PHOTO BY JACK CAMPBELL

*The Motor Enthusiasts' Magazine*

Maserati issued a more ambitious roadgoing sports car in 1951, the A6G, available with a variety of coachbuilt coupe and convertible bodies. A new 2.0-liter overhead-cam inline six sat in the basic chassis of the superseded A6/1500 series but delivered 100 bhp instead of 65. But that was no match for Ferrari in European formula racing, so Maserati substituted a twincam version with 150 horsepower for revised 1954 models dubbed A6G/2000. This engine was originally developed for racing, debuting in 1947. The cars it first powered, designated A6GS, were trim single-seat affairs with cycle-wing fenders. A two-seat "flared wing" version was also developed for sports-car contests, with body design by Gugliemo Carraoli. Completed in 1952, it was basically a prototype and the only one of its kind. It survives today as shown here. An improved "Series II" A6GS with modern slab-sided styling appeared in 1954.

Though not a true sports car, the Muntz Jet was descended from one: the Kurtis Sport. In the early Fifties, Earl "Madman" Muntz, the fast-talking Los Angeles radio and TV merchant who'd lately entered the car business, thought Americans would go for a sporty four-seater with luxury trim and gadgets. Investing $200,000, he bought rights to the Kurtis Sport design, stretched it to a 113-inch wheelbase, and dropped in Cadillac's new 160-horsepower overhead-valve 331 V8. Bodies were still made of aluminum, and Muntz claimed a brisk nine seconds 0-60 mph for his larger, heavier car. Features included a Muntz radio in a predictive center console and a removable hard top as well as a folding cloth roof. But sales proved difficult, so Muntz moved assembly from L.A. to suburban Chicago, switched to steel bodies with a three-inch-longer wheelbase, and used cheaper L-head Lincoln V8s. It didn't help, and the Jet vanished in 1954 after four years and just 394 units. Muntz admitted he lost $1000 on each one, so perhaps he really was "ca-raaaa-zy" after all.

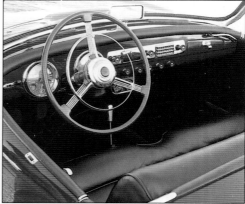

**Left:** The result of a chance encounter between Englishman Donald Healey and Nash Motors chief George Mason, the Nash-Healey bowed in 1951 as a well-appointed British-built roadster with a big American six. It impressed critics and in races like LeMans, but a steep $4100 price held sales to just 104. **Above:** The '52 edition stood to be more popular with a larger, more potent engine and new styling shaped with help from Italy's Pinin Farina, but only 150 were sold as price jumped to $5900. Sales inched up to 162 for '53, when a LeMans coupe was added in honor of continuing success in the 24-hour French classic. **Opposite page:** Only the coupe returned for '54, with price reduced some $1300 to $5100. But Nash was floundering by then and Healey had moved on to a new Austin-based sports car, so the Nash-Healey disappeared after a final 90 units. At least Nash ventured a genuine sports car at a time when most U.S. automakers couldn't see the point.

## DONALD HEALEY
### Made the Mundane Great

In his teens Donald Healey went from being an engineering apprentice at Sopwith Aviation to flying Sopwiths in World War I. Healey battled Zepplins over England, then flew bombers in France until he was shot down and injured. After the war he opened an auto-repair garage in his native Cornwall. He later took up rallying, becoming the first Englishman to win the Monte Carlo Rally. Healey's Rally success lead to a position with Triumph as director of experimental design. A fellow Triumph engineer said of Healey: "He was a great enthusiast. He had the personality to get the best out of a very good engineering team."

At the outbreak of World War II the military decided Healey was too old and too valuable for active duty, so he was charged with design work on planes and armored cars. After the war Healey built the first automobile bearing his name. Healey had wanted to stuff a Cadillac V8 in his new car, but Cadillac was unwilling to part with any of its precious post-war production. However, a chance meeting with George Mason of Nash proved more productive. The two car guys hit

it off immediately, (Healey seems to have been good friends with half the auto industry) and a deal was struck for Healey to build a Nash powered sports car. The Nash-Healey did well at LeMans and helped build Nash showroom traffic but proved too costly for long term sales success.

Healey's next project pirated components from the unexceptional Austin sedan to create a sports car priced between MG and Jaguar. The heads of Austin saw the Healey 100 at the 1952 London Motor Show and wanted to build it themselves. Healey was invited for drinks and in his words "...after too many dry martinis we shook hands. There was never any other agreement between us." The Austin-Healey was born.

Healey again used his gift for using mundane components as the basis for sports cars in 1958, creating the Austin-Healey Sprite. Much smaller than the "big" Healeys, it was a favorite of its creator because it made sports car ownership possible at a lower price.

Though occupied with building cars, Healey found time to set international speed records at Bonneville during the '50s.

In retirement, Donald Healey was a popular and gracious guest at Austin Healey events until his death in 1988 at the age of 89.

**Left and above:** L.A. sports-car dealer Bill Devin sold racy bolt-on fiberglass bodies starting in 1952. His novel modular molding system allowed varying dimensions of one basic design to fit a number of period stock chassis. This sports/racer uses a Crosley chassis and dates from 1956, four years after the final Crosleys were built. **Below left and bottom:** Designer and amateur racer Brooks Stevens took the hot rod-der-style "backyard" approach to building a sports car, but his Excalibur Js were thoroughly professional efforts. In the early Fifties, Stevens was a consultant to Kaiser-Frazer and thought its Henry J compact a good starting point for a low-cost race-and-ride machine. Stevens fortified the chassis and brakes and replaced the Henry J's weak four-cylinder engine with a 161-cubic-inch Willys six tuned up to 125 horsepower. Stevens built three Excalibur Js in 1952 and raced them for two years, racking up nine firsts, seven seconds, and four thirds in the SCCA's D-Modified class. One of those class wins came at the 1953 U.S. Grand Prix, where a Stevens car finished third overall. Though K-F said no to a showroom Excalibur J, Stevens kept modifying and racing the cars through 1958. One was outfitted with a supercharged Jaguar six and took the B-Modified class at the Elkhart 500 to win the national class championship.

**Top:** After selling his Kurtis Sport design to "Madman" Muntz, Frank Kurtis decided to one-up the Allard J2X with his own sports/racer, the 500-S. Announced in 1953, it was named for the Indy 500 won by Kurtis-built racers in 1950-51 and again in 1953-55. In fact, the 500-S was basically Frank's race car with a wider tube frame, two-seat body, and enough road equipment to be street-legal. It sold for about $4600 without engine; most buyers seem to have opted for potent Cadillac and Chrysler V8s. A kit version was available as the 500-K. Only about 20 turnkey 500s were built. Either way, these cars won a pile of races for local Southern California hotshoes.
**Above and right:** A "SoCal" contemporary of the Kurtis 500, the Woodill Wildfire was also sold as a kit and fully built for anywhere from $2000 to $4500. With its trim fiberglass body, the Wildfire weighed just 1500 pounds with "stock" six-cylinder Willys engine and could really fly. Many, like this Ford V8 powered example, were turned into effective weekend racers.

**Above:** Like the Nash-Healey, the Arnolt-MG was a British car with Italian style and a U.S. backer. Coachbuilder Nuccio Bertone showed an MG-based coupe and convertible at the 1952 Turin Auto Show as attention-getters for his then-ailing business. Attention he got from Chicago car dealer Stanley H. "Wacky" Arnolt, who astonished Bertone by ordering 100 of each. The chassis, basically that of the contemporary TD roadster, was shipped from England to Turin for body installation and final assembly. Bertone sent finished cars to Wacky's showroom. All that travel made for a stiff price, but Arnolt-MGs sold well, mostly in 1953-54. **Below:** Arguably one of the prettiest Fifties sports cars, the Siata 208S was certainly unexpected from a tiny Italian concern founded in 1926 to make hop-up parts for various Fiats. No less surprising was its 2.0-liter V8, a Fiat cast-off but very capable. A small engine supply limited production of this model to just 35 units, all built in 1952-53.

The 208S came about simply because Siata was able to buy 56 V8 powerteams from Fiat, which had built another 114 for its own short-lived sports car, the *Otto Vu* ("8V") coupe. But where the Fiat was ungainly, the 208S Spider was handsome. The design is now generally attributed to Giovanni Michelotti, who would earn wide fame in the 1960s with his work for Britain's Triumph. Siata also built a handful of 208S coupes. As might be expected of an Italian sports car, the Spider was all business. A trim 90-inch wheelbase and an alloy body with no cockpit frills held weight to just under a ton, so performance was brisk despite the engine's modest 105 horsepower. The strong chassis featured rigid box-section members and a highly advanced all-independent suspension with coil springs and double wishbones at each corner. Forecasting later race-car design, each spring operated by a rocker arm from the upper suspension wishbone. Another forward-thinking feature was aluminum drum brakes, which cooled faster and were thus more fade-resistant than conventional cast-iron brakes. For a time, the 208S was a Tinseltown status symbol, partly because you had to be a star or a studio mogul to go the $5300 price, which was then top-end Cadillac money. Even so, the cars were raced quite often and successfully. We suspect Chrysler's Virgil Exner was thinking of this Siata when he penned the Falcon "idea car" of 1955, which was very similar in its proportions, rear fenderlines, and in using a large, square grille.

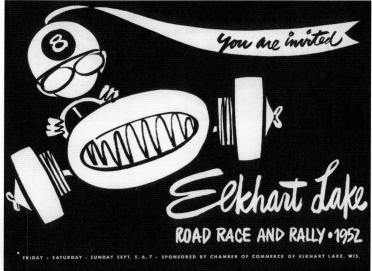

Official
**PROGRAM
50¢**
SEPTEMBER 6·7·1952

**Left and above:** These images from 1952 Elkhart Lake publications remind us how simply drivers dressed in those days and that sports-car racing was then starting to draw enough spectators to be a serious business. **Below:** Woody Woodill devised his Wildfire as a cheaper, more reliable alternative to the Jaguar XK120 he'd planned on buying. He later tried to persuade Willys and Kaiser-Frazer to build it for volume sale, but both companies passed. The Wildfire combined a fiberglass body, designed and first marketed by boat-builder Glasspar, with a special chassis dreamed up by ace hot rodder "Shorty" Post. Suspension and powertrain came from the contemporary Aero-Willys compact, but owners and Woody himself ad-libbed all sorts of modifications, fitting for a car sold mainly as a kit. Also, the basic design saw several changes from the 1952 debut to the end of "production" four years later. Among these was going from a two-piece flat-pane windshield to a single curved affair. Wildfires didn't come with a top or side curtains—after all, sunny Southern California was the target market—but some owners later rigged up their own. Wildfires starred in several period Hollywood movies, including the racing-themed *Johnny Dark*.

Inspired by a prototype sports car called Tojeiro, the Ace bowed in 1953 as the best thing in years from Britain's staid AC Cars. An elderly but able 2.0-liter overhead-cam six could take the 1685-pound roadster up to the magic 100-mph mark. Fine handling was provided by a stout tubular ladder-type chassis with a trim 90-inch wheelbase and 4-wheel independent suspension. The Ace fast rejuvenated AC's fortunes, enough for a companion coupe, the Aceca, to be added in late 1954. Today, the Ace is known around the world as the starting point for Carroll Shelby's awesome 1960s Cobras.

## ZORA ARKUS-DUNTOV
### The Father of the Corvette

Zora Arkus-Duntov did not invent the Corvette, but he will forever be known as its father. His passion and expertise helped transform Chevrolet's glamorous but mechanically deficient niche vehicle into a world-class sports car. By the time he joined General Motors, Zora had already lived a remarkable life. He witnessed the Russian Revolution in 1917, served in the French air force, narrowly escaped Nazi-occupied France just before WWII, developed his own overhead valve conversion for the Ford flathead V8, and raced at Indianapolis and LeMans all before he ever laid eyes on the first Corvette. When he saw it along with the rest of the world at the 1953 GM Motorama in New York City, he was smitten.

Duntov had already been exploring employment with several U.S. automakers, but the lure of working on the Corvette helped push GM to the top of his list. Starting at Chevrolet in May 1953 as an assistant staff engineer, he soon established himself as an in-house authority on sports cars and high performance. Throughout his two decades at Chevrolet, Duntov strove to keep Corvette at the forefront of technology and competition as America's only true sports car—other considerations be damned. When GM execs were preparing to kill the Corvette in 1954, Duntov fought to save it. Later, under his hands-on guidance, production Corvettes got cutting-edge technology like fuel injection, disc brakes, and independent rear suspension.

Zora couldn't have been more different from his GM colleagues. Born in Belgium in 1909 to Russian parents, he had lived in St. Petersburg, Berlin, Paris, New York, and London before moving to Detroit. English was his fourth language. He enjoyed tobacco, fine alcohol, and beautiful women and indulged in them frequently. His maverick nature was immediately jarring to many in the insular GM culture, where quiet subordination was usually the quickest way to advance. Zora was thrilled to have access to the vast resources of a huge corporation like GM but perpetually aggravated by its starchy bureaucracy. GM management frowned on Duntov's swashbuckling ways but recognized the value of his undeniable talents. The relationship was always volatile, but Duntov's single-minded conviction was never in question.

He worked for several weeks in the summer of 1956 in a body cast after breaking his back in a 'Vette testing accident. With clandestine projects like the Corvette Grand Sport, he defied GM's adherence to the Automobile Manufacturers Association ban on factory participation in racing. He butted heads famously with Bill Mitchell over the GM styling chief's insistence on the 1963 Sting Ray's split rear window. (Zora got his way in '64.) He never gave up his fervent lobbying for a mid-engined production Corvette that was never to be. Even after his mandatory retirement in late 1974, he remained devoted to the Corvette and took a great personal stock in its continuing development. He craved the spotlight and, in his later years, enjoyed basking in the admiration of countless 'Vette enthusiasts at public events. Zora Arkus-Duntov died April 21, 1996, at the age of 86. Fittingly, his cremated ashes reside in the National Corvette Museum.

**Left:** The brainchild of General Motors design chief Harley Earl, the Chevrolet Corvette bowed in January 1953 as a GM Motorama "dream car," then entered production in June as a result of enthusiastic consumer response. A novel fiberglass body sat atop a unique frame with a 102-inch wheelbase *a la* the Jaguar XK120, an Earl favorite. But the engine was a pedestrian Chevy six, albeit tuned up to 150 horsepower, and coupled only with Powerglide automatic. Sports-car purists sneered at that, as well as "Detroit" styling features like the wraparound windshield. Only 315 Corvettes were built for '53, all done in Polo White with Sportsman Red interiors. **Below and bottom:** Additional color combinations were added for '54, including black paint, and Chevy attended to workmanship glitches. But buyers evidently thought $3523 was too much to pay in light of the tepid performance and inconveniences like clip-in side curtains instead of roll-up windows. As a result, Corvette sales for the model year totaled just 3640 units, less than a third of what Chevy had planned. Worse, some 1500 cars were unsold at year's end. With that, GM brass were ready to axe Chevy's sports car.

**Top, upper left, and above:** News of Ford's "personal" two-seater, the Thunderbird, persuaded GM to keep the Corvette going for 1955, when Chevrolet's brilliant new 265-cubic-inch passenger-car V8 became an option. Coupled with a three-speed manual gearbox, another new extra that year, the V8 completely transformed the performance of Chevy's "plastic" sports car, weighing less than the old six but packing 30 percent more power. An exaggerated "V" in the Corvette front-fender script identified '55s so equipped—which was most of them. Despite that, and a price cut to $2799, model-year production was a mere 674, the lowest in Corvette history. **Left:** Though it looks like a period Ferrari, this car actually clothes a 1954 Corvette chassis with a custom body built by Ghia Aigle and designed by Giovanni Michelotti. It was built for the 1957 Geneva Auto Salon as a showcase for the coachbuilder, which was the Swiss branch of the famed Ghia works in Turin. Amazingly, the car recently turned up in Portgual and in excellent condition, its odometer showing only some 3800 kilometers, about 2356 miles.

Evolved from the Aston Martin DB2/4, the illogically named DB Mark III offered smoother looks and more power. It arrived in 1957 with 162 standard horsepower, 178 with optional twin exhaust and carburetors. Triple carbs and higher compression delivered 180/195 bhp in '58. Front disc brakes fast moved from optional to standard status, and electric overdrive as well as automatic transmission became available. Despite all the refining, the Mark III could be factory-ordered with special engine, close-ratio gearbox, heavy-duty suspension, and other equipment to be a competitive long-distance racer. Exactly 551 were built through 1959.

Likely prompted by his work with Nash, Donald Healey designed a sports-car proto-type around British Austin running gear for the 1952 London Motor Show. Leonard Lord, head of Austin-parent British Motor Corporation, liked it so much that he put it into production with a hard eye on the lucrative U.S. market. The Austin-Healey 100 lived up to its name with a genuine 100-mph top speed and looks to match. The engine, a 2.7-liter four with 90 horsepower, linked to a three-speed gearbox with electric overdrive on second and top; a four-speed unit, also with overdrive, was substituted in 1954 for an improved BN2 version (the original was BN1). That same year, Healey devised a lightweight racing model, the 132-bhp 100S (S for Sebring), but built only 50. A "deluxe" 100M followed, seeing 1159 copies. Overall, the Austin-Healey was a big success by British sports-car standards, offering Jaguar looks and performance for about $2100. Over 14,000 were sold through 1956.

" To stow away the hood (top), first release the securing hooks at each windscreen pillar. The hood will then spring away from the screen. Next undo the turn buttons and stud fasteners at the rear and side of the hood, and inside the door rear pillar, then pull the steel bar of the hood rear panel out of the two chrome clips on the boot top panel.

Bring the two main ribs of the hood frame together, folding the material inwards between them. Close the trellise frames at each side of the hood so that the front rail moves rearwards to meet the first rib. Again fold the material neatly between rail and rib. With the collapsed hood upright, ensure that the rear panel hangs straight down, then swing the whole assembly forward and downward to tuck away behind the seats.

Raising the hood is the exact reversal of this process. "

— Austin-Healy Owner's Handbook

Briggs Cunningham, scion of the Proctor & Gamble empire, was good at all sorts of sports, including racing. For the 1950 LeMans 24 Hours, he entered a mostly stock Cadillac and an odd Caddy-powered special dubbed "Le Monstre" by the French. The former finished 10th, the latter 11th. Cunningham then bankrolled a touring roadster, titled C-1, with a strong tubular chassis, 105-inch wheelbase, DeDion rear axle, and a potent 331 Chrysler hemi V8. Only one was built, but it set the stage for his next car, the C-2R shown here. Only three were built, all in race trim, though a road model had been planned. The C2-R was much like the C-1 underneath but wore a special body designed for high-speed racing. Briggs hoped to do better with them at LeMans but had to settle for 18th overall in the 1951 contest. Undaunted, Cunningham developed new cars for the French classic. The brutal-looking C-4RK coupe finished 4th in '52; C-4R roadsters ran 7th and 10th the following year and 3rd and 5th in 1954. Then came the horrific accident at LeMans 1955, and Briggs gave up on racing his own cars, though not racing itself—or LeMans.

Briggs Cunningham devised the touring C-3 mainly to qualify his race cars as "production"—and fend off scrutiny from the IRS. Only 27 were built in 1953-55: nine convertibles and 18 coupes. All used the basic C-2R chassis, Chrysler hemi V8, and handsome, well-appointed Vignale bodies designed by Giovanni Michelotti. Despite eye-popping $9000-$10,000 prices, demand for the C-3 exceeded Briggs' ability to supply.

# BRIGGS CUNNINGHAM
## Took Racing to the Streets

Not content to live the simple life, millionaire Briggs Cunningham restlessly sought challenges, pursuing new victories even in the wake of success. A car guy by choice, and competitor by nature, Cunningham not only owned, built, and raced cars but also promoted racing and found time to win the America's Cup as well.

By the time Briggs Swift Cunningham was born in 1907 his father had amassed wealth sufficient to guarantee the family's comfort in perpetuity. A financier who first invested in meatpacking, the senior Cunningham later helped fund a startup company founded by two gentlemen named Proctor and Gamble.

An avid driver, Cunningham was not content exploring the capabilities of existing automobiles and took to building makeshift racers. Running on private estate roads, Cunningham longed for the thrill of organized competition. Attracting a group of like-minded cronies, Cunningham founded the Automobile Racing Club of America (ARCA) in 1934 and actively promoted the sport. Cunningham never drove in these events however, honoring a request from his mother that he not engage in the dangerous activity.

Though not racing, Cunningham continued to build cars for the track. In 1940 his half-Buick-half-Mercedes creation, the "BuMerc" raced in what would be ARCA's last event before the war.

A licensed pilot, Cunningham served in the Civil Air Patrol during the war, monitoring the Atlantic coastal waters.

Following the war Cunningham found the competition he sought in the newly formed Sports Car Club of America (SCCA). Sanctioning street races in the New York town of Watkins Glen, the SCCA appealed to a broader audience than Cunningham's clubby and somewhat exclusive ARCA.

Freed by his mother's death, Cunningham was finally able to race the vehicles he had been building. Piloting his now infamous BuMerc, Cunningham placed second in his first SCCA event.

Now backing a complete team, Cunningham's efforts expanded to include assaults on Sebring and LeMans. Famous for fielding apparent underdogs, Cunningham became a popular target of the French press while at LeMans. Cunningham's 1950 entry, a nearly stock Cadillac, was dubbed the "Clumsy Puppy" by local newspapers. More egregious to the motoring press was Cunningham's 1951 entry: the Cadillac-powered "LeMonstre," featuring a decidedly ugly hand pounded body and an unapologetic American V8 rumble.

Not completely dedicated to racing activities, Cunningham managed to build a couple dozen street versions of his racers between 1953 and 1955. All the road cars featured Chrysler power and Italian bodywork.

The IRS would catch up to Cunningham by 1955, no longer allowing his racing-related costs to serve as business deductions. By that time however, Cunningham-built cars had performed impressively at LeMans, though failed to earn an outright victory.

With his driving career behind him, Cunningham took his love of cars to the street, acquiring the Northeast states distribution rights for Jaguar. Never having satisfactorily scratched his competitive itch, Cunningham made a few more attempts at LeMans, but now in Maseratis or Jaguars.

Cunningham continued to field and help finance teams, however. Running Jaguars and enjoying factory support, his team scored numerous successes, including an outright LeMans win in 1957, the same day Cunningham captained his personal yacht, the 12-meter *Columbia*, to an America's Cup victory.

Though hardly a rags-to-riches story, Briggs Cunningham was the consummate car guy. A self-challenger and restless tinkerer, Cunningham owned, built, and raced automobiles, all the while promoting motorsport at the amateur and professional level. Cunningham died July 2, 2003, only weeks after having been inducted into the Motorsports Hall of Fame.

*Briggs Cunningham, right*

**Above:** Replacing the MG TD in 1953, the TF was basically the same car with a nose and tail job, plus a new dashboard with gauges shaped like MG's familiar octagon badge. Contributing to the modernized look—which disturbed some purists at the time—were a more rakishly angled radiator, rear fuel tank and spare tire, plus headlamps moved out and down into the fender "catwalk" areas. Center-lock wire wheels returned at extra cost, something purists liked. Unfortunately for MG, the Triumph TR2 also arrived in 1953 offering better performance for the same money. MG responded during 1954 by enlarging the 1250cc four-cylinder to 1466cc for an updated model, the TF 1500. Small hoodside badges identified it, as shown here. **Left:** This early-Fifties ad suggests a practical gift idea for MG TD owners. Besides adding a "custom" touch, a metal tire cover made changing flats a bit less messy than leaving the tire exposed to the elements or using a canvas cover, which might get waterlogged in a downpour. The listed price seemed a bargain, even if painting was necessarily left up to owners.

**Above and right:** This view of the 1955 MG TF 1500 pictured opposite gives no clue that the cowl and cockpit were the same as on the TD. The 1500 engine boasted 17 percent more torque than the 1250 unit it replaced but made only six more horsepower—63 in all—and there was no getting around the car's poor aerodynamics. As a result, any TF drove much like any TD, and a 1500 might reach 85 mph versus 80 for a 1250 TF. The big improvement came in 0-60 mph acceleration, which dropped from near 19 seconds for the TF to about 16.5 for the 1500.

**Below:** After building two race-and-ride convertibles in 1951-52, San Francisco industrialist Sterling Edwards considered selling a road car but ended up building just two convertibles and three hardtop coupes. Like the sports/racers, all had fiberglass bodies with the European look Edwards admired. Mechanical components and body hardware were taken from a variety of American cars. This convertible used the 100-inch-wheelbase Henry J chassis, but other Edwards were built on 107-inch spans. All had V8s and GM Hydra-Matic transmissions. A very steep price—$6769 at first, later a princely $8000—implied very meager sales, and Edwards went back to his wire cable business.

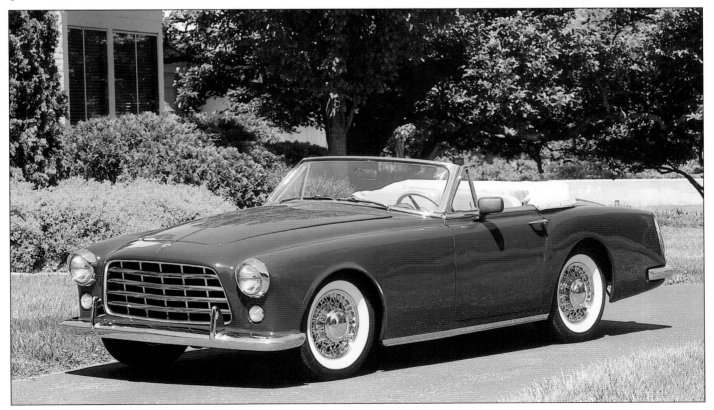

**Above, left, and right:** Evolved from a 1952 prototype called 20TS (aka "TR1"), the Triumph TR2 bowed the following year offering 100-mph performance for $2500, about the same as an MG TF and less than the equally fast Austin-Healey. This is one of 250 first-year examples, though production accelerated afterward. The TR2 featured a tight but well-organized cockpit and a simple but rugged 90-horsepower 2.0-liter four. **Below:** The TR2 was a hit in the U.S. and a popular weekend racer. This one seems to be getting a last-minute tuneup with a little help from Sun Instruments.

**Top:** Sir John Black, managing director of Standard-Triumph Motor Co., ordered his team to develop the TR2 after he failed to buy Morgan. Designed for strong export appeal, especially in the U.S., it was Triumph's first true postwar sports car. A steel body designed in-house by Walter Belgrove sat atop a conventional box-section chassis with a snug 88-inch wheelbase. Even so, the TR2 cut a particularly dashing profile. It also offered uncommonly good sports-car trunk space; the bobbed-tail "TR1" prototype had almost none. Sales got an early boost with a 120-mph run on Belgium's long, straight Jabaekke Highway and outright victory in Britain's 1954 RAC (Royal Automobile Club) Rally. **Right:** The TR2 had a few early bugs, but Triumph squashed them as fast as it could. Two early fixes involved stronger brakes and shallower doors, the latter to improve curb clearance. Triumph was also quick to offer extra-cost accessories, including a lift-off hardtop, as shown here, as well as radial tires, electric overdrive for the standard four-speed manual gearbox, and British-traditional center-lock wire wheels (as at top). Triumph built 8628 TR2s into 1955, when it changed over to a restyled and refettled version, the TR3. Most TRs ended up in America, just as Sir John intended.

> " Driving home from a Triumph convention in my TR2, I found myself in a long line of slow-moving Interstate traffic. We had traveled in single file for miles because of those annoying construction barricades. They were keeping traffic in the right lane, although there was clearly nothing wrong with the left lane, and no construction was going on. Mile after mile of these perfectly spaced barricades, with no construction or purpose... I couldn't resist. I had to slalom the TR2 back and forth around the barricades. After all, that's what Triumphs were made for! "

> – **Bill Lynn**
> Riverwoods, Illinois

**Top and above:** By the early Fifties, Britain's Rootes Group had acquired several makes in a bid to achieve the size and market power of British Motor Corporation, itself a pairing of Austin and Morris. Included in the Rootes stable was Sunbeam-Talbot, then known for orthodox but sporty sedans. Seeking to cash in on the growing two-seater market, Rootes added the Sunbeam Alpine in 1953. A touring convertible based on the S-T 90 sedan, it used the same 2.3-liter four-cylinder engine and 97.5-inch wheelbase chassis. Front-end sheetmetal and some interior hardware were shared too, but the Alpine cut a more raffish figure, if in a rather late-Forties way. With a modest 80 horsepower and fairly soft springing, the Alpine was no enthusiast's drive, but it was different and fairly rare in the U.S., as only some 3000 were built through 1955. Film buffs may recall this as the car Cary Grant and Grace Kelly took for a moonlight spin in the classic *To Catch a Thief.* **Right:** Everyone likes to personalize their cars, and everyone loves the holidays, hence the many December gift ads run by auto accessory houses. Here, a 1952 pitch for add-ons from Autocessories, one of "Wacky" Arnolt's many enterprises. Note in particular the quick-fill radiator cap and cutdown dual-pane racing windscreens, plus the ever-popular heater and driving lamps.

*Distinctive Gifts...*

every sports car owner will prize

...... Arnolt Autocessories

**MG ASSIST GRIPS**
These gleaming chrome-plated grab handles for the TC or TD MG fascia combine beauty with practical utility.

**IMPORTED MIRRORS**
Exterior styles for top-up driving include the graceful model shown above. Also rear view mirrors for suction mounting on windshield.

**IMPORTED ASHTRAYS**
These new smart-looking ashtrays will be especially appreciated in winter when driving with top up. Your choice of 3 lustrous chrome-plated models.

**TROUBLE LAMP**
Ideal for safe night road repairs. Plugs in any cigarette lighter. Interchangeable clear and red lenses for both sides of lamp.

**VALVE COVER**
This highly polished cast aluminum valve cover for MG cars effectively dampens engine sounds and "dresses up" the motor.

**WINDWING-WINDSCREEN**
Another famous Arnolt original—custom-tailored for sports cars. Fully adjustable and non-rattling. Folds flat against windshield when top is up.

**RADIATOR FILLER CAP**
A real racing type for MG. Cam and lever action . . . no threads! Opens in one motion, closes and locks in one motion. Finished in lustrous chrome.

**SPORTS CAR HEATER**
12-volt heater, designed and built by Arnolt specifically for sports cars. Tailored kit for installation in the MG. Adaptable to other sports cars.

**ARNO-LITE DRIVING LAMPS**
For safer night driving give this handsome chrome-finished Arno-lite driving lamp. May be used as a flood or spotlight and mounted in a low position on the central badge bar. (See below.)

Here are only a few of the distinctive gift suggestions that you will find in the new 1952 complete line catalog of Arnolt Autocessories. Send for your copy now and the name of the nearest Autocessories dealer! (Please enclose 25c to cover cost of mailing.) Address Dept. 12A.

**Autocessories, Ltd.** | DIVISION OF
WARSAW, INDIANA, U.S.A. | ARNOLT CORPORATION

Despite a lengthy, even shady birth, the Alfa Romeo Giulietta was a sales hit and a financial savior for the marque, introducing Alfa to a much broader audience, including many more Americans. It appeared in 1954 as a 2+2 Sprint coupe designed and built by Bertone. A sedan followed in '55, along with this neat two-seat Spider convertible shaped by Pinin Farina. All used a new 1290cc twincam four-cylinder engine, four-speed gearbox, aluminum drum brakes, coil-spring/double-wishbone front suspension, and a well-located live rear axle. Horsepower was 80 at first, but 1956 brought an available high-compression, twin-carb Veloce engine with 90 bhp. With a tight 88.6-inch wheelbase, fine balance and a very revvy engine, the Spider and Sprint won many friends on road and track alike. Indeed, for many people they remain the very essence of what Alfa Romeo is all about. As one writer noted, "The handling of these cars was so nimble and predictable that it took a real idiot to get one off the road." Max Hoffman was so impressed with the Giulietta that he became Alfa's U.S. distributor, adding the marque to his ever-growing stable. He listed the Spider and Sprint at about $3000, a bit pricey by Detroit standards, but not for the dynamic ability and driving satisfaction you got.

"I came to my love of Alfas the usual way, heart before head. I remember seeing my first one as my family wandered past a dealership window when I was about thirteen. It was a Giulietta Spider—bright red, naturally—and they had the showroom floor kind of elevated so my bulging, thirteen-year-old eyes were staring right into that…face!

Of course I read all the (Giulietta) road tests, and phrases like "little jewel," "delightful," "surefooted," and "falls readily to hand" were invariably peppered throughout the prose. And then I got a ride in one and fell in love. It was softer, smoother, and more sensual than any equivalent British sportscar. Feline where they were canine. Feminine where they were masculine. Far more mistress and temptress than buddy or chum. And what a song from that all-alloy twincam motor as it snarled up through the gears and gurgled back through the Webers on over-run. No question about it, this car had a pulse! Sure, I heard all the horror stories about reliability, dealership service departments and bodywork so prone to rust that it fizzed like Alka-Seltzer if you left it out in the rain. But that was all right, because they were—and are—so marvelous to drive."

— Burt Levy
Oak Park, Illinois

By 1953, Chicagoan "Wacky" Arnolt was a vice-president of the Italian Bertone coachworks and looking for a new sports-car project. A visit with Bristol of England secured a sturdy box-section chassis with 96-inch wheelbase and a 2.0-liter six-cylinder powertrain, both with prewar BMW origins. The resulting Arnolt-Bristol sold mostly as this stark Bolide roadster, a ready-made "club racer" with hand-crafted Bertone body, priced at $4250. With 130 horsepower, the sleek 2000-pounder could do 0-60 mph in about 10 seconds. It was a worthy racer too, winning the 2.0-liter class at the 1955 Sebring 12 Hours. Bertone also designed a companion fastback coupe, but it accounted for only two or three of the 142 Arnolt-Bristols built.

## STANLEY "WACKY" ARNOLT
### Brought the British home

Son of a Chicago bookbinder, Stanley Arnolt played football at the University of Wisconsin while earning an engineering degree. Unable to find desired work in the auto industry, Arnolt went into business for himself. In 1939 he set up shop in the Northern Indiana town of Warsaw building small marine engines. Arnolt expected the engine would be useful for navy lifeboats and other small support craft. As the world was being drawn into World War II, military contracts poured in. Arnolt's expanded to include other naval products and business flourished. Things only got better after VJ Day as consumer products such as battery chargers, dinette sets, and row boats were added to the company's range.

Somewhat impulsively, in 1950, Arnolt ordered 1000 Morris Minors from the British Motor Corporation, ostensibly making him the Midwest distributor. Eventually handling almost every English make available, he opened a large dealership in his native Chicago. He also distributed Solex carburetors and Borrani wire wheels while manufacturing a line of sports car accessories. Often wearing a suit, cowboy boots, and hat, "Wacky" Arnolt, as he was called by friends, cut a colorful figure in the Fifties sports car world. He had an electric organ in his office and relaxed by playing hymns. He was a keen business man whom *Road & Track* saluted for his contribution in establishing the sports car market in America.

Arnolt never did anything by half measures. Wearing his cowboy hat, he walked into the 1952 Torino Auto Show where a Bertone bodied MG coupe and convertible caught his eye. He ordered 100 of each. That chance encounter probably saved Bertone. Near bankruptcy, the sale not only provided much needed funds but also attracted the other business. Arnolt had MG

ship TD chassis to Torino and sold the finished products in Chicago as the Arnolt-MG.

MG dropped the TD after '52, so Arnolt came up with something new—the Arnolt-Bristol. Bristol built luxury coupes using a 2-liter six. Arnolt had Bertone design and build a lightweight roadster body. Arnolt made an assault on the 1955 12 Hours of Sebring and finished first, second, and fourth in its class. René Dreyfus, one of Europe's top Grand Prix drivers in the Thirties, was cajoled out of retirement to be the team captain. Not only was his experience valuable, but he attracted extra publicity. Dreyfus said of Arnolt: "What a wonderful companion he was, exuberant, expansive, warm, generous, a good good man...cowboy hat and boots, the big smile, the open manner, everyone he met liked him."

After the Sebring victory, the Arnolt-Bristol wasn't as successful as the experts had predicted. In '58 Arnolt's co-driver at Sebring was killed in a crash. After that, Arnolt lost interest in racing, although the program continued through 1960. Production ended in '58 and the last unsold Arnolt-Bristols were auctioned off in 1963. Stanley Arnolt died on Christmas Eve of the same year.

**Top and above:** It may look Italian, but the Doretti was basically an upscale Triumph TR2 built in 1954 by a descendant of the British Swallow company that sired Jaguar. Priced around $3000, it was named for Dorothy Anderson Anthony, whose father arranged for Swallow to make a special steel-tube understructure, and whose husband handled sales at his Hollywood import-car emporium. Only about 100 Dorettis were built before Triumph decided to stop supplying components to a competitor. **Right:** The second luxury *grand routier* masterminded by French industrialist Jean Daninos, the Facel Vega bowed in 1954 with a conventional chassis, U.S. Chrysler V8 power, impeccable workmanship, and effortless high-speed performance. A follow-up Sport or FVS hardtop coupe bowed in 1957 with wraparound windshield, a 325-bhp 330 V8, and a staggering $7000 price tag. The FVS saw only 227 copies. Most were sold in the U.S., either through Charles Hornburg in Hollywood or Max Hoffman in New York.

" Long ago I owned a Ferrari Lusso. I enjoyed this sweet little coupe for eight years, then sold it for twice what I paid. I'd heard similar stories from other owners, and I don't doubt a well-maintained Lusso can still make you a profit.

Those eight years sure were fun. The thing I remember most was the fabulous sound you'd get going through a tunnel at 3500 rpm. That 12-cylinder Ferrari rap always gave me goose bumps and a big grin. I'd always try to accelerate hard to peak cylinder pressure, then shift up and do it again. No way you can drive a Ferrari and not smile.

The 1963 Ferrari 250 GT/L Berlinetta Lusso was a curious combination of ratty bodywork and elegant, superbly designed high-alloy engine parts. Red paint, chrome wire wheels, and that prancing horse on the nose were expected, but I did a lot of mechanical and cosmetic restoration over the years and always discovered something amazing. "

— Robert H. Gurr
Los Angeles

The first of Ferrari's famous 250 GTs bowed in 1954 with a "second-series" Europa coupe powered by a 3.0-liter enlargement of the proven Colombo V12. The chassis followed previous practice save a wheelbase trimmed nearly eight inches to 102.3, plus twin coil springs instead of a single transverse leaf for the double A-arm front suspension. Pinin Farina was Ferrari's preferred coachbuilder by now and created most of the styles offered, though other *carrozzeria* contributed a few. Among the best this simply named Cabriolet, introduced in 1957. A slightly modified "Series II" version took over in 1959. With 220-260 horsepower depending on model, the Fifties 250s could do 0-60 mph in 7-8 seconds and comfortably beat 110 mph all out. Enzo Ferrari had always viewed selling road cars as simply a way to finance his beloved racing cars, but the 250 line proved that he was finally committed to satisfying a small but demanding clientele year after year.

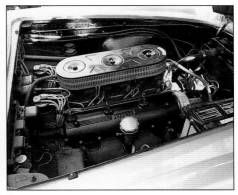

**Above and above left:** Elegant if not exciting in appearance was this notchback coupe version of the Ferrari 250GT. Introduced in late 1958, it was shaped by Pinin Farina, which also crafted the body (and its other styles) for the Maranello firm. PF also did several one-off variations on this theme over the style's three-year lifespan. Production totaled some 350, the highest by far of any 250GT model—but then, as Ferrari expert Dean Batchelor once noted, the PF coupe was the "standard production Ferrari road car" of its day. **Lower left and below:** Ferrari's first serious attempt at a regular-production touring car was the 250 Europa, announced in 1953. Only 17 were built through '54. Most were coupes, and most of those were the Pinin Farina style shown here. Unlike the later 250GT Europa, this Ferrari used a 3.0-liter version of the "long-block" Lampredi V12 that was intended to deliver better mileage in Europe, the target market, where gasoline was very expensive. Chassis design was shared with the larger, concurrent 4.0-liter America series, but only the longest, 110.2-inch wheelbase was available. Though larger and more lavish than previous Ferraris, the 250 Europa was a genuine sports car, if not a pure race-and-ride machine. Like all early Ferraris, it's long been a high-priced collector's item, and 10 of the original 17 survive today.

**Above and left:** Replacing the C-Type as Jaguar's factory racer, the slinky D-Type was lower, wider, and more aerodynamic. It was also faster, thanks to a 10 percent weight paring and further modifications that coaxed at least 250 horsepower from the XK twincam six. Construction involved a complex multi-tube front structure and separate unitized center and tail sections. Unveiled in 1954, the D-Type proved its mettle right away, winning the 1955 LeMans 24 Hours—and the '56 and '57 contests as well. Exactly 87 were built, including 18 team cars, of which a dozen were the so-called long-nose type. The rest had the short-nose body shown here. **Below:** Some D-Types had a distinctive fin trailing back from the integral driver's head restraint. A good many were sold to privateers who kept on racing them long after the car's factory career had ended. Here, a D-Type goes inside a Mercedes 300SL roadster in late-decade production-class action.

**Above and right:** Jaguar's great competition success of the 1950s was owed in large part to the commercial success of the roadgoing XK120. In 1954, Jaguar issued an improved version, the XK140. The 120 roadster had gained coupe and convertible companions since introduction, and all three styles returned in the new series. So did the respected XK twincam six, but horsepower rose to 190 standard, 210 optional. This convertible is one of 2740 built through 1957. Roadster production totaled 3347. **Below and bottom:** Though it looked much like previous XKs, the 140s offered more cockpit space from a driveline moved three inches forward, plus higher rooflines and reworked dashboard and footwells. Other changes included more precise rack-and-pinion steering to replace recirculating-ball and—a nod to the U.S. market—an optional Borg-Warner automatic transmission, though only some 800 cars were so equipped. This coupe is one 2797 built during the model's three-year run. Remarkably, XK140s cost little more than counterpart 120s—around $3200—so Jaguar's sports cars still represented strong value for money.

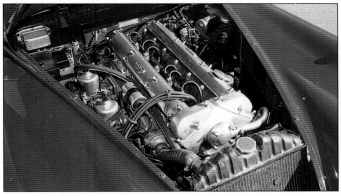

**Above and right:** Among the raciest sports cars ever, the Jaguar XKSS was essentially a roadgoing version of the LeMans-winning D-Type, with only the barest concessions to off-track driving. Among them were a larger windshield, windshield wipers, an opening door for the passenger, and a rudimentary folding top. Yet the D-Type was surprisingly tractable and civilized on the street, so the XKSS was too. It was also about as swift, capable of 0-60 mph in under 5 seconds and a sub-14-second standing quarter-mile. Unfortunately, a mere 16 of these cars were completed when Jaguar decided to end production of both the SS and D-Type following a disastrous factory fire in February 1957. **Below:** Despite its greater rarity, the XKSS went racing just like its track-bred sister, usually running in production classes, occasionally as a sports/racing prototype. Though no one knew it at the time, the XKSS forecast the general look of the future roadgoing E-Type. Also predictive was the hood/front fenders assembly that tilted up to provide fast, easy powertrain access, a boon in the heat of competition. In this scene, however, driver well-being seems the chief concern.

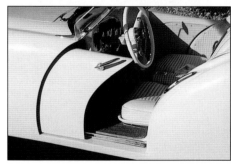

**Top and above:** Produced only for 1954, the Kaiser-Darrin featured a sleek two-seat fiberglass body with novel sliding doors, a well finished cockpit, and a three-way folding top with Thirties-style landau irons. The 100-inch-wheelbase chassis was borrowed from Kaiser-Frazer's Henry J compact but carried a 161-cubic-inch Willys six. Designer Howard A. "Dutch" Darrin conceived this *boulevardier* sports cars as a sales and image booster for fast-failing K-F, but a steep $3668 price and rumors of K-F's imminent demise held sales to just 435. Most survive today. **Right:** A rare example of a rare breed is this Zagato coupe version of the Maserati A6G2000 series, which saw just 61 total copies in 1954-57. All models ran Maserati's first roadgoing twincam engine, a 2.0-liter six with 150 horsepower. That was half again as much as the slightly smaller single-cam unit of the predecessor A6G series and enough to improve 0-60-mph times to 10-12.5 seconds. Allemano also built coupe bodies for this chassis, while Frua supplied both coupe and convertible styles.

**Top left and right:** One of the most recognized and coveted of sports cars, the Mercedes-Benz 300SL "Gullwing" coupe was evolved from the 1952 SL prototypes that won that year's LeMans 24 Hours and marathon Mexican Road Race. U.S. import-car baron Max Hoffman convinced Daimler-Benz to offer a production model by ordering 1000 of them. As on the racers, the flip-up doors stemmed from the need to preserve rigidity in a high-sided multi-tube space-frame chassis, but they were distinctive and would be much copied in later years. The only engine was a 3.0-liter six with mechanical fuel injection. Horsepower was a stout 240, fed through a four-speed gearbox. Unveiled in early 1954, the Gullwing sold for a princely $7000-plus. That and its semi-handbuilt nature conspired to limit production to around 1400 units. **Above and left:** Replacing the Gullwing in 1957, the two-seat 300SL Roadster was a true convertible with wind-up windows and an even stiffer price—near $10,000. Mercedes engineers modified the space-frame for conventional doors and added a trunklid. Lower-body styling was otherwise identical with the coupe's. So were cockpit furnishings, which were plush for a sports car and beautifully crafted. Weight went up by about 250 pounds to 3000, quite reasonable for a ragtop.

**Left:** The 300SL Roadster offered more predictable handling than the Gullwing, thanks to a modified swing-axle rear suspension with a lowered center pivot point and a transverse "camber compensator" spring. The payoffs were greater roll stiffness and less rear-wheel "jacking" in hard cornering. Coil springs continued all around, with twin A-arms and an anti-roll bar up front. The SL six made 10 more horsepower and somewhat more torque in the Roadster, which helped offset the model's added weight. Like the Gullwing, the Roadster body was made of steel except for aluminum doors, hood, and trunklid. A lift-off hard top was available to supplement the folding cloth top. The SL Roadster was always very exclusive, with just 1858 built through 1963. **Below:** Being sired by race cars, 300SLs have always been excellent production-class racers in their own right. Here, two Gullwing coupes try to outrun one another in a latterday "historics" event.

" In the fall of 1961 my daily driver was a 1952 Oldsmobile Rocket 88 sedan, but finances finally allowed for the purchase of a sports car. I was about to make a deposit on a Porsche Carrera 2 when a friend of mine called to say he had spotted a 300SL Gullwing in front of Moss and Sons Mercedes Motors in Detroit. The next day I went to look at the car and found several dents. A young fellow, the owner's son, came out. I asked what they wanted for the car. He said, "We're going to fix the dent in the hood and some other small things and sell it for $7000. I responded, "How about if I buy it 'as is' for $5000 cash?" The next day I owned a 1956 300SL Gullwing, something I'd never have dreamed of when I was finishing up at art school barely three years before!

The car now has 91,000 miles. It starts immediately, winds to 4000 rpm without stumbling and gets 18 mpg at 100 mph! I love the car. It has actually given me less trouble than a couple of late-model Cadillacs I own. It is the only collector car I can afford, but if you can only have one, the Gullwing is the one to have. "

— Syd Mead
Los Angeles

**Left:** In 1947, after nine years of working for the Orsi family in Modena, the three remaining Maserati brothers returned to their native Bologna and to the sports/racing cars they loved, forming a new company with the acronym OSCA. By the early Fifties, OSCA was turning out the MT4, a stark two-seater powered by twincam four-cylinder engines of 1100 to 1500cc. Light, strong, and surprisingly quick, MT4s were consistent winners in their displacement classes and occasional outright victors. In fact, an MT4 driven by Stirling Moss and Bill Lloyd won the 1954 Sebring 12 Hours. *Road & Track* tested a 1500cc car in 1955, recording 7 seconds 0-60 mph and 120 mph all out. Though never numerous, MT4s are still racing and winning. Production wound down in the early Sixties, after which OSCA was sold and then closed. **Lower left and below:** The Mercedes 190SL bowed at about the same time as the exotic 300SL it faintly resembled but cost less than half as much, about $4000. Like so many period sportsters, this two-seat convertible borrowed the basic chassis and running gear from a volume sedan (the W120 "Pontoon" of 1953). Wheelbase was trimmed to 94.5 inches. The engine, a 1.9-liter overhead-cam four, delivered 105 horsepower through a four-speed manual gearbox. Like its big brother, the 190SL had swing-axle rear suspension, but wasn't as twitchy. And it was decently quick, doing 0-60 mph in 13-14 seconds. An optional lift-off hardtop was available, as was a fixed-roof coupe model a few years on. Immediately popular, especially in the U.S., the 190SL saw surprisingly few changes over a nine-year life-span and 25,881 units. It even made money for Mercedes, which the bigger SLs didn't.

"Termite jokes aside, everybody loves the reactionary, fingernails-imbedded-in-the-past eccentricity of a Morgan. They're just not like other sportscars. And if they look a bit cobbly with their knobs and louvers and buckled leather straps, so much the better to the Morgan faithful. They love the purebred, bulldog toughness that exudes from that jutted out lower jaw and the graceful chrome waterfall grille cascading into it. But the real joy of a Morgan is in the driving.

From the inflatable seat cushions to the push/pull shifter to the sliding pillar front suspension (think of a cross between a door hinge and a pogo stick) to the wood framing that supports the bodywork, the Morgan abounds in clever—if oxcart—engineering. But the result is marvelous to drive.

You can feel the car wind itself into corners and just as gently unwind itself on exit like the flex of a fine fly rod. Amazingly, Morgans have proven to be excellent racecars, taking on and beating more modern, more powerful cars with embarrassing regularity. One reason is that Morgans behave exactly the same on all corners, fast or slow, and that sort of honesty gives the driver confidence to take it to the edge."

— Burt Levy
Oak Park, Illinois

Though it seemed stuck in the 1930s, Morgan was relatively innovative in the Fifties. Most of the changes occurred in 1951, when the 4/4 roadster gave way to a longer Plus 4 with a 96-inch wheelbase. Styling was modestly updated with faired-in headlamps astride a "fencer's mask" radiator that was lower and more raked than the old "flat rad." As ever, Morgan built its own chassis, a simple ladder-type with sliding-pillar front suspension, and bodies, which had steel panels over traditional wood framing. Running gear and other chassis bits came from larger British automakers. Engines were pushrod fours purchased fron Standard-Triumph: a 68-bhp 2.1-liter through 1954, then the new 2.0-liter TR2 unit with 100-115 bhp. Seating was available for two or four, the latter via a very small rear seat.

**Above:** Instead of trying to be a true sports car like the Chevrolet Corvette, Ford's new 1955 Thunderbird was a sporty "personal" two-seater designed for comfortable cruising and hassle-free ownership. A 102-inch wheelbase was one of their few common features. The T-Bird body, for instance, was made of steel, not creaky fiberlass, and there were expected Detroit conveniences like roll-up windows, a power top, and optional air conditioning. The Ford also arrived with V8 power, a modern 292 making 193 horsepower with three-speed stickshift or 198 with optional self-shift Ford-O-Matic. After trouncing the 'Vette with 16,155 sales for model-year '55, the Thunderbird returned for '56 with a standard "continental" outside spare tire, smoother-riding suspension, optional stick-over-drive, and available 312 V8s with up to 225 bhp. This Ford archive photo shows a new '56 posed casually in a company parking lot as a reference for catalog illustrators. Sales for the model year slipped a bit to 15,631. **Left and below:** A handsome restyle made the '57 the best-looking of the "early Birds" in the view of many fans. Optional seatbelts and padded dashboard returned from '56 among several safety-enhancing "Lifeguard Design" features.

**Above:** A lift-off hard top, usually with distinctive "porthole" windows, was a popular option throughout the two-seat Thunderbird's three-year run. The '57 was the last and most numerous of the flock at 21,380 units, due to an extended model year. It was also the priciest "early Bird" at $3408 basic, versus $2944 for the '55. **Right and below:** T-Bird engines expanded to four for '57: a 212-bhp 292 with stickshift, a 245-horsepower 312 with stick-overdrive and automatic, and optional 312s with 270 and 285 bhp, the last via twin four-barrel carburetors and 10:1 compression. Hotter still was a supercharged 312 with 300 or 340 bhp, intended mainly for racing. Cars so equipped were nicknamed "F-Bird." This red beauty is one of 208 originally built. Its wire wheels were not a factory option but are period-correct, being available from accessory makers like Kelsey-Hayes. Two-seat Thunderbirds never raced much, but a few showed their stuff. A modified '55 swept production sports-car classes at that year's Daytona Speed Weeks with a two-way average of 124.633 mph, faster than all comers bar a Jaguar XK120. A pair of '56s were faster still on the Florida sands, and a '57 reached 138.775 mph. Questing for higher sales and profits, Ford blew up the T-Bird into a luxury car for '58, and the two-seaters became "instant classics."

**Above:** Porsche's first sports/racer surfaced in 1953 as the Type 550, a.k.a. 1500RS and simply Spyder. A new four-cam flat-four engine arrived in '54, along with a "customer" model, the 550S, priced at $5500. Further improvements yielded the 550A by mid-1956, as shown here. With 135 horsepower for just 1200 pounds, Spyders could hit 120 mph and were exceptionally reliable in the long-distance races they won with crushing regularity. **Left:** Evolved from the Spyder, the RSK 718 appeared in 1958 with a new suspension and better handling, plus 142 bhp. Top speed was up to 155. A 1.6-liter unit with 148 bhp featured in the refined RS60 replacement for 1959. **Lower left and below:** Launched in 1955, the MGA was a complete break with the classic T-Series it replaced. Wheelbase was the same, but the sleek new body was now all-steel, a first for an MG sports car. A new 1500cc pushrod four delivered 72 bhp. There were no wind-up windows and the top was still a trial, but the MGA was a big advance and, at $1600-$1700, sold quite well against the rival Triumph TR3. Nearly 59,000 were built through 1959, with the U.S. again taking the majority.

> " (To start) Place the gear lever in the neutral position and see that the handbrake is on. Pull the carburettor choke control out the stop (sic), switch on the ignition, and press the starter switch button. When the engine has become sufficiently warmed up, turn the choke control and allow the control to spring back to the half-out position and turn to lock in this position. After one or two minutes of driving, as the engine warms up, it will be possible to permit the control to return home without causing the engine to run without undue hesitation. If the battery has been allowed to get into a run-down condition, it is better to use the starting handle. "

– Triumph Sports Car
Instruction Book

**Above:** Though most foreign marques eventually got around to setting up a national U.S. distribution arm, advertising in the early Fifties was often left to individual dealers. This ad extolling the Triumph TR2 is but one example. **Right and below:** Arriving in late 1955, just in time to battle the new MGA, the Triumph TR3 improved on the TR2 by adding five horsepower and filling the grille cavity with a bright eggcrate. It also added a little weight, but a running change to more efficient "high-port" cylinder heads added another five horses for 100 total. Triumph also attended to the TR's weak brakes by standardizing front discs for model-year '57, a first for a regular-production British sports car. The rear drum brakes were upgraded too, and the rear axle was strengthened. All this provided a timely sales lift, boosting calendar-year export deliveries from 4726 units in 1956 to 10,151 in '57. Helped by a slightly longer model run, TR3 sales were 55 percent higher than the TR2's at 13,378 through 1957.

**Above, above left, and left:** After three successful years, British Motor Corporation replaced the Austin-Healey 100/4 with the thoroughly revised 100 Six. Styling didn't change much, but wheelbase was stretched two inches, to 92, to make room for a token rear seat. Under the hood was a 2.6-liter corporate six with 102 horsepower, but it was a heavy lump that further dulled speed and handling. Things improved some in late '57 when a reworked 117-bhp engine was substituted and a lighter two-seat model reinstated. Though a bit slower than the 100/4, the Six was no less popular, with 14,439 built through 1959. **Below:** Sports cars aren't made for going off-road like an SUV, and veering off the track is no way to win a race. Here, an Austin-Healey 100 Six raises a dramatic dust cloud in getting back on course after some sort of mishap, perhaps a corner taken just a shade too quickly.

Bavarian Motor Works struggled to resume its auto business after World War II, offering an odd mix of high-priced sedans and inexpensive license-built microcars. Yet somehow, BMW managed a sleek two-seat convertible in late 1955. Designated 507, it borrowed the basic chassis and running gear of the then-current 502 "Baroque Angel" sedan and related 503 sporty coupe, but a trimmer 97.6-inch wheelbase supported handsome styling by German-American industrial designer Albrecht Goertz. With a 3.2-liter V8 sending 150 horsepower through a four-speed gearbox, the 507 took just 8.8 seconds 0-60 mph and could do over 120 mph, impressive for the 2900-pound heft. In a sense, this was BMW's Thunderbird, but also an answer to the Mercedes 300SL—and just as costly at about $9000. Only 253 were built, mostly by hand, through 1959.

**Left and below:** Chevrolet's Corvette became a much more serious sports car with a stem-to-stern redesign for 1956. Harley Earl and his GM designers conjured tasteful new styling for the fiberglass body, which now boasted roll-up windows and distinctive bodyside "cove" identations, often two-toned. Chevy's 265 V8 was uprated to 210 base horsepower, 225 optional, and a three-speed manual gearbox returned from late '55 as the standard transmission. Recently hired engineer Zora Arkus-Duntov made handling equal to straightline performance, which was fierce: as little as 7.5 seconds 0-60 mph and over 120 all out. Sales turned up smartly to 3467 units, helped by a modest price increase to $3149. **Above:** The rejuvenated 'Vette was a formidable track racer, but you still had to remember to put gas in, preferably in the pits.

**Above and left:** Corvette had more fire for '57 with a V8 enlarged to 283 cubic inches. The five versions offered 220 to a thumping 283 horsepower, the last via "Ramjet" fuel injection, a costly $500 option. Only 240 "fuelie" '57s were built, each wearing i.d. badges on fenders and trunklid. A late-season four-speed gearbox option and stump-pulling axle ratios trimmed 0-60 mph to as little as six seconds. Total Corvette sales moved up to 6339 for the model year. **Below:** Corvettes began piling up racing trophies in '56, winning SCCA's national C-Production championship and finishing 9th in the Sebring 12 Hours. This photo shows one in action at Pebble Beach, California, where a 'Vette ran 2nd behind a Mercedes 300SL. In '57, Corvettes placed 1-2 in class at Sebring and won SCCA's national B-production crown among numerous impressive showings.

**Above and left:** The Porsche 356A was constantly improved after its late-1955 debut, thus enhancing its appeal. These second-generation models were roomier, better insulated, and more nicely trimmed than earlier 356s. The flat-four engine, now at 1600cc, offered 60 horsepower in Normal trim or 75 in Super tune. In 1958, the high-output twincam Carrera engine also became a 1600 and more durable with it. **Below:** Another wholesale makeover resulted in the replacement 356B series, unveiled in late 1959. Styling was subtly altered with heftier bumpers, raised front fenders, and new wheel covers. Engines didn't change much, but brakes switched from cast-iron to cast-aluminum to improve fade resistance in hard driving and to reduce unsprung weight for better handling. As ever, the coupe was the mainstay seller, but the standard cabriolet, shown here, remained especially popular in the U.S., as did the sportier Roadster version, formerly Convertible D. Though prices inched upward, the B-series would prove the fastest-selling 356 yet.

Replacing the 375 America as Ferrari's "deluxe" touring sports car, the 410 Superamerica bowed in late 1956 with a larger, 5.0-liter version of the "big" Lampredi V12, plus a new coil-spring/A-arm front suspension. Horsepower was 340 at first but went to 360 with 1958's Series II revisions and the mildly updated Series III models of 1959. As before, senior Ferraris were high-performance GTs with bodies designed and built virtually to order, so prices could approach a breathtaking $20,000. This heroically tailfinned 410 coupe is one of 36 bodied by Ghia in 1956-59. It looks much like Chrysler's 1956 Dart show car, which Ghia also built at the behest of Chrysler styling chief Virgil Exner. The similarity was likely no accident, as Ghia had already built several Exner-designed Chrysler "idea cars."

## BATTISTA PININFARINA
### That singular man

At their best, sports cars represent power and grace, and no designs consistently express these qualities better than those from the house of Pininfarina.

The feral Ferrari 250 GT Short Wheelbase Berlinetta, the charming Alfa Romeo Giulietta, and the incomparable Cisitalia 202 are artistic achievements. These and scores of other sublime automobiles are the work of a stocky, animated, inspired stylist and coachbuilder from Italy.

"Pinin" was a nickname. It meant "the little one" and fit nicely the youngest of 11 children born to the Farina family of Turin. In 1961, when he was 68, Battista "Pinin" Farina legally changed his last name to Pininfarina. By then, Pininfarina was already an international byword for the pinnacle of automotive form, proportion, and detail.

His journey to greatness began at age 11, with work in the bodyshop of his brother Giovanni. By 17, he had designed a car for Fiat, by his early 20s, a trainer plane for the Italian air force, and by 1920, he was in Detroit, drawn by a fascination with the pace of American industrial enterprise. He turned down a job offer from Henry Ford and returned to the family business. He raced cars briefly, and in 1930, founded Carozzeria Pinin Farina. It was a visionary undertaking that applied new thinking and technology to high-end coachbuilding and design. Cars from Alfa Romeo, Lancia, Hispano-Suiza, and Fiat were among hundreds that sported prewar Pinin Farina bodies. Innovation was evident in their aerodynamically integrated styling elements and, in some cases, their early use of all-metal framework.

The breakthrough came in 1947, with a skin for the tiny Cisitalia 202 two-seat GT. Spare, organic, and highly influential, the shape of this coupe united automotive design and contemporary art. Indeed, it's in the permanent collection of New York's Museum of Modern Art.

Bentley, Rolls-Royce, Peugeot, even Nash enjoyed Carozzeria Pinin Farina work in the 1950s. But it was with Ferrari that the design house made its deepest impact. Starting with the elegant 212 Inter cabriolet of 1952, the chrome strip "pininfarina" signature has adorned nearly every road car from Maranello.

Pininfarina officially transferred management of his firm in 1961 to son Sergio and son-in-law Renzo Carli. But his philosophies were always evident, especially in the Ferraris. Among the embarrassment of riches are graceful 250 GT Berlinetta Lusso of 1963, the sexy 365 GTB/4 Daytona of '68, and 1969's Dino, which established the look of most every midengine Ferrari to this day. The firm remains a pillar of automotive design and construction and operates the Pininfarina Aerodynamic and Aeroacoustic Research Center.

Battista Pininfarina died in 1966, his life the subject of numerous honors, his work the object of dozens of books and countless lines of adoring prose. Few were in better position to speak than Enzo Ferrari himself. Ferrari considered Pininfarina a friend, and one of his few equals. "That singular man," he called him. "His car bodies are simple and clean, being reduced to the essential lines...actually nothing sensational, but his style will always preserve its personality and will never look dated."

Swedish aircraft maker Saab branched out into cars starting in 1950 with the 92 sedan, a stout little fastback two-door with front-wheel drive and a two-stroke two-cylinder engine. Encouraged by the 92's success in European rallying, Saab explored the idea of a sporty open version. The result, called Sonnet Super Sport, broke cover in 1955, but went no further than six prototypes, such as the one pictured here. Perhaps influenced by U.S. trends, the Sonnet employed a fiberglass body with tilt-up front and rear sections. The chassis was a specially designed light-alloy affair with deep side members. The contemporary 93 sedan donated a 33-horsepower two-stroke three-cylinder engine to drive the front wheels through a three-speed manual transmission with floorshift. Styling, by Saab's own Sixten Sason, also reflected period American trends with a curved windshield, a hint of tailfins, and low-slung stance. No thought was apparently given to a folding top, odd for a land not known for sports-car weather. Then again, it might not have been deemed necessary, as the Sonnett was conceived mainly for rallying.

**Above:** Sweden's other automaker was little more successful with a sporty convertible, Volvo building just 67 P1900s in 1956-57. Inspired by an executive trip to the sports-car-crazy U.S., the P1900 used a fiberglass body styled by California's Glasspar and an X-member steel chassis with 95-inch wheelbase. The 1.4-liter B14A four-cylinder engine came from Volvo's mainstay PV444 sedan (which resembled a 1940s Ford) but was tuned up to 70 horsepower. All but one P1900 was exported to the U.S. before new management killed the project as unprofitable. **Right and below:** A more potent Ace roadster and Aceca coupe bowed in 1957 with a more powerful 2.0-liter six-cylinder. The engine was basically that of the prewar BMW 328 but came from Bristol of England, which had acquired design and manufacturing rights for its own costly touring models. Four states of tune delivered 105-130 horsepower through a Bristol four-speed gearbox with optional overdrive. The Ace/Aceca-Bristol didn't replace the AC-powered versions but were much scarcer with 466 and 169 built, respectively.

Bowing in mid-1957, the XK150 was Jaguar's response to growing U.S. demand for more comfortable and refined sports cars. Only a coupe and convertible were planned at first, but the roadster, shown here, was reinstated within a year, albeit with roll-down windows in conventionally shaped doors. All three models were wider and heavier than counterpart XK140s and thus slower, as horsepower was unchanged. But Jaguar responded to that too, first with a 250-bhp 3.4-liter S version in 1958, then a pair of 3.8s offering 220 (base) and 265 (S). The added power offset the 150's added weight, so a 3.8 S could do 0-60 mph in about 7 seconds and top 135 mph. Overdrive was standard on S-models, optional otherwise, but every XK150 was built with servo-assisted four-wheel disc brakes by Dunlop, a competition-proved advance that was also welcome in these heavier cats. Typical fuel economy was 18-20 mpg in American driving, more than acceptable in an age of quarter-a-gallon gasoline. Despite its somewhat dowdier appearance, the 150 was the most popular XK of all, with nearly 9400 built through 1961. The 3.8 and S models are the rarest of the breed.

**Above:** S-model XK150s weren't identifiable without getting close enough to read the small badges on the doors, but their extra muscle was evident from behind the wheel. S-engines used triple SU carburetors instead of two, a special straight-port cylinder head with 9.0:1 compression versus 8:1, and wilder cam timing. **Right:** The XK150 redesign made the roadster look more like the convertible, but it was easier to tell them apart when you put the tops up. The convertible's more thickly padded roof folded into a bulky stack atop the body, while the roadster top remained skimpier and had to be removed for open-air driving.

# KJELL QVALE
## West Coast Pioneer

Kjell Qvale's British Motor Car Distributors, Ltd. building stands on Van Ness Avenue in San Francisco. It was originally built in 1925 and served as a Packard dealership. The walls of Kjell's office are covered in exquisite wood paneling and photos and paintings of prized race horses. It's an appropriately regal place of business for one of America's oldest and most revered dealers of high-end European cars.

Kjell Qvale (pronounced "Shell Kah-vah-lee") has been in the import car business ever since 1947, when he opened the first MG dealership on the West Coast. The young Norwegian was in on the ground floor of a promising new trend. American servicemen had taken note of all the zippy foreign cars they had seen in Europe during World War II, and many were anxious to get zippy little foreign cars of their own. Car-crazy Californians were especially eager to partake in this newfound form of automotive enthusiasm, so the market was ripe for entrepreneurs like Qvale. Kjell sold 75 cars in his first year, and his operation expanded quickly from there. Before long, BMCD was the largest distributor of British cars in the United States, handling Austin-Healey, Bentley, Jaguar, Jensen, Lotus, Rolls-Royce, and Triumph. Kjell's scope soon expanded beyond British cars: in 1953, Qvale's Riviera Motors became the first Volkswagen distributor in Northern California, and in 1955 Volkswagen made him distributor for the entire Northwest. Other European makes followed.

In the early uncertain days of foreign automakers in the US, savvy

dealer/distributors like Qvale provided vital feedback, helping offshore manufacturers better tailor their products to American consumers. Power steering, modern radios, and better heaters became available in part because of dealer prompting. Kjell's efforts at building his business also helped develop the burgeoning American sports car scene. He was a founding member of the Sports Car Club of America, helped organize the original Pebble Beach sports car races, and had a hand in the design of the Laguna Seca road course—it was Kjell who suggested the inclusion of the race track's famous "Corkscrew" turn.

While most car dealers would be content with a lucrative network of dealerships, Qvale's entrepreneurial spirit led him to grander ventures. In 1970, Kjell bought Jensen Motors, where he collaborated with Donald Healey on the Jensen-Healey. The car's initial quality bugaboos gave it a bad reputation, and the company itself never quite recovered, folding in 1976. In the 1970s and '80s, Kjell's sons Bruce and Jeff assumed larger roles in the family business. Jeff became the president of BMCD, and Bruce President and CEO of Qvale Automotive Group. The Qvale family made another run at manufacturing in 1998, signing a deal with DeTomaso to produce and distribute the new Mangusta roadster. The partnership with DeTomaso dissolved in 2001, and the car was renamed Qvale Mangusta. Today, the 13-store Qvale dealer group still thrives, handling mostly European luxury makes. Kjell Qvale, youthful and active in his eighties, still comes in to work, as the proud patriarch of a legacy that has spanned more than half a century.

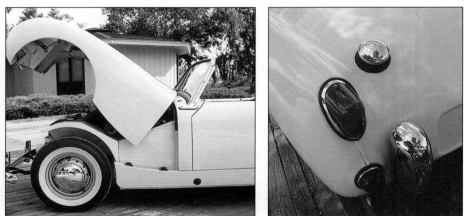

> **"** Another (adjustment) method is to listen to the hiss of each carburetter with a piece of tube, on end which should be placed adjacent to the carburetter intake and the other in the ear, then adjust the throttles until the hiss is equal. **"**
>
> –To Adjust the Carburetters: Austin Healey Owners Handbook

Conceived by British Motor Corporation as a little sister to its MGA and Austin-Healey Six, the Austin-Healey Sprite arrived during 1958 at around $1500, about $1000 below the MG. Weighing just 1460 pounds on an 80-inch wheelbase, it had just the basics, though a front-hinged "clamshell" front end provided very easy access to the little 43-horsepower, 948cc four-cylinder engine. Many other components also came from BMC shelves. Retractable headlights had been planned but were rejected as too costly, resulting in the "bugeye" face that many buyers found irresistible. Though just able to touch 80 mph in stock form, the Sprite was easily and cheaply modified for racing, and many owners did so. Some 49,000 were built in all through 1961.

No, this isn't a Ferrari but a Bocar XP-5, one of several sports/racing models built by the Denver, Colorado, company, started in 1958 by one Bob Carnes. The XP-5 appeared in 1959 as a sleeker version of the previous year's SP-4. Both used a steel-tube inner structure with fiberglass body panels and a 90-inch-wheelbase chassis available with race-tuned Pontiac 370 or Chevrolet 283 V8s. The suspension was evidently lifted from the lowly VW Beetle, the wire wheels from Jaguar. Carnes built fewer than 100 Bocars before closing shop in 1960. There was also a larger XP-6 with a supercharged Chevy V8 allegedly making over 400 bhp. It listed for a lofty $11,700 versus $11-grand for the XP-5. Both were fast, but saw only limited competition success.

## MAX HOFFMAN
### The Man Behind the Machines

Behind every great man, the saying goes, there's a great woman. Though a relic of more sexist times, the line proved true more often than not. The same concept of greatness advanced by some unseen muse can be applied to the quiet machinations of a certain automobile importer. The truth is that behind some of the greatest sports cars ever brought to American shores, there was Max Hoffman.

By the mid-1950s, Austrian-born Maximillian Hoffman owned and operated the largest import-car dealership in the United States. Hoffman's New York-based operation handled almost exclusively makes and models not already available through established channels. Considered opportunistic by some, brilliant by others, Hoffman's ability to identify what sports-car shoppers wanted was uncanny.

A shrewd and hard-working businessman, Hoffman had high expectations for himself and his employees alike. A stickler for formality, he kept business on a last-name basis, insisting his employees address him as "Mr. Hoffman." Hoffman in turn, referred to all his employees as "assistants."

A successful importer of American cars to Europe, Hoffman fled his homeland in 1941 because the political situation had become "uncomfortable." Hoffman had planned to reenter the car business immediately upon reaching America but was forced to wait out the war—amassing a small fortune in the costume jewelry business while waiting.

Using his jewelry money, Hoffman set up a dealership on Park Avenue in New York. Obtaining cars from war-weary Europe was difficult at first, but Hoffman soon established a reasonably regular supply of product.

Through the years, Hoffman imported a seemingly endless parade of Europe's lesser known classics, including Allard, Cisitalia, Delahaye, Facel-Vega, HRG, Jowett, Lancia, and Lagonda.

Famous for working without contracts, Hoffman often ordered models in round lots of 500 or 1000, paying cash for the order, and moving on to the next promising make and model when the supply went dry.

Hoffman's relationship with manufacturers firmed up when dealing with larger makes interested in reclaiming their pre-war American presence. Upon hearing that Mercedes-Benz was waffling on whether or not to produce a street version of its hyper-successful 300SL racer, Hoffman signed a deal promising to purchase the first 1000 cars produced. The promised order sealed the deal for Mercedes, which delivered its first SL to Hoffman in 1954.

Similar Hoffman deals brought to the U.S. BMW's lithe 507, Alfa's stunning Giuletta, Porsche's 550 Spyder, and several Jaguars.

While most of these makes eventually established their own U.S. distribution networks, it was Hoffman who first coaxed them into the U.S. Using his own money, Hoffman imported, marketed, sold, and serviced now legendary makes that at the time were only magazine fodder in the U.S.

An active auto importer into the '70s, Hoffman amassed the bulk of his personal fortune by selling back distribution rights to the manufacturers. Hoffman received $2 million from Mercedes in 1957 and $16 million from BMW in 1976, with countless smaller deals in between. Max Hoffman died in 1981. Legendary for his business, marketing, and importing acumen, Hoffman was truly the man behind the (European) machines.

**Above and left:** To the dismay of many critics, the Chevy Corvette returned for 1958 measuring two inches wider, 10 inches longer and 2000 pounds heavier than the svelte '57. It also sprouted four headlamps, needless chrome trim, and dummy hood louvers. But engines were as potent as ever, performance options no less numerous, and there was a roomier cockpit with a more driver-focused dashboard. Defying a generally downbeat market, Corvette sales went up for '58 to 9168 units. The total went to 9670 for 1959, when Chevy removed some of the glitz and tied down the rear axle better, which aided handling. **Below:** On paper, the longer-wider-heavier 'Vettes looked less competitive for racing, but proved otherwise by winning two more national SCCA B-Production class championships in 1958-59. The car pictured here was one of many contestants for the crown in those years. A Corvette also won the GT class and finished 12th overall in the 1958 Sebring 12 Hours, while another set a new sports-car speed record in that year's Pike's Peak Hill Climb. So much for the critics.

"It's a kick to teach yourself how to drive at 12, and even better in a '60 TR3A. My father bought the little black-over-yellow darlin' new, when I was seven. We lived in the Ohio countryside on a road of tire-smoothed gravel in tar, with narrow shoulders that wanted to dump you into the weedy ditches where frogs lived.

The old man'd be happily ruminative in his hammock, a Ballantine Ale in one hand, a Chesterfield in the other, while I putted around the yard or in the road, grinding the gears, overcompensating with the steering, braking too hard, stalling it, grinning my head off.

By 14 I was piloting the TR at 70 mph along the ruler-straight asphalt of nearby Mulberry Rd., where hot rodders occasionally annihilated themselves, where a horse and a pickup collided one summer night with awful results, and where I learned why sports cars are better, much better, than other cars, and almost as sweet as memory."

– David J. Hogan
Arlington Heights, Illinois

Triumph had prepared a new sports car for the late Fifties, but management rejected it as uncompetitive. Designers and engineers went back to their drawing boards after dressing up the TR3 with hopes that it could hang on a while longer. The result appeared in early 1958 and has since been dubbed "TR3A" by Triumph enthusiasts, though it was not advertised as such. Changes were relatively few and mostly cosmetic. The main ones were a "wide-mouth" grille and exterior door and trunk handles, though the latter had been available in a "GT Kit." The following year brought a 2138cc enlargement of the base 2.0-liter four, which had a little more torque but no more horsepower, which may explain its comparative rarity. Brakes were slightly revised a bit later in 1959. Despite all this, the 3A sold better than previous TRs, drawing 58,236 customers through 1962. Though the new TR4 was out by then, the older car held on through '62 and another 3331 sales as the TR3B with the 2.1-liter engine and the TR4's new four-speed gearbox.

British travel-trailer maker Berkeley had unused factory space. Engineer Lawrie Bond had ideas for a tiny sports car. The two joined in the 1956 Berkeley B60. Berkeley was experienced with fiberglass and aluminum, which made up the body and chassis of a petite 700-pound, 70-inch-wheelbase roadster. An air-cooled two-stroke motorcycle twin drove the front wheels by chain. Larger engines took horsepower from 15 to 18 and then 30 for the B90 of 1958, which sold in the U.S. for $1750-$1850. But sales were limited everywhere by poor build quality and price competition from the more grown-up Austin-Healey Sprite, so Berkeley left the U.S. after '59 and folded in 1961. This B90 has been retrofitted with a newer Honda motorcycle engine.

" To a 12-year-old with bulging, gee whiz eyes and a nascent lust for speed, it (the Berkeley) didn't look nearly as tiny and ridiculous as it does today. In fact, it was about the coolest thing I'd ever seen!

And it got even cooler when the mechanic who'd just finished tuning it asked me if I'd like to go for a ride. I still remember the flimsy, "I can't believe this is a real car!" feel of the door and seat cushion and the ungodly ringing, popping, splattering noise that 3-cylinder, two-stroke Excelsior motorcycle engine made when he fired it up. The sound hammered your eardrums until it rattled your spine. And then he snicked the stubby, motorcycle-style sequential shifter into first, chirped the tires with a quick pop of the clutch, and off we went, careening around the parking lot lamp posts and alley trash barrels, the tires snatching for traction on the broken concrete and the sound absolutely shattering off the viaduct walls every time the pipes aimed in that direction. Don't think he ever got it out of 2nd gear, but even so I was certain that Berkeley was the fastest car on the face of the earth. "

— **Burt Levy**
Oak Park, Illinois

**Right:** Berkeley followed the B90 in 1959 with the facelifted, 40-bhp B95 and 50-bhp B105. They were the fastest Berkeleys of all, but still needed a lengthy 15 seconds to do 0-60 mph. It thus took bravery—and patience—to drive any of these toy-like roadsters in heavy, fast-moving U.S. traffic, let alone on the track, yet a few hardy souls did race the cars. SCCA put them in its smallest-displacement class, J-Production, hence the "JP" on the B90 in this period action shot. Though engines were tweaked or replaced for racing, the chassis also needed modifying, as its front drive and swing-axle rear suspension were far from ideal. But a Berkeley was a cheap way to go racing, and you still see a few buzzing along in vintage-car competition today. Maybe that's just as well, as a Berkeley isn't happy on the road, being noisy, cramped, and a real handful in a stiff crosswind. At least it's super-easy to park. **Below:** Looking for the perfect gift for the sports-car lover in your life? Perhaps a logo lighter or watch is in order. Long before the satin Ferrari jacket, marketers were capitalizing on owners'—or would-be owners'—desires to more closely associate themselves with their favorite marques. While the lighter below represented a minimal investment, the watch listed for $37.75 in the mid-'50s, about $300 in 2003 dollars—suitable only for the most dedicated enthusiasts. Now prized artifacts, auto memorabilia fans buy, sell, and collect such treasures with the same fervor as enthusiasts seeking out low-mileage unrestored classics. Note that Corvette stands alone as the single domestic logo option available.

Looking like a half-scale late-Fifties Lincoln, the Shamrock was a short-lived attempt at manufacturing an export-worthy sporty car in Ireland. Indeed, the period Detroit styling implies that America was the target market. The two-seater convertible body was made of fiberglass, likely for reasons of low cost and easy manufacturing. The same factors dictated a "bought-in" engine, a 1.5-liter four supplied by British Motor Corporation, probably the same 72-horsepower unit found in the contemporary MGA. Plans called for a lift-off hardtop, as shown above, to be available as either standard or optional. The photo at the left suggests the Shamrock would have had the same overall size as the contemporary 100-inch-wheelbase Rambler American—and that some styling elements were still in flux even as publicity efforts got underway. The documents reproduced below suggest a good many other details had yet to be settled too. But it didn't matter, as the project never got off the ground and only four cars, all prototypes, were built in 1958-59. Where are they now? Only St. Patrick could say.

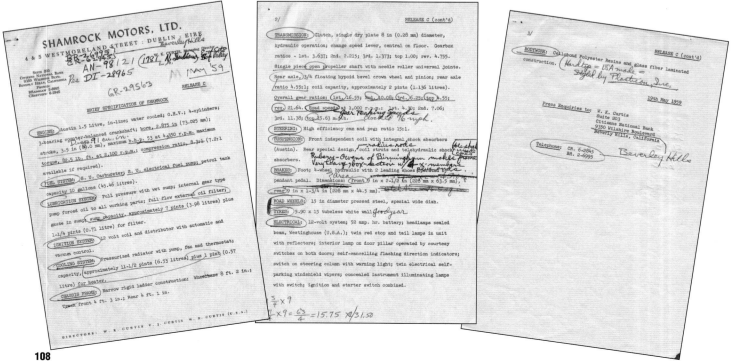

The war-ravaged Japanese auto industry was still rebuilding in the late Fifties, when it began sending a trickle of orthodox cars and trucks to the U.S. Ambitious Nissan, though, had been building sports cars since 1952. By decade's end, the original Datsun Sports had evolved into the S211, quaintly badged Fairlady. Like other period Japanese cars, much of its engineering was owed to the British automakers that had helped the native producers get back to business, but the little four-cylinder four-seater was no less export-oriented than any MG or Triumph. Though quite ordinary in design and build quality, the S211 was a faint sign of a Japanese assault on the U.S. market.

**This page and opposite:** Long regarded as one of the finest race-and-ride sports cars ever made, the Ferrari 250 GT SWB Berlinetta premiered in October 1959 to replace the longer 250GT "Tour de France" coupe offered since 1956. Ferrari by now virtually owned the yearly race around the perimeter of France, hence the earlier car's nickname. The newcomer was even better suited to road racing, being lighter on a tighter 94.5-inch wheelbase. *Ferraristi* use "SWB"—short wheelbase—to distinguish it from the predecessor "TDF." The SWB introduced several internal improvements to the 250 GT-series' 3.0-liter overhead-cam Columbo V12 that added 20 horsepower for a total of 280. As usual, drive was through a four-speed manual transmission. Emphasizing the SWB's dual-purpose nature was a wide variety of available axle ratios ranging from a relatively rangy 3.44:1 to a screaming 4.57:1. Ferrari's chassis designs in the Fifties progressed much more slowly than its engines, so the SWB retained a familiar, proven suspension layout comprising coil springs and twin A-arms in front and a live rear axle located by semi-elliptic leaf springs and trailing arms. Four-wheel disc brakes, however, were new for roadgoing Ferraris, being phased in for long-wheelbase 250s earlier in 1959. Pinin Farina, still Enzo's favorite coachbuilder, gave the SWB Berlinetta purposeful two-seater styling that still turns heads after more than 40 years. Doors, hood, and trunklid were rendered in aluminum, the rest of the body in steel, though a few full alloy-bodied cars were built. PF also created a new Spyder California on the SWB chassis for introduction in late 1960. Only 57 were built, versus 175 Berlinettas. Scarce though they were, the SWBs compiled a distinguished record on the track and were always thrilling on the road, with 0-60 mph available in 6.5-7.0 seconds on the way to a top speed of 140-150 mph. Factor in the timeless look and it's no wonder that these 250 GTs now command six-figure collector-market prices—and sometimes more. In the opinion of many, sports cars just don't come any better than this.

**A**merican scholars have been dissecting the 1960s almost since the decade ended, and they still debate what happened then and why. But though the analysts may differ in their conclusions, all could agree on one point: The Sixties was an extraordinarily eventful era that profoundly transformed American life.

Consider all that occurred in those 10 short years. A confrontation over Soviet missiles in Cuba that took the world to the brink of a nuclear abyss. The assassination of a charismatic president, his younger brother, and two revered leaders of the historic African American civil-rights movement. The awesome sight of man walking the moon. The awful daily pictures of soldiers dying in Vietnam. Increasing protests and riots at home.

Millions of postwar-born "baby boomers" came of age, often with a rebellious spirit that shocked the older generations. Catchphrases captured the issues and spirit of the times. "Make love, not war." "Do your own thing." "Don't trust anyone over 30." "Black is Beautiful!" "Tune in, turn on, drop out." "The whole world's watching!" A growing counterculture was led by "hippies" and "flower children" sporting bell bottoms, long hair, and "love beads." Anything cool was now "groovy," "boss," or "far out." Miniskirts and the Beatles landed in a friendly "British invasion." Sex was more openly discussed with the advent of The Pill, women's lib, and *Playboy* magazine. Space-age technology gave us pocket-sized transistor radios for playing Dylan and The Doors, the Stones and "Motown." It was quite a time.

So, too, for America's automotive scene. Perhaps the most significant change there was the sharp market growth that occurred once all those "boomers" started buying cars. From a decade low of 5.8 million units in 1961, total U.S. car sales reached an all-time high of nearly 9.4 million in 1969—a near 31-percent increase over previous-best 1955. This and changing public tastes prompted U.S. automakers to branch out from traditional "standard" models, first with European-inspired "compacts" for 1960, then somewhat larger "intermediates."

By 1962, the richer competitive field had sprouted all manner of specialty models with some of the features and flair of European sports cars. Chevrolet had uncovered the "youth market" car with the bucket-seat Monza version of its rear-engine Corvair compact, but Ford would have the decade's single biggest automotive success. Though the Mustang was basically a humble compact Falcon with a snazzy body, its combination of high style, low price, and numerous options started a buyer stampede to what became known as the "ponycar." In its first 16 months, starting in April 1964, the Mustang attracted nearly 691,000 enthusiastic customers. Once more, rivals rushed to copy a "better idea." By decade's end, some ponycars could also be "muscle cars," the big-engine high-performance breed born at mid-decade with the midsize Pontiac GTO, which quickly inspired its own herd of imitators. U.S. automakers had resumed their Fifties "horsepower war" after a brief ceasefire in the early Sixties, and performance again reigned supreme—appropriate for the "go-go" era.

Performance also loomed large among genuine sports cars, but so did a greater emphasis on comfort, convenience, and style, a necessity for manufacturers given the U.S. market's ever-growing economic clout. Even at decade's dawn, Americans had rejected a number of small-time Fifties sports cars as well as Detroit decadence. The import ranks would dwindle further after 1967, when new federal safety and emissions standards began virtually mandating special "U.S. versions" that only the more able, well-financed companies could manage. "Fed regs" also instantly killed off old favorites like the classic Austin-

Healey that couldn't meet the new rules without ruinous expense and effort, if then.

Despite that ominous turn, Americans still had plenty of exciting sports cars to choose from, many now coveted collector's items. Jaguar kicked things off in 1961 with the E-Type, as sensational as the XK120 was in its day, maybe more so. The only thing familiar about it was the respected XK twincam six-cylinder engine, and that was improved. As if in reply, Chevrolet unveiled its own stunner for 1963. Like the E-Type, the Corvette Sting Ray boasted independent rear suspension, reflecting a period sports-car trend, plus styling that rivaled the Jaguar's for pure sex appeal. The replacement 1968 "Shark" was dismissed as just a rebodied Sting Ray with more gadgets but had its own appeal and would prove exceptionally long-lived.

Meanwhile, a wily former racing driver named Carroll Shelby was stuffing potent Ford V8s into British A.C. Ace roadsters to create some of the hairiest production sports cars ever. Shelby loved stark, elemental machines, and his Cobras were precisely that. Engines quickly progressed from 260 to 289 V8s and finally a monster 427 big-block. Acceleration thus ranged from fierce to incredible, but the Cobra also had the stamina to be a world championship racer. Only very expert drivers could tame it, which was the whole point.

Having established itself in the Fifties on both road and track, Ferrari continued offering thoroughbred sports cars in the Sixties, issuing new models most every year. A few quickly became marque icons, particularly the all-conquering 250 GTO and later 365/GTB4 Daytona. Ferrari also explored new territory with the smaller, more affordable V6 Dino, one of the first road cars with the midengine layout that had recently revolutionized open-wheel racing car design. Maserati hit its stride with a series of conventional but fast and handsome V8-powered grand tourers. And Italian tractor baron Ferruccio Lamborghini began building high-performance sports and GT cars designed by some of the best talent around. His aim was to outdo Ferrari, and in some ways he did. Among the volume Italian marques, Alfa Romeo's successful Giuliettas carried into the Sixties as improved Giulia models. The roadster and a nifty new coupe became perennial America favorites. Even mass-market Fiat, never known for sports cars, entered the fray.

The costly, racing-inspired Mercedes-Benz 300 SL was dropped after 1962 for a smaller sedan-based two-seater that was more tourer than pure sports car, capable though it was. This left Porsche as Germany's premier sports-car builder, and it went from strength to strength. After honing the original 356-series to near-perfection, Porsche introduced the stronger, faster six-cylinder 911, which ultimately proved a car for the ages.

Not surprisingly, Britain still delivered more popularly priced sports cars than any other country, and Americans liked most every one. In this era, British Motor Corporation alone offered the aforementioned "big" Healey, a restyled Austin-Healey Sprite, a new MG Midget companion, even an MGB with—gasp!—roll-up windows. A resurgent Triumph initially countered with its small Spitfire and TR4 roadsters, then followed up a few years on with interesting variations of each. Britain's Rootes Group weighed in with the Alpine, which later got a Ford V8 transplant to become a Tiger. Newcomer Lotus sent over the tiny Elan roadster and a quirky but capable midengine coupe called Europa.

With all this and more, the 1960s were great sports-car years in the U.S., despite the many problems the nation endured. Of course, the fun and excitement wouldn't end when 1970 rolled in, but a new decade would bring historic problems of its own, and the automotive world would never be the same.

**1960** Ferrari premieres 400 Superamerica at Brussels • Ferrari wins LeMans, first of five straight victories • A Chevy Corvette finishes 8th overall at LeMans • Ferrari 250GTE bows as Maranello's first 2+2 • New Aston Martin DB4GT Zagato offers British brawn, Italian beauty • Ferrari scores fifth straight win in grueling Tour de France • New Porsche 356B arrives with more power • Updated Sunbeam Alpine Series II boasts larger engine **1961** Carroll Shelby turns AC Ace into Ford-powered Cobra • Jaguar launches stunning E-Type • Austin-Healey Sprite redesigned, gets MG Midget clone • Austin-Healey 3000 Mk II introduced with improved mechanicals • Chevrolet Corvette gets a "taillift" • Datsun of Japan launches MG-like Fairlady 1500 roadster • Interim MGA 1600 gets several "Mk II" updates • Triumph begins building TR4 • Volvo launches P1800 • SCCA expands to sanctioning professional races **1962** Maserati brings out Sebring 2+2 to replace 3500GTI • Lotus Elan bows with fiberglass body on novel "backbone" chassis • Engine transplant turns Alfa Romeo 2000 models into 6-cyl 2600s • Facel Vega introduces suave Chrysler-powered Facel II • Fiat 1500 evolves into more potent 1600S Cabriolet • Corvette-powered Iso-Rivolta gives Italy a new sporting marque • MGB stuns purists with unibody design, wind-up windows • Porsche offers its hottest road car yet in 356B-based Carrera 2 • Rare Sunbeam Alpine Harrington LeMans fastback coupe offered • Triumph adds new, low-cost Spitfire roadster

One-time royal car-maker Daimler was in dire straits by 1959. Owner BSA, of motorcycle fame, thought a sports car designed for American tastes would generate the cash needed to turn Daimler around. The resulting SP250 boasted a finny fiberglass body, a chassis and suspension mimicking those of the Triumph TR3, and England's first production V8, a 2.5-liter with hemi heads and 140 horsepower. With standard 4-speed gearbox (optional automatic was added in '61), the 2220-pound SP250 could do 0-60 mph in just 10.2 seconds and reach 120 mph. But despite such good performance, an unusually spacious cockpit with token rear seat, a roomy sports-car trunk, and amenities like wind-up windows, sales were shaky. So was the body. Help arrived in mid-1960 when Jaguar bought Daimler and gave the SP250 a much stiffer body, plus suspension changes to improve the skittish handling. But nothing seemed to help, and Jaguar dropped the sporting Daimler in mid-1964 after just 2468 units.

**Top and above:** Still largely relying on posh *grand routiers*, France's Facel-Vega entered the Sixties with an updated FVS, the HK500. The main change was a larger, 383-cubic-inch V8, again from Chrysler but a "wedgehead," not a hemi. Horsepower was a stout 360 with twin four-barrel carburetors, good for 140 mph all out and 0-60 mph in a brisk 8.4 sec. Famed American road-tester Tom McCahill said the HK500 was "sexier than the Place Pigalle," but a king's-ransom price of near $9800 assured limited sales—fewer than 500 through 1961. **Right:** Seeking broader sales in the rich U.S. market, Facel founder Jean Daninos added a mid-priced two-seat convertible in 1959 to battle the likes of the Alfa Giulia and Triumph TR. Called Facellia, it was handsomely furnished and neatly styled on a trim 96.5-inch wheelbase, but cooling problems dogged its new 1.7-liter, 115-bhp four-cylinder engine, which soured buyers on all Facels and forced the firm into bankruptcy. After 500 units, the Facellia was given a 1.8-liter Volvo four in 1963 to become the Facel III. It drew 1500 sales, still far from enough. A last-gasp Facel 6 version with a debored Austin-Healey six found just 26 takers before Daninos bowed to fate and closed shop in early 1965.

**1963** Porsche turns to further-improved 356C series • Race-bred, midengine Ferrari 250 LM wows at Paris • Alfa Romeo Giulia bows to replace Giulietta models • James Bond gets his car in Aston Martin's new DB5 • Chevrolet unleashes all-new Corvette Stingray • Facel Vega struggles to stay afloat with Volvo-powered Facel III • New engine turns Fiat 1200 into 1500 Cabriolet • Maserati Mistral debuts • Mercedes issues sophisticated all-new 230SL • Shelby Cobra gets "Mark II" updates • Sunbeam Alpine Series III arrives • Ford 289 V8 turns Britain's odd TVR coupe into U.S.-market TVR Griffith • SCCA stages U.S. Road Racing Championship, its first pro series **1964** Ferrari 330GT 2+2 replaces interim 250 model • Ferrari bows new "deluxe" GT in 500 Superfast • Italian upstart Lamborghini launches V12 350GT • midengine Porsche 904GTS racer finishes 100-unit run; a few take to the road • Ferrari unveils 275 GTB/GTS • Austin-Healey 3000 Mk III offers more power, refinement • BMC issues improved Austin Healey Sprite Mk III, MG Midget Mk II • Facel Vega bids *adieu* with Healey-powered Facel 6 • High-power Ferrari "275" LMs win 10 major international races • Lotus Elan updated to Series 2 form • Sunbeam bows "definned" Alpine Series IV, scorching V8-powered Tiger • Triumph announces a spiffier Spitfire, the Mk 2 **1965** Lotus adds Elan coupe • Toyota shows slick 2000GT prototype • AC goes GT with posh Cobra-based 428 coupe, convertible

### Is it too chic to be champ?

The loveliness of a Sunbeam Alpine is only skin deep. Underneath it's all muscle and brawn and racing nerves.

It wasn't looks that cleaned up at the Riverside Grand Prix, where the Alpine swept Class "F" in the "Enduro." Or at Le Mans, where it took first, too, with an efficiency average of 91 mph and 18 miles per gallon for 2194 miles in 24 hours.

It streaks from 0 to 60 in 13 seconds, flicks off a quarter mile in 19, hugs corners like a lover!

But for all its snap and snarl, it treats you tenderly—with wind-up windows, weather-tight soft top (optional hard top), restful foam-cushioned seats, a usable jump seat, and thoughtful little touches that add lots to your driving comfort.

At only $2595*, no wonder the race is to your Sunbeam Alpine dealer's!

**SUNBEAM ALPINE**

*EAST P.O.E. SLIGHTLY MORE IN WEST. HARD TOP, WIRE WHEELS, WHITE WALLS OPTIONAL, EXTRA.*
GOING ABROAD? ASK YOUR ROOTES DEALER ABOUT OUR OVERSEAS CAR DELIVERY PLAN.
A BETTER BUY BECAUSE IT'S BETTER BUILT BY **ROOTES** MAKERS OF HILLMAN/SUNBEAM/SINGER/HUMBER

**Above:** Britain's Rootes Group introduced a new Sunbeam Alpine on the eve of the Sixties, and it was a true two-seat sports car instead of a midsize tourer. Early ads like this played up period-trendy American-inspired styling and conveniences like wind-up windows, standard heater, and easy-operating soft top. The initial engine was a 78-horsepower 1.5-liter four, borrowed from corporate bins like many other components. The new Alpine was heavier and not as quick as the MGA and Triumph TR it targeted, but it was more rigid, thanks to a unitized structure, and it was priced right at an initial $2600. It sold well at home and abroad, especially in the U.S. **Below:** Arnolt-Bristol sales limped along until 1963, ending with the death of "Wacky" Arnolt. This racy Bolide is one of about 100 total A-Bs known to survive. Wacky sold all his cars at a loss. Today they're pricey collectibles.

**Top and above:** Ferrari's short-wheelbase 250GT chassis always seemed to inspire Italy's *carrozzeria*. One of the best efforts was the Spyder California, new in 1960. Pinin Farina, *Il Commendatore*'s favorite coachbuilder, patterned the design on its earlier long-wheelbase SC, but trimmer proportions made it look even better. The SWB Spyder was advertised as "ready to race," but few owners did. The car was just too pretty to risk. Too rare, as well, as only 57 were built through 1963. No wonder they've become among the most sought-after—and expensive—collector Ferraris. **Right:** Ferrari issued a new "deluxe" GT in early 1960, the 400 Superamerica. Suspension changed little, but standard four-wheel disc brakes greatly improved stopping power over the previous 410 SA. Equally notable, the burly "big-block" Lampredi V12 was abandoned for a new 4.0-liter version of the mainstay Colombo engine with a thumping 400 horsepower. Most 400s were built with this *aerodinamico* coupe bodywork by Pinin Farina, but PF also ran off a few cabriolets. Production ended in 1964 at just 54 total, including 29 interim "Series I" 400s and 19 further refined "Series II" versions.

# nineteenSIXTIES

• Aston Martin trades DB5 for more lavish new DB6 • Chevy Corvette trades "fuelie" engines for big-blocks, adds disc-brake option • Datsun evolves 1500 roadster into 100-mph 1600 version • Italy's Iso adds burly Corvette-powered Grifo 2-seat GT • "Mark III" Shelby Cobra bows in 289 and ultra-fast 427 models • Maserati issues its first V8 road car, the new Mexico 2+2 coupe • MGB GT coupe joins traditional roadster • Porsche makes history with new 6-cyl 911 and 4-cyl 912 • Sunbeam Alpine reaches pinnacle with Series V version • Improved Triumph TR4A boasts independent rear suspension **1966** Two-seat Ferrari 330 GTC introduced • Racing Ford GT40 wins LeMans, breaks Ferrari win streak • Ferrari launches 275 GTB/4, its first twincam road car, and ragtop 330 GTS • Triumph launches Spitfire-based GT6 fastback • BMC again ups engine size and power for Austin Healey Sprite Mk IV, MG Midget Mk III • Alejandro deTomaso displays sleek Mangusta • Lamborghini adds faster 400GT and sleek, sexy mid-V12 Miura • Lotus unveils lightweight midengine Europa coupe • Maserati replaces Mistral with sleek, sexy V8 Ghibli • Saab tries another "sports car" in Sonnet II coupe • TVR issues MGB-powered Grantura 1800S • SCCA launches Trans-Am race series; Alfa Romeo, Ford Mustang are class champs **1967** Toyota 2000GT begins limited production • Ford GT40 again beats Ferrari at LeMans • The biggest Ferrari yet debuts in 365 GT 2+2 • Datsun introduces improved 2000 roadster with 5-speed gearbox

After three successful years, the little Austin-Healey Sprite exchanged its "bugeye" look for more conventional styling that would persist for the next decade. The redesign grafted a squarish nose and matching tail onto the existing center body section, leaving wheelbase at 80 inches. Also carried over were suspension, rack-and-pinion steering, 4-speed gearbox, and British Motor Corporation's 43-horsepower 948cc A-Series four-cylinder engine. "Bugeye" fans might have been doubly disappointed that the play-it-safe look was shared with a nearly identical new MG Midget, but BMC was delighted to see total sales reach 15,000-20,000 a year. A 54-bhp 1098cc engine and front disc brakes arrived for 1963's Sprite Mark III/Midget Mark II. The following year brought 59 bhp, wind-up windows, and the taller windshield shown here. A 65-bhp 1275cc A-Series was substituted for 1967's Sprite Mk IV/Midget Mk III. As the above ad suggests, these entry-level sports cars were easily modified for racing, and many owners cut their competition teeth in a Sixties "Spridget." They're still buzzing around road courses today.

**Right and below:** The first MG Midget since 1934 differed from the '61 Austin-Healey Sprite mainly in having a grille with vertical bars instead of mesh, plus slightly nicer trim to justify a $150-$200 higher price. But either "Spridget" was a cheap ticket to the world of true sports cars, listing at well under $2500 through decade's end despite escalating period inflation. This pre-1964 "Mark I" Midget has the original sliding side curtains, plus accessory wire wheels and cockpit tonneau. Both versions featured an external trunklid, something new for the Sprite. **Bottom left:** The Midget was a bit less popular than the Sprite, with world production of 61,707 through 1969 vs. 71,920. This U.S. ad, circa 1966, seems to suggest that MG heritage was a reason to prefer the Midget over the less costly Sprite. **Bottom right:** For less air drag and more speed, "Spridgets" often raced with bolt-on hard tops available from the factory and many outside suppliers. Of course, it also made life a lot less taxing for drivers.

this midget casts a giant shadow

# nineteenSIXTIES

Ferrari unwraps "junior edition" Dino 206 GT with midships V6 • Lotus issues stretched Elan +2 coupe • Mercedes 250SL offers larger engine • Six-cyl MGC roadster and coupe start troubled 2-year run • Porsche 911 adds potent S coupe, "Targa" semi-convertible models • Sunbeam Tiger swaps 260 Ford V8 for a hotter 289, then disappears • Triumph TR gets 6-cyl power as TR250 for U.S., TR5 PI elsewhere **1968** Ford takes third straight LeMans victory • Ferrari shows soon-to-be-legendary 365 GTB/4 Daytona • Shelby Cobra production ends • American Motors bows AMX as Corvette-rival "muscle" sports car • Stylish Aston Martin DBS ousts DB6 • Ferrari replaces 330 GTC/GTS with big-bore 365 versions • Fiat starts over with new 124 convertible and 2+2 coupe • Lamborghini adds sleek Espada 2+2 and new-style Islero 2-seater • Lotus Elan evolves to Series 4 specs • Morgan goes mad with V8-powered Plus 8 • Opel GT bows with "baby Corvette" looks, econocar price • Triumph GT6 Mk 2 offers new rear suspension, safer handling • TVR fights on with Grantura Mk IV, V8-powered Tuscan • Volvo 1800S upgrades to 2.0-liter engine **1969** Aston Martin adds more-potent V8 version of DBS • Chevrolet Corvette acquires "Stingray" badges • Ferrari announces an improved Dino, the 246 GT • Maserati offers fastback Indy as a second 2+2 • Porsche 911s shuffle models, engines in "wide-body" update • Triumph's senior sports car transformed into TR6 • Volvo switches to fuel injection for revised 1800E

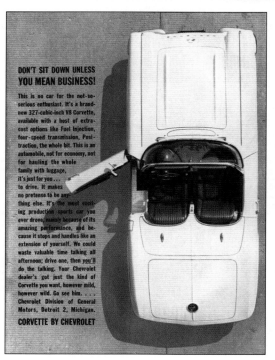

**Above:** Chevrolet had considered a radical all-new Corvette for 1960, but circumstances dictated hanging on to the existing 1958-59 design. However, new GM styling chief Bill Mitchell freshened the car's appeal for 1961, remodeling the rear into a shapely "ducktail" and substituting simple mesh for the 'Vette's trademark grille "teeth." Other changes included standard sunvisors and a wider choice of axle ratios. Though base price was up to $3934 and powertrains were basically unchanged, Corvette sales improved by nearly 700 units to set another record at 10,939. **Left:** This '61 Corvette ad shows how well the "ducktail" blended with the existing body, evident even from overhead. The new rear end was shaped much like that of the Stingray special that Mitchell had lately been racing. Regular Corvettes were still piling up track successes. One car entered by Briggs Cunningham finished an impressive 8th overall at LeMans 1960, and a near-stock '61 came home 12th in that year's Sebring 12 Hours.

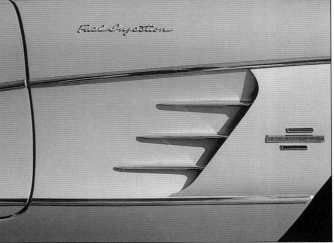

**Top and above right:** The '61 Corvette had less chrome than previous "four-lamp" models. The '62 was cleaner still, dispensing with bright "windsplits" and two-toning in the bodyside coves and gaining a black grille insert. Discreet fender script marks this '61 model as having one of the ever-rare "fuelie" 283 V8s, which that year delivered 315 horsepower. With available four-speed manual transmission and one of the shorter axle ratios, a 'Vette would scorch 0-60 mph in well under 6 seconds and top 130 mph. The '62s were faster yet, thanks to a larger 327 V8 offering from 250 bhp to a mighty 360. With that—and some suitable race prep—Corvette was the '62 national champ in two hard-fought SCCA classes, A- and B-Production. The 'Vette also finished ahead in the sales race, setting another record with 14,531 units. **Right:** Besides a slightly larger trunk, the 1961-62 "ducktail" introduced a tidy quartet of four taillamps, a treatment that would be a Corvette hallmark for years to come. **Above:** All 1958-62 Corvettes had a big semicircular speedometer above a round tachometer flanked by fuel and temperature dials. Earlier 'Vette gauges were spread across the dash, but these were near the driver's normal sightline, desirable in a high-performance sports car.

" Big Ed drove out past the edge of town and gave it a quick blast in second and third. Jeez, was that car ever Fast. "THAT'S EIGHTY," Big Ed hollered over the wind noise, "AND WE'RE NOT EVEN OUTTA THIRD YET!" Right at that exact moment, with hair whipping in my eyes and the howl of that big twin-cam six filling my ears and the dotted white lines on the highway coming at me like tracer bullets, right then I fell in love with Jaguars. "

– From *The Last Open Road* by Burt Levy

A singular sensation on its 1961 Geneva, Switzerland, debut, Jaguar's slinky E-Type—called XKE in the US—picked up the general look and modified unit construction the firm had first employed for its late-1950s racing D-Type and roadgoing XKSS. Styling was again the work of Malcolm Sayer and overseen by company founder Sir William Lyons. **Top:** Initially, the E-Type came with the same 3.8-liter six and all-disc brakes of the XK150, while gaining independent rear suspension. A bigger-bore 4.2-liter took over in 1964. This added 23 pound-feet of torque (to 283) but left horsepower unchanged at 265. Starting in late 1967, modifications were phased in to meet federal regulations resulting in the Series II of 1969. **Left and above:** Larger bumper and taillights of the Series II, but with triple carburetors of the Series I, identify this convertible as a 1968 Series "1 1/2" US model, as do the "safety" rocker switches on its dashboard.

**Above:** Unlike the earlier XK-series notchbacks, the E-Type coupe was a sleek fastback standing seven inches lower on a 96-inch wheelbase vs. a 102. A side-hinged rear door, as on this Series I, made for easy luggage access. **Right:** Not surprisingly, E-Type racers preferred the coupe for being lighter and more aerodynamic than the convertible. These Jags remain a common sight in modern "vintage" racing. **Below:** Series I E-Types had covered headlamps and "ears" on their knock-off hubs—lost on the Series II due to federal regulations. Initial U.S. price was about $5500, a bona fide bargain for such a beautiful, agile sports car able to run 0-60 mph in 7 seconds or less and reach as much as 150 mph. No wonder sales soared. Jaguar built 15,490 of the 3.8-liter E-Types, followed by 41,740 of the 4.2-liter cars. The latter included a 2+2 coupe added in 1966 with a 105-inch wheelbase and a higher, more ungainly roofline. **Above right:** Pennzoil was one of several auto-related companies that sought to use the E-Type's popularity to burnish their own images—and sales.

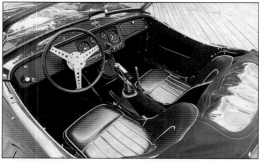

**Above and left:** Elva was little known in America, and then mainly for small, affordable sports-racing kit cars. But the small British concern also offered a petite roadgoing roadster, the Courier, in 1958-61. A fiberglass body sat on a tough tube-steel chassis with a solid rear axle and, on most examples, a four-cylinder MGA engine. Very few Couriers came stateside, and few were ever built: only 400-700 estimated. Elva folded in 1968 after 13 years, but ended U.S. exports in 1960. This '61 Courier Mark II was thus a private import. **Below:** For 1962, Triumph sold both an updated, old-style TR3B and the rebodied TR4 on the same 88-inch wheelbase. Besides handsome new styling by Giovanni Michelotti, the TR4 boasted wind-up windows, the first for a sporting Triumph, plus Britain's first dashboard air vents. Accessories included a new-style hard top with a center section that lifted out to make a "surrey" top. This car shows the normal folding roof but also bumper "overriders" and wire wheels, two popular factory-fit accessories.

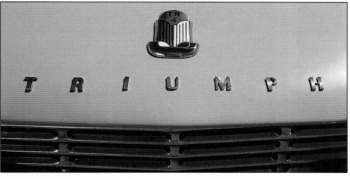

**Top and above:** Though the TR4 used the basic TR3 chassis, it handled somewhat better thanks to three-inch wider front and rear tracks, plus adoption of more precise rack-and-pinion steering. But the suspension was still quite stiff, so ride was as rocky as in any TR3, and bump-steer remained a problem. Also, the TR4 was heavier and thus no faster despite a 2.1-liter four-cylinder engine, which provided little more oomph than the TR3's 2.0. Even so, the TR4 sold well, helped by its new looks and fully synchronized four-speed gearbox, plus a roomier, better-furnished cockpit and reasonable $2850 U.S. starting price. Over 40,000 were built through 1964. But newer, more modern rivals were pushing hard, so Triumph responded in '65 with the improved TR4A. Besides a sturdier chassis, the big news was *de rigueur* independent rear suspension with coil springs and semi-trailing links, which improved ride and banished wayward cornering behavior vs. the prior leaf-sprung solid axle. The 4A also gained a few horsepower, to 105 total, which boosted top speed by about 8 mph to 110 and reduced the 0-60-mph sprint time to just under 10 seconds. Critics applauded the 4A, but it didn't win over that many buyers who weren't already TR fans. **Right:** The TR4 extended Triumph's triumphs in rallying and on racetracks. In fact, it so dominated the E-Production class in SCCA road racing that it was moved up to D-Production in '63, which it more or less owned for three years. This trackside photo, which looks to be a post-race victory pose, shows the fairly simple modifications typical of period "club racing," including a cut-down windscreen, small rollover bar, and headlamps removed or capped rather than taped over.

WE ARE BY NATURE
A PRACTICAL PEOPLE

That's true. ■ But there is more to owning some cars than
just plain being practical. ■ There's the feeling you get when
you know somebody is looking . . . when your friends talk . . .
when they ask questions. ■ The pride, compliments, questions,
fun — that's all part of owning a sports coupe. ■ So we've
put them all together in our new P1800. Solid and sturdy
materials. Careful and meticulous workmanship. Styling
that's lush. And Volvo sports car handling that makes driving exciting. ■ There are large doors and well-padded bucket

seats and mile-long leg room. The jump seats in back handle
the kids, packages, dogs. The padded dash has all the various
instruments you'll ever need. There's trunk space enough for
a two-suiter, a gal's garment bag and week-end case, and a
set of golf clubs. ■ We've even added things you might not
think of: Pirelli sports car tires, overdrive, undercoating,
seat belts. ■ What the looks don't show, driving will. That's
how you'll know we Swedes are practical.
Volvo Distributing, Inc., Englewood Cliffs, New Jersey.

**VOLVO P1800** SPORTS COUPE

**Top and above:** Volvo's second try at a two-seater,
the P1800 coupe bowed in 1961 with a conventional chassis, 100-bhp 1.8-liter pushrod four, and
four-speed manual gearbox with overdrive. Though
not a true sports car, it did liven up the Swedish
automaker's sensible-shoes image, as a few ads
playfully noted. The evolutionary 1964-67 1800S
and 2.0-liter 1968-71 1800E offered refined
styling, more power, up to 115-mph all out and
0-60 mph in as little as 10 seconds vs. 14. **Right:**
Two racing Alfa Romeo Giulietta Spiders in the
midst of a Sunday afternoon fender-bender. No. 15
is still recovering from its shunt with No. 66. Both
cars drove on, but not much farther.

**Above:** We don't know what caused this Alfa Giulietta Spider to head off track in a cloud of dust. Perhaps it had to do with whatever is heading into the trees behind. **Right and below right:** Alfa Romeo introduced Giulia models in 1962 to supplement its successful Giulietta sedan, coupes, and Spider, which continued through mid-decade. Though little changed dimensionally, the Giulias boasted improved suspension and handling, a standard five-speed gearbox instead of a four-speed, and a torquier 1570cc all-aluminum twincam four instead of an iron-block 1290. The result was a quicker, better-handling small Alfa that was even more agile and fun to drive, yet also easier to drive in the daily cut-and-thrust. Horsepower rose from 80 to 104 with single carburetor and from 115 to 122 for the available twin-carb Veloce engine. Save a hood scoop, the Giulia Spider retained its predecessor's near-timeless Pinin Farina lines through 1966, after which it stepped aside for a more adventuresome PF design, the Duetto. Though the chassis would last well beyond the Sixties, many regard the early Giulias as some of the best Alfas ever.

**Above and left:** Replacing previous small Alfa coupes in 1963, the elegant Giulia Sprint GT made a star of its designer, Giorgetto Giugiaro, then on staff at Bertone. This '67 carries the 1570cc Giulia twincam four. A lower-priced, tax-beating 1300 Junior version was available in Europe; a few came to the U.S. Like other Giulias, the Sprint GT would evolve into the 1970s with interim changes to powertrains, styling, and equipment, but the basic 2+2 body persisted throughout. **Below:** A handsome new body transformed Facel Vega's HK500 into the 1962 Facel II. More aerodynamic than its predecessor and a whopping 400 pounds lighter, it also packed more punch, with FV's Chrysler-sourced 383 V8 up to 355 horsepower with available Torqueflite automatic or 390 with standard four-speed manual. With all this, a Facel II could reach 150 mph and do 0-60 in just 8.3 seconds. It was arguably the best Facel yet but still far too costly to generate the funds needed to save Jean Daninos' struggling company. Only 180-184 were built before Facel ended operations in 1965.

**Right:** A standout even among Ferraris, the 250GT Berlinetta Lusso arrived in late 1962 as the 250GT/L. Lusso and L stand for "luxury," yet this Pininfarina model was actually intended to replace the race-and-ride SWB berlinetta. Lussos did race—they were Ferraris, after all—but seldom. As with the 250 Spyder California, most owners simply couldn't stand the idea of putting racing numbers on such masterful rolling sculpture. As with many other period Ferraris, Lusso bodies were built by Scaglietti, by now virtually a Ferrari subsidiary. Only 350 were built. **Below right and bottom:** The SWB's true successor was the 250GTO, announced in early '62. Though it used the same basic chassis, the GTO—"O" for *homologato,* approved for GT-class racing—had less weight, more power from a race-proved 3.0-liter V12, and superior aerodynamics. New U.S. world driving champ Phil Hill teamed with Olivier Gendebien to win the GT class and place second overall at both Sebring and LeMans in '62. Only 39 GTOs were built through 1964, including a few 4.0-liter and "Series II" models, plus special-body Prototype-class racers. Surprisingly docile yet very fast—5.9 seconds 0-60 mph, 0-100 in 14.1—the GTO still reigns supreme among collectible Ferraris.

**ENTER THE DAY OF THE FROG**

**LOTUS**

**Above and right:** England's Colin Chapman, of Formula race-car fame, unveiled a more practical roadgoing Lotus in late 1962. Like his earlier Elite coupe, the Elan roadster used a fiberglass body, but also a strong new steel "backbone" chassis with petite 84-inch wheelbase. The chassis forked at each end to carry brakes, steering, all-independent suspension, and a British Ford four-cylinder engine with Lotus-designed twincam head. Despite just 1588cc and 105 horses, the 1515-pound Elan could top 110 mph and do 0-60 in 9 seconds or less. It was also a wizard handler and loaded with charm. A coupe version and longer "+2" models arrived later, but tiny Lotus couldn't build any Elan fast enough to meet demand. **Below:** After 15 years of rapid growth in motorcycles, Honda of Japan launched its first four-wheeler in 1963, the S500 roadster. About the size of an Austin-Healey Sprite, it showed motorcycle heritage with chain drive to each rear wheel and a high-revving twincam four making 44 bhp from just 531cc. The replacement S600 of 1965 offered 57 bhp before giving way in '66 to the 70-bhp 791cc S800, which also came as a coupe. Honda built fewer than 15,000 of these cars through 1968. None were officially exported to the U.S.

**Top and center:** Replacing the MGA in late 1962, the logically named MGB used a similar suspension and the same B-Series four-cylinder engine, albeit enlarged to 1798cc. New were modern unitized construction, classically simple styling, and a roomier cockpit with...wind-up windows. The last bothered some MG diehards, but the B was as quick as Triumph's new TR4, pleasant to drive, and priced right at around $2500 on introduction. An instant sales success and a widely popular "club racer," the B would see no major design changes over a long 18-year career. **Above:** The MGB got a hatchback coupe sister in 1965, the B GT. Though not as popular, it did good business, with every sale a plus. Italy's Pininfarina reportedly helped with the styling. For 1968, both MGBs finally got a fully synchronized four-speed gearbox—no more "crash" first gear—as well as MG's first optional automatic transmission, though the latter would draw only some 5000 customers through 1973.

❝ MGBs are tough little cars. I taught myself to shift on a '67 roadster. After driving briefly around the yard I thought I learned all you needed to know: where the gears were and that you didn't downshift into an unsynchromeshed first gear until you came to a complete stop. Once on the road I couldn't get the stupid grin off my face because the car was so much more fun than big Seventies cars I was used to. I lost the grin when I attempted a downshift to second and found reverse. The car was moving forward and then backward. It was one of my smoother shifts of the day. There has never been any problem with the rear end. Syd Enever (MG engineering chief) once said he built the MGB heavy so that after losing a few layers of rust the driver would still have a safe car in a crash. I put that theory to test while driving about 60 mph one night and saw the profile of a Black Angus cow in the road. I was unhurt, and the car was repairable. The cow didn't fare as well... ❞

– Jack Stewart
Evanston, Illinois

Unveiled in 1962, the Maserati Sebring was basically a short-wheelbase version of the existing 3500GTI, which continued into '64. Sebring, of course, referred to the famous 12-hour annual road race in Florida, and this new Maser was very much aimed at the U.S. market, offering air conditioning and even automatic transmission, both firsts for Maserati. A trimmer 98.4-inch wheelbase supported handsome 2+2 coupe bodywork supplied by Vignale and designed by the prolific Giovanni Michelotti. Suspension, standard front disc brakes, and standard five-speed ZF gearbox were carried over from the 3500GTI. So was a 235-horsepower 3.5-liter twincam six. But only until spring 1964, when an upsized 3.7-liter with 245 bhp became available. The following year introduced a "Series II" Sebring with the larger engine, minor styling changes and, in a few cases, a 4.0-liter engine with 255 bhp. All Sebrings had functional heat-extractor vents on the front fenders. Series Is, as shown here, had low-set twin "gills" versus a high-set louvered panel on Series IIs. Respective production was 346 and 98 through 1966, so the Sebring was a fair sales success by Maserati standards. Top speed was at least 135 mph, with 0-60 mph clocking at just over 8 seconds.

Triumph answered the Austin-Healey Sprite and MG Midget in 1962 with a slightly larger budget sports car, the Spitfire. Triumph's small Herald sedan donated an all-independent suspension, backbone-type chassis, and 1147cc four-cylinder engine, but the Spitfire had 63 horsepower, unitized construction, 83-inch wheelbase, and dashing lines by Giovanni Michelotti. Despite tricky cornering behavior with its swing-axle rear end, the Spitfire was an instant hit, outselling the Sprite and Midget combined. Optional overdrive, wire wheels, and removable hardtop arrived in '63, then a Mark 2 with 67 bhp and nicer trim for 1965. The 1967 Mark 3 boasted a 75-bhp 1296cc engine, bigger brakes, spruced-up cockpit, improved soft top, and, in a nod to the U.S., a raised front bumper. The Spitfire would be even further evolved into the Seventies.

“ *...I always carried the "Standard Triumph spare kit," jumper cables, coat hanger, brake fluid, and full tool kit. I carried a rubber hammer under the seat to jar the tach needle into action from its resting place. But let me not focus on the challenges... Soon a family came and a Porsche 911, and the Spit was driven less and less. As the Spit continued to rust, I ended up selling her to a guy who promised he would restore her. Two years later I saw my poor little Spit still leaning to one side with shades of brown all over her. The Porsche was OK but could not match my little Spit for sheer Fun. The lesson I learned again was "always stay true to your first love."* ”

– Online owner posting—*My Spitfire Pub*

**Above, right, and lower right:** When heart trouble forced him to retire from racing, Carroll Shelby decided to offer his idea of a "pure sport car," the lightning-quick Cobra. The first 75, built in 1962, were stiffened-up British A.C. Ace roadsters powered by Ford's then-new 260-cubic-inch V8 with 260 horsepower. Fast as they were, Shelby wanted more, so the next 51 had the larger 289 engine rated at 271 bhp, up to 380 in race tune. Another 528 were built as improved Mark II models through 1968. **Below:** Though tricky to drive, the Cobra 289 was an almost unbeatable race car. It virtually owned SCCA's A-Production class from 1963 on. Even street versions could do 0-60 mph in 5.5 seconds and 0-100 in 14. **Opposite page, top:** Even more brutal, the Cobra 427 appeared in 1965 with bulged fenders that added seven inches to overall width, plus a big-block Ford V8 conservatively rated at 390 bhp. Exactly 348 of these beasts were built over two years, each capable of 0-60 mph in just 4.2 seconds.

## CARROLL SHELBY
### The Snake Charmer

Carroll Shelby wasn't the first to drop a American engine into a lightweight British sports car chassis. Allard J2s and J2-Xs used a variety of Yankee V8s, and Nash-Healeys had Nash six power—all in the early 1950s. But no British/American hybrid, before or since, has achieved the legendary status of Shelby's Cobras. The man behind the cars was a tenacious Texan who parlayed his good ol' boy charisma, technical skills, and shrewd business sense into a storied career that has spanned more than four decades.

Born in 1923 in Leesburg, Texas, Shelby served as an Army Air Corps flight instructor during World War II and made an ill-fated run at chicken farming before trying his hand at sports car racing. His first race was in 1952, piloting an MG-TC. Shelby's flair for self-promotion was evident early on—in 1953, Carroll was running late to the racetrack and didn't have time to change out of his work clothes. When he noticed the reaction his farmhand attire garnered at the track, Shelby made it a point to wear "Texas tuxedo" coveralls as his trademark. Throughout the 1950s, Shelby raced successfully in Europe and the US in many of the great sports cars of the day: Allards, Aston Martins, Austin-Healeys, Maseratis, and Ferraris. A natural racer, he would often steal a quick snooze before a race started, saying, "Wake me up when it's time to grid." The high point of his driving career was winning the 1959 24 Hours of LeMans, co-driving with Ray Salvadori in an Aston Martin DBR. But a heart condition forced Shelby to quit racing in 1960, and he soon focused his efforts on building sports cars instead.

In September 1961, Shelby learned that England's AC Cars was losing the engine supplier for its two-seat roadster and saw a golden opportunity. He convinced AC to provide him cars and then talked Ford into providing him their new small-block V8s. In 1962, the first Cobras hit the streets and racetracks. In 1965, the GT-350 Mustang and brutal 427 Cobra debuted. Wheeled by the best American drivers of the day, Shelby's cars racked up highly-touted racing victories. His mystique quickly grew to epic proportions. Here was a Stetson-topped cowboy who had an honest chance at sticking it to Europe's best in big league, international competition—a big crock of fichptve-alarm Texas chili crashing a tea and crumpets party. Shelby and his cars were brash, unrepentantly overpowered, and unabashedly American. Star-spangled sports car buffs were all too eager to celebrate the exploits of their homeland hero, and Shelby's place in sports car history was secure by the end of the decade.

As the sixties drew to a close, so did Shelby's racing operation and his association with Ford. Carroll went on to oversee a string of coarse but potent turbo Dodges in the 1980s, serve as a consultant for Dodge's landmark Viper in the 1990s, and today is still active building "continuation" Cobra replicas and the modern Series I sports car.

Classic dual-purpose sports cars became increasingly rare as the Sixties passed, but Alfa Romeo kept the faith with the exotic Giulia GTZ. Announced in 1963, it used the running gear and basic chassis of other Giulias but was thoroughly optimized for competition. "T" stood for *Turbolare,* Italian for tubular, a reference to the shape of the members making up the car's complex but very strong inner structure. "Z" denoted Zagato, the free-thinking coachbuilder who designed and supplied the unusual coupe bodywork, made mostly of lightweight aluminum. Weight-watching also dictated a no-frills interior and snap-in door windows, though a heater was included. Aerodynamics prompted a low nose, smooth fastback shape, and sharply cut-off "Kamm" tail. The GTZ also differed from other Giulias in having a fully independent rear suspension instead of a heavier live axle and in replacing rear drum brakes with discs, which mounted inboard to reduce unsprung weight. All brakes were race-car large and supplied by Girling. With all this, a GTZ tipped the scales at just 1450 pounds, some 500 pounds less than a conventional Giulia Sprint GT coupe. Alfa offered both racing and road models. The latter carried the hotter 129-horsepower Veloce version of Alfa's 1570cc twincam four. Though not a world-beating major-league racer despite a good power-to-weight ratio, GTZs were usually class contenders, yet were also surprisingly usable on the road. Only 112 were completed through 1967, when the model was dropped.

**Above:** Actor Sean Connery poses with the Aston Martin DB5 that was also made a star by the early James Bond films. Bowing in 1963, the DB5 kept the basic look and 98-inch wheelbase of the prior DB4 but used a twincam six enlarged to near 4.0 liters and 282 horsepower. An optional 325-bhp Vantage engine arrived in '64. There was also a Volante convertible with the same lightweight Superleggera construction by Touring of Italy. Though much heavier than a DB4, Mr. Bond's car could still top 140 mph. **Below and right:** New in 1959, the Austin-Healey 3000 sported a larger 2912cc six, front-disc brakes, and minor trim changes. Two-seat and 2+2 models continued on a 92-inch chassis. Horsepower went from 124 to 132 for 1962's Mark II, which soon became the 3000 Convertible with wind-up windows, attached folding top, and no two-seat option. A plusher Mark III arrived in early '64 with 148 bhp, revised suspension, and top speed up to 120 mph. The line ended in 1967, mainly because it couldn't meet new U.S. regulations. **Bottom:** But the big Healeys still have many fans, including those who go in for "vintage" racing. Here's one dueling with an Alfa.

**Above right, below right:** New from stem to stern, the 1963 Corvette Sting Ray was lighter, stronger, and more striking than America's sports car had ever been. More capable too, with first-time independent rear suspension and a returning lineup of 327 V8s with up to 360 horsepower in top fuel-injected form. A sleek fastback with unique split window—for this year only—joined the traditional convertible. Both rode a tauter 98-inch wheelbase, yet offered more room, comfort, and convenience. No wonder Corvette sales broke the 20,000 barrier for 1963 and would keep heading up to reach nearly 28,000 by 1966. Numerous interim improvements helped keep demand strong, including a gradual design cleanup that eliminated the '63's dummy hood vents, for example. Speed freaks cheered the arrival of big-block 396 V8 power for 1965, followed by bored-out 427 Turbo Jet options with up to 425 bhp, good for 0-60 mph in less than 5 seconds and 140 mph all out. Optional front disc brakes gave '65 and later models the stopping power to match their performance. The Sting Ray was hailed in its day as the best 'Vette yet, and many still think that's true some 40 years later. **Below:** Some people seem to have *all* the fun, like this group taking in the action at Road America circa 1967 from the appropriate vantage point of a shiny Corvette. Sting Ray's "ducktail" was evolved from that of the final 1961-62 "solid axle" models.

**Left:** A racing Sting Ray coupe leads a pair of Ferraris in a mid-Sixties Road America moment. Though the Shelby Cobra was usually the car to beat in period major-league road racing, Sting Rays scored a good many trophies, including SCCA B-production national championships in 1963-64 and high finishes at Daytona and Sebring in '66. **Below:** The '67s were the last and cleanest Sting Rays, represented here by a lovingly restored 427 ragtop. Any big-block 'Vette is now a prime collector's item. You'll pay a six-figure price for one of the mere 20 cars fitted with the mighty 560-bhp L88 option with special aluminum cylinder head and lofty 12.5:1 compression ratio. Not that they often change hands. **Bottom left:** All Sting Rays featured a well organized "dual cowl" dashboard with large speedometer and tachometer and a center section containing a clock, minor controls, and radio, which mounted vertically. Air conditioning joined the 'Vette options list for 1963. **Bottom right:** Chevy's big-block was taller than the small-block V8. A bulged hood with functional hood air scoop was provided to add clearance.

**Above and left:** Maserati continued its assault on the GT market in 1963 with the Mistral, basically a two-seat Sebring on a tighter 94.5-inch wheelbase. This hatchback coupe was offered along with a spider convertible, both styled by Pietro Frua. Respective production was 828 and a mere 120 through 1970. Most Mistrals had 3.7- or 4.0-liter twincam sixes rated at 255 horsepower. **Middle left:** Staid German automaker Glas added a four-cylinder GT coupe starting in '63, but it didn't improve the troubled company's outlook. BMW took over in 1966, giving the model a "twin kidney" grille and the 105-bhp engine from its compact 1600Ti two-door sedan. BMW built 1255 of its version in 1967-68, versus some 800 for the Glas original. **Bottom left and below:** Though based on an everyday sedan, Fiat's second attempt at a sports tourer sold quite well in Europe and the U.S. It bowed in 1959 as a two-seat cabriolet offered as the 1200 with a 58-bhp pushrod four and as the 1500S with an 80-bhp twincam version. Engine swaps in 1963 created a replacement 72-bhp 1500 and twincam 90-bhp 1600S. Twincam models had Alfa brio, if not breeding, and were somewhat more affordable. Some 43,000 were built through 1966.

**Above:** Regardless of brand, tire companies pitched sports-car enthusiasts in the Sixties with promises of improved performance, cornering ability, and wet-weather roadholding no matter what the car. Ads like this are still a staple of major car-buff magazines, only the tires are a lot lower and wider now. **Right and below right:** As if to answer charges of being hopelessly stuck in the Thirties, Morgan added a more contemporary car in 1963, the Plus 4 Plus. Not only was it the company's first coupe, its smooth "bubbletop" body featured rust-free fiberglass outer panels and a separate trunk with external lid, all pretty radical for the tiny British specialist. But though "mod" enough for Carnaby Street, the Plus 4 Plus had Morgan's usual steel-and-wood inner body construction and a chassis that hadn't been fundamentally altered in decades, the same 96-inch-wheelbase platform that served Morgan roadsters. The engine wasn't that new either, being the four-cylinder 2.1-liter Triumph TR4 unit that dated from the mid-Fifties. But with 100 horses, only 1820 pounds, and much less air drag, the Plus 4 Plus could see 110 mph and run 0-60 mph in about 12.5 seconds. Trouble was, Morgan loyalists thought the coupe too modern, while non-Morgan owners were put off by the ox-cart ride and crude details like manual sliding door windows. As a result, production was halted in 1966 at just 26 units out of a planned 50. Thus stung, Morgan hasn't tried anything this daring since. And why should it, when each year brings long waiting lists for its Thirties-style roadsters?

The 904 GTS was conceived in 1962 as Porsche's latest GT-class endurance racer but could be used on the road given a skilled, tolerant driver. A sturdy box-rail chassis with 90.6-inch wheelbase and all-independent suspension supported a smooth fiberglass body shaped by "Butzi" Porsche, grandson of the great Ferdinand and designer of the milestone 911, which also broke cover in 1963. A five-speed 911 transaxle teamed with an engine sitting just behind the two-seater cockpit. The package was sized for the legendary 2.0-liter Carrera flat-four from the outgoing 356 series, but some 904s got six-cylinder 911 engines, and one or two were built with racing flat-eights. Though a bit heavier than planned, the 904 was fast enough and could go the distance. In 1964 alone, team entries ran 1st and 3rd in the Targa Florio, 3rd overall in the Nurburgring 1000 Kilometers, 3rd *through* 6th in the Tour de France, and were five of the top 12 finishers at LeMans. Only 100 were built over two years. A good many survive today and are still going strong on road and track alike.

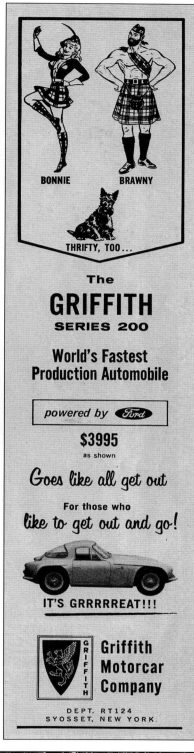

In 1962, TVR was a small British sports-car maker not well known in the U.S. except to the likes of Jack Griffith, whose New York shops prepped racing versions of TVR's stock-in-trade model, the bobtail Grantura coupe. Just for fun, Griffith tried replacing the normal MGB four-cylinder engine with a Ford 289 V8 and found it would fit with a little work. He took the idea to cash-short TVR, which was happy to send over engineless Granturas for what Jack sold starting in 1963 as the TVR Griffith 200. Both versions wore a fiberglass body over a stout tubular backbone chassis with double-wishbone suspension and trim 85.5-inch wheelbase, but the 1905-pound Griffith packed much more power: 195 base, 271 optional. With its four-speed Ford gearbox, it could do 0-60 mph in under 6 seconds and top 150. A replacement 400 bowed in early '64 with a flat tail and better engine cooling, but events were against it and Jack gave up the following year after selling some 300 units. A few Griffiths, like this 200, were reverse-exported to Britain, complete with left-hand drive.

143

> " Quite honestly, I would have to say Ferrari (is my favorite car.) No particular one, just Ferrari. They had 12 cylinders, were very powerful, very fast, and very fun to drive. Ferrari is certainly the car I had the most fun with. Of course, they too have their faults. "
>
> – Ferruccio Lamborghini

**Top and above:** The Ferrari legend grew with the 1964 arrival of the 275 GTB coupe and GTS spider. Both used a 260-horsepower 3.3-liter V12, plus Ferrari's first rear transaxle, a five-speed, and first independent rear suspension. This early berlinetta shown here got a longer nose and detail styling changes in late '65. A twincam engine with four valves per cylinder and 300 bhp highlighted the further-improved 275 GTB/4 models of 1966. Series production totaled 940 through 1967, of which 730 were coupes. **Left:** Among the coupes was a handful of racing 275 GTB/Cs with aluminum bodies and hotter engines. Like many period Ferraris, they're a common sight in vintage races today.

Ferrari got serious new competition with the March 1964 debut of the two-seat Lamborghini 350GT coupe, which earned immediate rave reviews for its vivid V12 performance and top-notch handling, courtesy of chief engineer Giotto Bizzarrini. Two years later, Lamborghini added this 400GT with cramped "+2" rear seating and subtle styling alterations on the same 100.3-inch wheelbase, plus a V12 enlarged from 3.5 to 4.0 liters and from 280 to 320 horsepower. Both models shared classic all-round double-wishbone suspension, all-disc brakes, and smooth bodywork by Touring of Milan. The 400 also boasted a Lamborghini-built five-speed gearbox designed by redoubtable engineer Gianpaolo Dallara. Though not yet a sales threat to Maranello—fewer than 400 total through 1968—the upstarts from Sant'Agata served notice on Enzo. Or, as *Road & Track* put it, "Watch Out, Ferrari!"

# FERRUCCIO LAMBORGHINI
## The Fighting Bull

As sports-car giants go, he was not cantankerous, manipulative, or obsessed. Maybe it was because his sense of identity didn't depend wholly on the automobiles that bore his name. He was, after all, an industrial tycoon long before he started building cars. Still, the story of how Ferruccio Lamborghini decided to construct high-performance exotics shows he certainly was spirited.

One of the richer tales in the sports-car canon, it holds that around 1962, Lamborghini, already a millionaire maker of farm equipment, was having mechanical trouble with one of the Ferraris he owned. He sought to complain directly to Enzo Ferrari. In some accounts, Lamborghini is denied an audience with *Il Commendatore*. In others, an imperious Enzo advises him to stick to driving tractors. All picture an outraged Lamborghini storming off to create his own damn sports car.

If not exactly historically accurate—there are doubters—building prestige GTs was a natural step for Ferruccio Lamborghini. Here was an enthusiast of means who couldn't find just the right car to please an ambitious, self-made man of demanding technical sensibility—a man like himself.

Born to farmers near Bologna in 1916, Ferruccio was from boyhood captivated not by the soil but by machines. He modified Fiats, even raced briefly. Duty in the Italian army motor pool honed his skills. Emerging penniless from World War II, he saw an opportunity. From discarded Allied equipment he cobbled up simple tractors, winning

sales traveling the countryside and challenging competitors to pull-offs in dusty town squares. Of such wit and will emerged an agricultural-equipment manufacturing company, then an industrial-heating and air-conditioning concern. For the emblem of his growing corporate empire, Lamborghini chose a charging bull.

It was the sign of his Taurean birth, but it also symbolized his forthright approach. Lamborghini's formula was to gather top-grade people, show faith in their skills, and work and laugh along with them. Visitors to his villa found the stocky, square-jawed mogul tanned and smiling, dressed, as one said, "in the rough clothes of a working man, and wearing carpet slippers because he was at home."

Applying the same strategy to carmaking, Lamborghini harnessed sharp young automotive talent, including Ferrari engine designer Giotto Bizzarrini, and in 1963, built them a factory. Today, Lamborghini is associated with the wildest midengine supercars. Under Ferruccio, its main goal was refined grand-touring coupes. But the enterprise was never a big commercial success, producing less than a dozen separate models and only a few thousand cars on its founder's watch.

By the late '60s, Ferruccio's attention and patience were spread thin, his businesses frustrated by cutthroat international competition and labor unrest. In the early 1970s, he sold controlling interest in Automobili Ferruccio Lamborghini to Swiss business interests, and by age 58, had shed most of his other holdings to retire to his lush vineyard estate. He died there peacefully in 1993. Lamborghini the marque survived a slate of owners, including the Italian bankruptcy court, German, French, and Indonesian caretakers, even the Chrysler Corporation, before landing in 1998 at Volkswagen/Audi. All built exotic cars of bold spirit, each named for a fighting bull.

**Left:** Porsche began a new era with the 911, which bowed in 1963 but didn't reach U.S. customers until early '65. Like the 356 models it replaced (and fronts in this photo), it used a rear-mounted air-cooled "boxer" engine and all-independent torsion-bar suspension. But the engine was a new 148-horsepower 2.0-liter flat-six, and the unitized coupe body was an artfully fresh design by company scion "Butzi" Porsche on a slightly longer, 87-inch wheelbase. Critics hailed the more refined 911 as fully worthy of its higher price, initially $6500 U.S. But that was too rich for some buyers, so a four-cylinder version was added in mid-'65, the $4700 912. A hotter 180-bhp 911S followed in late '66, the first of many variations on what would prove to be one of the most enduring sports-car designs in history. **Below:** Despite its many improvements, the 911 was clearly evolved from the 356 and thus immediately accepted as a true Porsche by marque enthusiasts. Here, a group of Midwest fans brave a rainy day at Road America for a new-versus-old comparison shortly after the 911's U.S.-market debut.

**Right:** Almost before its paint was dry, the 911 took over from the 356 as Porsche's production-class warrior for road racing, rallies, and hillclimbs. In SCCA it first ran in D-Production and easily won the 1966 national championship. It was then lofted into C-Production, as shown here, and owned that class in 1967-69. The 911 scored many other early-days triumphs, including outright victory in the 1968 Monte Carlo Rally. Porsche helped its racers with numerous competition parts and ready technical assistance. **Below and bottom:** As with the 356, Porsche relentlessly pursued perfection with the 911, making considered changes most every year, some large, most small. The original design wasn't visibly altered through 1968, but models expanded to include the S, a lower-priced 911T detuned to 110 horsepower, and semi-convertible Targa versions with lift-off roof panel. All 911s (and the 912) offered a well-furnished 2+2 cockpit, an obviously driver-centered dashboard, solid German workmanship, the unique sound of a precision air-cooled engine, and a look that would stand the test of time.

**Above:** Aimed squarely at the U.S., the Sunbeam Tiger bowed in 1964 as a beefed up Alpine with a small-block Ford V8 instead of a tame four. At around $3500, it seemed like budget Cobra. And in fact, Carroll Shelby did much of the engineering. Performance was brisk with the initial 164-horsepower 260 V8, thrilling with the 200-bhp 289 substituted for '67—as little as 7.5 seconds 0-60 mph. By that point, though, parent Rootes Group had sold out to Chrysler, which had no use for a Ford-powered car and dropped the Tiger after fewer than 7100 were built. **Left and below:** After conjuring supercars for Ferrari and Lamborghini, maestro engineer Giotto Bizzarrini built one on his own, the GT Strada 5300. Actually, it was much like the 2+2 Iso Grifo A3L coupe he'd just designed, with a 327 Corvette V8, steel platform chassis, and a rakish Bertone-built body shaped by Giorgetto Giugiaro. But the Strada was a two-seater, had aluminum body panels instead of steel, and was built in both semi-open (*left*) and fixed-roof guises. No more than 100 were built, all by hand. Each was a flyer, able to see 145 mph and run 0-60 in 6.4 seconds.

**Above:** A follow-up to the sedate Rivolta 2+2, the two-seat Iso Grifo was the kissin' cousin of Giotto Bizzarrini's GT Strada 5300, with a similar chassis and Corvette power but a steel body, somewhat different looks, and a two-inch-longer wheelbase (98.4 inches). Deliveries began in 1965 with a choice of 300 and 365 horsepower and five-speed manual or GM automatic transmissions. A "7-Litre" model was added in 1969 with a Chevy 427. A facelift, shown here, carried the Grifo to 1974, when it became a casualty of the first Energy Crisis. Exactly 412 were built. **Right:** Fiat's most successful sports tourers yet bowed in 1968 as a two-seat Spider and 2+2 Sports Coupe based on the Italian giant's mass-market 124 sedan. The Pininfarina-styled spider, shown here, would endure for over 15 years with no fundamental change save engines. Sixties models used the 124's original 1438cc twincam four, tuned up to 96 bhp. Popular then and now, these Fiats are pleasant, relatively practical, sporty cars that cost less than comparable Alfas.

**Above:** Maserati dusted off a nine-year-old racing engine to power its first V8 road car, the Mexico, a 2+2 coupe bowing in 1965. An expansive 103.9-inch-wheelbase chassis from the recently launched Quattroporte sedan supported rather bland standard coachwork by Vignale, but a few cars inevitably got custom bodies, like this example designed by Pietro Frua. Though heavier than previous six-cylinder Masers, the Mexico had more power—290 in top-spec form—so it was a bit quicker, doing 0-60 mph in as little as 7.5 seconds. **Right:** Also new in '65, the Porsche 912 looked much like the six-cylinder 911 but gave up frills and outright acceleration in exchange for a lighter base price in the $4700-$5000 range. Even so, it sold reasonably well, with some 30,300 built through 1969. **Below:** The 911S arrived in the U.S. for 1967 with pretty five-spoke alloy wheels that pared five pounds from each corner. Other upgrades included firmer damping, vented front disc brakes, and rear antiroll bar, all of which made for phenomenal cornering power. **Below right:** Knock-off wheel hubs were invented to speed tire changes in races, but many roadgoing sports cars had them as well. If yours didn't, aftermarket companies were happy to oblige.

**Above and right:** At Ford's behest, Carroll Shelby turned the hot-selling Mustang "ponycar" into a serious race machine, the GT-350. Modifications abounded, including a stripped-down fastback body, beefed-up chassis, and a tuned 289 V8 rated at 306 horsepower. A track-ready R-model packed at least 325 bhp. Both were high-performance bargains at $4547 and $5950, respectively. Shelby built 562 GT-350s for '65 and 2378 of the similar '66s, including 936 GT-350H models like this. The "H" stood for Hertz, which lost a bundle on weekend rentals. **Below:** All '65 GT-350s and many '66s wore white paint set off by big, blue Ford/Shelby racing stripes. R-models won three straight SCCA B-Production national championships (1965-67). Here's one looking to pass a Corvette Sting Ray on the outside in period action at Laguna Seca Raceway near Monterey, California.

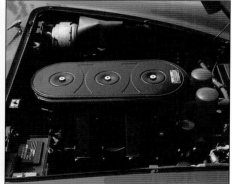

**Top and above:** In 1966, Ferrari mated the rear-transaxle 275 GTB chassis with the 4.0-liter V12 of its recently introduced 330 GT 2+2. The resulting 330 GTC notchback coupe and 330 GTS spyder convertible wore smart new Pininfarina bodies that continued for the replacement 365 GTC/GTS that arrived in 1968 with a 4.4-liter V12 making 20 more horsepower, 320 in all. This 365 GTS is one of only 20 built in a series total of some 900. **Left:** Pininfarina shaped another 1966 newcomer, the Alfa Romeo Duetto, which replaced the coachbuilder's 12-year-old Giulietta/Giulia spider design. The rounded nose and pointy tail harked to a 1959 show car evolved from the Disco Volante series. Some Alfa traditionalists didn't like the new look, but the Duetto got instant Hollywood-star sales appeal when Dustin Hoffman drove one in the hit film *The Graduate.* Like other Giulias, Duettos used the familiar 1570cc twincam four until 1969, when the series switched to a slightly torquier "1750" engine—actually 1779cc. At that point, the Duetto name was dropped in favor of Giulia Spider, later just Alfa Spider.

Rebuffed when it tried to buy Ferrari, Ford created the GT40 to exact revenge in international long-distance racing. The basic midengine design originated in Britain but was heavily reworked by Carroll Shelby and other Americans after a troubled 1964 debut season and scant success in '65. Ford reached the pinnacle in 1966 with smashing 1-2-3 finishes at LeMans and Daytona, thus eclipsing Ferrari at last, then repeated as world manufacturers champion and LeMans winner in 1967-69. Only 130 racing GT40s were built. Of these, 15 were Mark II versions powered by Ford big-block 427 V8s prepared by Holman & Moody of stock-car racing fame. The similar-looking Mark I used Ford's 289 small-block V8, also competition-tuned. There were also a few "Mark III" versions with long-nose bodies, detuned engines, and basic road equipment. This car is one of several Mark II replicas offered in the late 1990s by Holman & Moody scion Lee Holman. Fittingly, it was crafted with original GT40 tooling, which had somehow survived over the years in Britain, where the storied racers were built.

**Above and below left:** Ferruccio Lamborghini produced an instant icon with his second supercar, the sleek, sexy P400 Miura. It hit the road in 1966 with a 350-horsepower 4.0-liter V12 sitting amidships in a light but strong platform chassis. The styling, by young Bertone designer Marcello Gandini, turned heads everywhere but also caused unnerving high-speed aerodynamic lift. Then again, the Miura was amazingly fast. *Road & Track* clocked 0-60 mph at just 5.5 seconds and no less than 180 mph all out. Despite a huge $20,000 price, Lamborghini built 475 Miuras through 1969, over four times the number planned. The following year brought a tweaked 370-bhp P400S, shown here. It saw 140 copies over less than two years. **Below left and bottom:** Though pushed out of the spotlight by the Miura, Lamborghini's 400GT wasn't exactly slow, scaling 0-60 mph in about 7 seconds and good for at least 150 mph. Production was halted in 1968 after some 250 were built.

Lotus followed its Elan roadster in 1966 with the Europa, a coupe built to the same weight-conscious formula but with a four-cylinder Renault powertrain mounted amidships, as in the newest racing cars. The "breadvan" styling wasn't so racy, but the Europa was surprisingly brisk and very agile.

# COLIN CHAPMAN
## The Lean Operator

Armed with a passion for cars and £25 borrowed from his wife-to-be, Anthony Colin Bruce Chapman formed one of the most storied and eclectic car companies of the latter-half of the 20th century.

The son of a hotel manager, Chapman was born in 1928. While studying engineering at London University, Chapman also found time to learn to fly and drive an old Austin-based racer. In 1948 Chapman joined the Royal Air Force, again making time to build and race. After leaving the RAF Chapman found day work with an engineering firm and built race cars in a rented garage by night. In '52 he borrowed just enough money from his longtime girlfriend (later wife) Hazel Williams to form Lotus Engineering Co., Ltd.

Chapman's early cars found success on the track, and Lotus had plenty of work building copies for eager drivers. The Lotus Mark VI (later revised and renamed Seven) was especially successful and could be driven on the street—as Patrick McGoohan did in the opening sequence of the '60s television series The Prisoner.

Chapman was not only an innovative thinker and brilliant engineer, but also had the ability to attract talent—in spite of notorious stinginess. Nearly as careful with pounds as he was with Pounds, Chapman was fanatical about making components as light as possible. If a lightweight component could perform two functions instead of one—all the better. Sometimes flaws in materials or construction caused slender parts to fail, but when everything held together the racers were unbeatable.

In 1958 Chapman applied his racing prowess

to his first dedicated road car, the Elite. The Elite set high standards for handling but was expensive to produce and failed to make the company money.

Lotus's next road car, the Elan, of 1962, was cheaper to make, yet shared Elite's qualities of handling and performance. The Elan was a hit for the small company, racking up 15,000 sales in 11 years.

While making money from street cars, Lotus remained heavily involved in racing. Though technically influential in many racing venues, Lotus's impact on Indy Car racing was perhaps most dramatic. First entering the series in 1963, Lotus's success with its rear-engined entries sparked a field-wide conversion that led to the near elimination of front-engine cars by the 1965 Indianapolis 500—which Jim Clark won driving a Lotus. Lotus racked up similar successes in Formula One, scoring seven Constructors' Champion-ships by the late Seventies.

Taking notice of Lotus's engineering prowess, other car builders tapped into the firm's brain trust, providing a more steady source of revenue for Lotus than the firm's low-volume car lines.

Sadly it was a design contract with the ill-fated DeLorean Motor Company that may have hastened Chapman's death. Engaged to help bring the fledgling sports car to market, Lotus was implicated with DeLorean on charges of mishandling British government funds.

Stress from his legal problems combined with a series of recent racing failures conspired to compromise Chapman's health, and he died in December 1982 from a massive heart attack. The last-of-an-era in many ways, Colin Chapman managed to "compete with the big boys" combatting size and resources with technical prowess and rigid frugality. A tribute to its founder, Chapman's scrappy little Lotus is still known for its lean engineering and handling expertise.

*Jim Clark and Colin Chapman (right)*

**Above and left:** Mercedes-Benz dropped both its existing two-seaters in 1963 for a new SL with improved handling, comfort, and refinement, plus modern styling and adequate, though not awesome, performance. The debut 230SL had a 2.3-liter overhead-cam six with 170 horsepower. A short-lived 2.5-liter 250SL took over for model-year '67, followed in '68 by a 180-bhp 2.8-liter 280SL. Interim changes were minor and evolutionary. This 250SL wears the available "pagoda roof" lift-off hardtop, so called because of its shape when viewed from dead-on. **Below:** Maserati looked to the Seventies with its new 1969 Indy 2+2 coupe. Carefully sized between the four-place Mexico and the two-seat Ghibli (new in '66), it was a shapely hatchback with a 102.4-inch wheelbase and the Mexico's original 4.1-liter twincam V8, tuned for 260 bhp. The first Maserati with unit construction, the Indy was styled and assembled by Vignale, which would build 1136 through 1974.

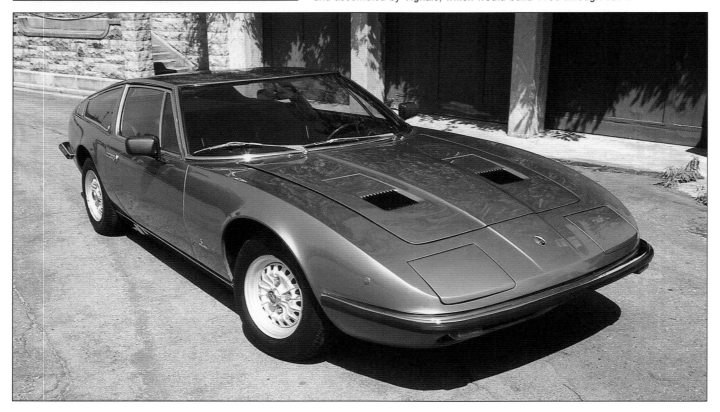

Saab took 10 years to try another sporty car, but this time the Swedish automaker actually built it for sale. Like the prototype Sonnet I roadster, the logically named Sonnet II borrowed the chassis and two-stroke front-drive powertrain of Saab's mainstay sedan. Fiberglass was again chosen for the body, only it was a new coupe style that strained to look racy. Still, the Sonnet II was obviously more practical, with a roomier, better-furnished cockpit and genuine luggage space, accessed by a panel in the tail. But though curb weight was a svelte 1565 pounds, it was too much for the 60 horsepower of the 841cc "triple" borrowed from Saab's sporty 96 Monte Carlo sedan. Saab responded in 1968 by substituting a narrow-angle 1.5-liter V4 purchased from Ford of Germany. This required a higher hood bulge for clearance (*top*) and had only five more horses, but its extra torque improved low-end response. Even better, the four-stroke V4 sounded more like a "real" engine. Alas, dumpy looks, relatively high price, and inept advertising—who wanted to drive a "toy"?—conspired against the Sonnet II in the U.S. market it was created for, and only 1868 were built through 1970—all likely at a loss.

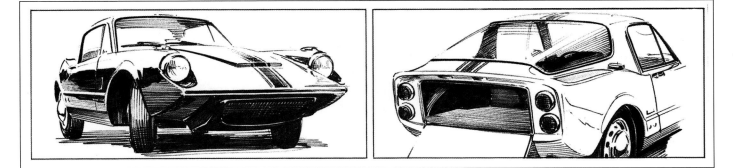

**Below and bottom:** Perhaps the ultimate in raw sports-car power and performance, the legendary Shelby Cobra 427 has been widely replicated—no surprise, as only 348 originals were built in 1965-67. Though some of the copies have been quite faithful, Carroll Shelby has jealously guarded the car's name and design, even bringing lawsuits against counterfeiters. A few 427s were actually fitted with Ford's low-stress 428 passenger-car V8, whose gross horsepower is usually quoted as 355. This, however, is a genuine 427, conservatively rated at 390 bhp. **Left:** Cobras have always thrilled crowds at race-tracks. Though they still typically command six-figure prices as collector cars, they often compete in vintage events, evoking memories of a now-distant sports-car era.

**Right:** Triumph raced Spitfire-based fast-backs in 1963-64, taking 1-2 in class at LeMans '64. In late 1966 came a similar roadgoing version, the GT6, but with a smooth 2.0-liter inline six instead of a small four and a $3000 initial U.S. price. The lower body was basically Spitfire, but the coupe offered greater luggage space beneath its liftup rear hatch, plus closed-car refinement and rigidity. Though heavier than it looked, the GT6 was quicker than the Spitfire—and the rival MGB GT—running 0-60 mph in around 12 seconds and up to 106 mph all out. Often viewed as a sort of mini Jaguar E-Type, the GT6 proved fairly popular, with 15,818 built through mid-1968. **Top and above:** The GT6 Mark 2 boasted better handling from a new-think independent rear suspension, plus upgraded cockpit furnishings and a higher-set front bumper to enhance crash protection. Front and rear side-marker lights identified U.S.-market models, which were labeled "GT6+." Horsepower remained at 95 despite a new camshaft, cylinder heads, and manifolds. World sales totaled 12,066 through 1970.

**Above and left:** A first cousin to Ferrari's famed midengine Dino coupe, the Fiat Dino bowed in late '66 as a Pininfarina-designed two-seat Spider on an 89.8-inch wheelbase. A Bertone-bodied 2+2 fastback on a 100.4-inch span followed in early '67. Both used a front-engine/rear-drive format and a 2.0-liter twincam engine with around 160 horsepower. Improved 2.4-liter models appeared in 1969 with 180 bhp and independent instead of live-axle rear suspension. Fiat built some 5000 of its Dinos through 1972. Few came to America as new cars, in part because they weren't engineered for the first U.S. safety and emissions regulations that took effect in '68. **Below:** Serving notice on the Cobra and other high-power sports cars, the DeTomaso Mangusta ("mongoose") appeared in late 1966 with purposeful midengine coupe styling by Giorgio Giugiaro and a Ford small-block V8 tuned for over 300 horsepower. Only some 400 were built.

**Top and above:** The Mangusta was the second sports-car project brokered by Argentinian Alejandro deTomaso after he gave up racing and moved to Italy with dreams of becoming a manufacturer. His first car, the small, Lotus-like Vallelunga roadster of 1964, attracted little attention. Not so the Mangusta. Low, wide, and menacing on a 98.4-inch wheelbase, it used a strong "backbone" steel chassis, with box-section and tubular members for carrying the powertrain, double-wishbone coil-spring suspension, and beefy all-disc brakes. The Ghia-built body nestled around very broad tires, which were wisely wider at the rear to suit a tail-heavy weight distribution. Dramatic gullwing sections behind the cramped two-seat cockpit provided race-car-like access to the midships Ford V8 and five-speed ZF manual transaxle. Though several hundred pounds heavier than a small-block Cobra, DeTomaso's mongoose had similar power potential and far better aerodynamics. Top speed was a claimed 155 mph, yet price was around $11,500, thousands less than a Ferrari or Lamborghini with comparable performance. Though the basic design was quite impractical for a road car, the Mangusta attracted enough orders to launch DeTomaso as a serious new sports-car marque. It also attracted the attention of America's Rowan Controls company, which soon bought DeTomaso and Ghia as well, thus assuring the future of both.
**Right:** Not all car waxes are alike—or so we've been hearing for decades. This mid-Sixties pitch for the fancifully named Car-Skin makes the usual claims for an advanced formula that's easy to apply and gives unsurpassed shine. *Motor Trend* apparently endorsed it, perhaps because Car-Skin placed an ad there. *MT* is still with us, but where is Car-Skin?

**Above:** Seeking to broaden its market, Lotus added the Elan +2 coupe in 1967. It was engineered much like two-seat models, but wheelbase was stretched 12 inches (to 96) to make room for a token rear seat. Soon after its debut, Lotus offered all Elans with a "Special Equipment" twincam four making 115 horsepower, 10 more than standard. Despite extra weight, the +2 performed and handled much like smaller Elans, but sales would prove somewhat disappointing at just under 4800 through 1974. **Left and below:** W113 was the internal designation for the square-cut Mercedes-Benz SL line of 1963-71. A discreet trunklid badge is about the only way to distinguish an early 230SL from the later 250 and 280 SLs, though U.S.-required side-marker lights and round headlamps mark this example as a post-1967 280. Note the subtle concave dip in the windshield header.

**Above:** Like so many MGBs over the years, this one is set up for a very specific sort of Sunday afternoon drive. **Right:** Transplanting a 3.0-liter BMC six into the MGB produced the MGC, a short-lived would-be successor to the Austin-Healey 3000. Offered as both a roadster and this GT coupe, the MGC was interesting but unimpressive. About half the total 8999 built (4256 being coupes) were sold in the U.S. **Below and bottom left:** An accessory rollover bar suggests this Sunbeam Tiger takes part in the occasional club race or a rally. Single-bar grilles mark Series I models. Series IIs used a cross-hatch insert. **Bottom right:** A finned early-Sixties Sunbeam Alpine slips past a rare two-cylinder French Deutch Bonnet.

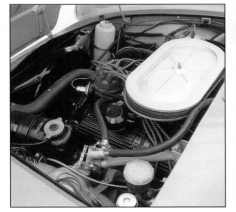

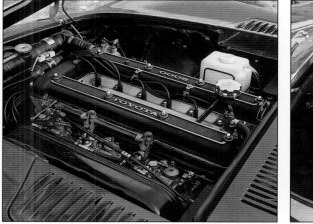

The Toyota 2000GT would have been impressive coming from an established European sports-car maker, let alone a Japanese outfit that in the Sixties was only beginning to make its mark with family cars. Inspired by a prototype designed by motorcycle maker Yamaha and refused by Nissan, the GT was heavily engineered along European lines, appearing in 1965 with a Lotus-style backbone chassis, Dunlop four-wheel disc brakes, rack-and-pinion steering, and all-round double-wishbone coil-spring suspension a la Jaguar E-Type. The hatchback coupe, which also mimicked the E-Type, was by Count Albrecht Goertz, who'd shaped the late-Fifties BMW 507. A Yamaha-designed 2.0-liter twincam six sent 150 horsepower through a five-speed manual gearbox. Low and sleek on a 91.7-inch wheelbase, the 2000GT was fairly fast and fully equipped but more an image-building experiment than serious money-earner. Only 337 were built through 1970. None were officially sold in the U.S., though a few did come in as private imports. The asking price was very steep anyway: an estimated $6800. A few convertibles were built for the James Bond film *You Only Live Twice*, thus setting the stage for more-affordable, if far less exotic, sporty Toyotas in the Seventies.

**Above:** With growing U.S.-market demands for greater refinement—and the demands of new U.S. emissions standards—the four-cylinder Triumph TR4A gave way to the six-cylinder TR250 for 1968. Changes were otherwise few, including weight but also horsepower, as twin carburetors and mild tuning were retained for the 2.5-liter six. But the 250 was only a one-year stopgap, though fairly successful with 8484 sold. Other markets, meantime, got a similar but much faster TR5 with fuel injection and 150 horsepower. **Right and below:** Despite its newfound power the 250 was a stylistic clone of the TR4 series. Fresh styling would arrive with the TR6 in 1969.

**Above and right:** Though it amounted to just a new body atop the existing Sting Ray chassis, the 1968 Corvette was profitable eye candy that pushed Chevrolet's sports car to another sales record: 28,566 units. Convertible and coupe continued, but the latter was transformed from a fastback to a notchback with a novel "T-bar" roof. Twin roof panels clipped to a central bar and the windshield frame and a structural rear "hoop" tied to it. The result combined roadster-like breeziness with coupe-like rigidity. The rear window was removable too. Buyers liked these innovations, and for model-year '69 the coupe outsold the roadster for the first time in 'Vette history. Though the '68s were just Corvettes, the '69s revived the Stingray name—as one word. Sales kept heading up, reaching 38,762. Among them was this T-top coupe with a big-block 427 V8 rumbling through optional side exhaust pipes. **Below:** Like previous Corvettes, the new "shark" generation immediately began tearing up American racetracks—witness this starting-grid squadron in 1969. Among early triumphs were GT-class wins at the Daytona Continental in 1968-69; an impressive 6th overall in the '68 Sebring 12 Hours, and 7th overall at Watkins Glen in 1969. Time to buy another trophy case.

Corvette's 1968 redesign was planned for model-year '67 but delayed by development problems. Some of those weren't fully sorted when the car hit showrooms, notably cooling capacity with the optional big-block engines and a disappointingly lower level of fit-and-finish. A 1965 show car, the Mako Shark II, provided an exaggerated preview of production styling, hence the "shark" nickname that attaches to this design generation. Critics generally applauded the new look, but not the tighter cockpit that went with it. Wheelbase remained at 98 inches, but adding seven inches to overall length, plus more weight, did not seem like progress. Neither did some rather gimmicky new features, such as wipers concealed beneath a cowl panel that popped up when the wipers were switched on—except, sometimes, on very frosty mornings. On the plus side, the '68 introduced an electric rear-window defroster and flow-through "Astro Ventilation" that did away with door vent windows. And wider standard wheels made for wider tracks that improved cornering ability. Performance was as fierce as ever. Small-block 327s offered 300 standard horses or 350 optional, while big-block 427s packed 390, 400, and 435. A 400-bhp 427 could deliver 0-60 mph in 5.7 seconds and a blazing quarter-mile of 14.1 seconds at 102 mph, but even the 350-bhp small-block was good for 7.7 seconds to 60, the quarter-mile in 15.6 seconds at 92 mph, and 128 all out. To its credit, Chevy was quick to address the '68 Corvette's problems. The '69s thus boasted a bit more cockpit space, improved workmanship, and a torquier, more emissions-friendly small-block enlarged to 350 cubic inches. As before, big-block cars like this '68 T-top coupe came with a bulged hood to clear the air cleaner. Headlights were still concealed but now popped up into view instead of swiveling.

**Above:** Ferrari unveiled another instant classic in 1968 with the 365 GTB/4, which the press somehow quickly dubbed Daytona. Replacing the 275 GTB/4, it used a similar rear-transaxle chassis and an identical wheelbase but offered even higher performance thanks to a V12 enlarged from 3.3 to 4.4 liters, which took horsepower from 300 to 352. At just under $20,000, the Daytona was the costliest street Ferrari yet, but also the fastest. *Road & Track* verified the factory's claimed 174-mph top speed and timed the standing quarter-mile in just 13.8 seconds at 107.5 mph. The body design was hailed as one of Pininfarina's best, one reason for the car's long-legendary status. This berlinetta is an early European version with clear headlamp covers. U.S. models initially wore rather warty-looking exposed lights, but all later Daytonas were treated to hidden headlamps in a smooth body-color nose. **Left:** The Daytona wasn't much changed otherwise, but 1969 introduced a companion spider convertible that's even more sought-after now than the coupe. Designated GTS/4, it saw only 127 copies versus nearly 1300 berlinettas. That was far too few to satisfy demand, which is why some Daytona coupes have since been decapitated to pass as spiders, an important point now for would-be owners—and judges at the ritzy car shows where these Ferraris gather.

**Above and left:** Appearing in early 1968, the Morgan Plus 8 raised many a purist eyebrow with its GM-designed 3.5-liter V8 purchased from Rover, which had bought the production rights. To handle its 50 extra horsepower (initially 148 total), the vintage four-cylinder Plus 4 chassis got a two-inch wheelbase stretch (to 98), plus wider tires on modern cast-alloy wheels, matched by broader fenders and axle tracks. The cockpit was also modernized, with U.S. safety rules in mind. Weighing little more than a Plus 4, the Plus 8 could outdrag a Jaguar E-Type at under 6 seconds 0-60 mph, though the bluff, traditional styling held top speed to "only" 125 mph. Not surprisingly for a Morgan, the Plus 8 is still being built, slowly and carefully. The last 35 years have brought occasional small power increases and other detail updates but no basic change to its unique "Thirties muscle car" character. **Below:** Another look at the Triumph GT6, this one a British Mark 2. As with the U.S.-bound GT6+, new rear suspension geometry improved control of wheel motions and thus stability in hard cornering.

Uncharitable types might have called it a sedan, but the Lamborghini Espada was a high-performance luxury GT unlike anything available at archrival Ferrari. Bowing in 1968, it rode a rangy 104.3-inch wheelbase that allowed Lambo's V12 powerteam to ride far enough forward to provide a true four-place interior. The long, low body wore a near horizontal fastback roofline above a clipped tail with a glass insert—handy when parking. Bertone supplied the body to a design by Marcello Gandini, who had shaped the midengine Miura and the 1966 Marzal show car that served as the Espada's template. Gianpaolo Dallara, who'd also worked on the Miura, engineered a new lower-cost chassis for the Espada, but with the expected double-wishbone/coil-spring suspension and disc brakes. Announced with a 325-horsepower 4.0-liter engine and five-speed manual gearbox, the Espada was a true supercar, good for 0-60 mph in around 7 seconds and at least 140 mph maximum. The V12 would be tuned up to 350 bhp in 1970, then 365 in 1972, by which time the car had received various cosmetic updates inside and out. Shown here is a post-1972 "Series III," the only Espada with an inward-curving "cockpit" dashboard. A very desirable machine then and now, the Espada lasted a full decade. Too bad that just 1217 were built.

Ferruccio Lamborghini himself is said to have outlined the basic shape for his new 1968 Islero, essentially a restyled version of the 2+2 400GT. The actual design work, however, was done by freelancer Mario Marazzi, who'd recently left then-struggling Carrozzeria Touring. Though it looked conservative next to the contemporary Miura and Espada, the Islero was clean, purposeful, and a more practical design for daily driving, especially in visibility, entry/exit, and ergonomics. It was also roomier than the 400, yet preserved all its sterling qualities, including terrific acceleration and faithful handling. Performance got even hotter in 1969, when the 4.0-liter V12 was boosted from 320 to 340 horsepower for the Islero S, which also sported some minor appearance changes. But with Lamborghini going great guns by now, the Islero was only a stopgap, lasting through just two years and a total of 225 units, 100 of them S-models. Like other Lambos, they've since become prime collector cars, sedan-like looks nothwithstanding.

**Above:** It took a sharp eye to spot the changes, but the Porsche 911 returned for '69 with a 2.2-inch longer wheelbase, which helped improve weight distribution, plus subtle wheelarch flares to go with thicker disc brakes and wider wheels. This 911S coupe was priced from $7895 in the U.S. **Left:** The 911's air-cooled flat six was available three ways for '69: with twin carburetors and 125 horsepower for the base 911T; with 160 bhp for a new fuel-injected 911E; and in high-compression 190-bhp 911S tune, also *mit Einspritzung.* Top speeds now ranged from 110 to 140, yet any 911 could return reasonable fuel economy if driven with restraint—which most owners found hard to do. **Below:** Porsche made it easy, though not cheap, for 911 owners to go racing. Besides the usual suspension upgrades, the late-Sixties options list showed a pair of engine kits that together added some 15 bhp to a 911S. As always, the Porsche's tidy size and great agility were as helpful on the track as they were on the street.

**Right:** From the first, on *autobhan* or interstate, the Porsche 911 was a fine long-distance companion as well as an entertaining curvy-road sports car. The rear-engine layout and resulting tail-heavy weight distribution sullied straightline stability in gusty crosswinds and could cause sudden oversteer in hard cornering, but the 911 rewarded those who knew how to use it properly and were sensitive to its unique characteristics. Among '69 models, a five-speed manual gearbox was newly standard for the S and optional for the T and E in lieu of a four-speed. Porsche also offered "Sportomatic," a clutchless manual that did not prove very popular, even in the U.S.

# FERRY PORSCHE
## Kept it Simple

Literally piggybacking on the strength of his father's "Beetle," Ferry Porsche contrived to build an extraordinary car from ordinary parts. Sharing his father's preference for steady improvement over radical change, Ferry created the first true Porsche from an amalgam of existing pieces including the Beetle's heart, its air-cooled four-cylinder engine. From that first car came a company that, more than 50 years after its founding, maintains a reputation for building technically brilliant and mechanically engaging sportscars that is rivaled only by Ferrari.

The Porsche most people know today is the life's work of the good Herr Docktor's son, Ferdinand "Ferry" Porsche. Like his father, he was passionately dedicated to innovation and careful, considered improvement in pursuit of "driving in its purest form," and his impact on the auto world was just as great.

Working as engineer for his father's engineering firm, Ferry was swept into the torrents of the Third Reich when the Nazis appropriated the company in 1941. Under Hitler's thumb Porsche's company worked on both war-related designs and civilian efforts that included Der Führer's pet project, a "people's car," known later as the Beetle.

Later, with the Allies closing on Berlin, Hitler ordered the senior Porsche and his engineers to the relative safety of sleepy Gmund, Austria, where they immediately set up shop. Soon after the Nazis fell from power, the resilient design firm was free again to pursue civilian business. Complicating the company's revival however was the senior Porsche's arrest and detainment by the French in 1945 on charges of Nazi collaboration. Ferry himself had also been arrested at the same time but was released a few months later.

Yet despite his father's absence and what Ferry described as "very primitive conditions," the company prospered. At first the company focused on contract projects for other concerns, but then in 1948 Porsche introduced its first car, the 356. Though working with only 40 horsepower from its Beetle-based rear engine, the first Porsche-brand car was widely applauded for its low weight, agile handling, and quick steering.

Acquitted of all charges, the senior Porsche was released from France in 1950, two months after his 75th birthday. Though he returned to work, the war-weary old man was a ghost of his former self, never recovering his prewar spirit. He died soon after, having lived long enough to see the first car that bore his name.

Even without his father, Ferry brought Porsche to the peak of commercial and competiton success in remarkably short order, then assured the company's legacy with one of the most successful and most storied sports cars of all time, the 911.

Though joined by other vehicles through the years, the 911 became the foundation on which Porsche forged his company's reputation. Using the same rear-engine/rear-drive layout as the 356, the 911 advanced the design with a purpose-built six-cylinder engine and modern teardrop design. Fueled by a passion for steady improvement, the 911 received few major updates, evolving slowing over time, ever improving.

Ferry Porsche was 88 years old when he died in 1998—ironically, the same year a water-cooled engine was installed in a 911 for the first time. Though the new engine was a radical departure from the car's long-standing design, it is one Ferry would likely have approved if he believed it was the next logical step in improving the 911.

**Top and above:** Ferrari's first V6 road car was born in 1967 with the midengine Dino 206GT. The replacement 246GT of 1969 offered better performance via a larger, 2.4-liter twincam V6 with 175 horsepower, plus iron instead of alloy construction for greater durability. Shown here is the 246 GTS, a slightly heavier, targa-top model added in 1972 but otherwise identical to the coupe. Dinos did not wear the Ferrari badge, though some cars have been so adorned since. They were certainly in keeping with Ferrari's design and engineering heritage. **Right:** For 1969, Triumph's senior sports car received another restyle, only this one was created by Karmann of Germany, not design consultant Giovanni Michelotti. It was effective nonetheless, with a completely new nose and tail on the existing central body. Thus did the TR250/TR5 morph into the TR6.

Besides a new look front and rear, the Triumph TR6 restyle extended to the accessory lift-off hard top, which got a more contemporary square cut and greater glass area, as shown here. Unfortunately for U.S. fans, the TR's latest makeover did not bring extra power, let alone the fuel injection available in Europe. Come the Seventies, however, Americans would be treated—if that's the word—to the large black rubber bumper guards in evidence here, a cheap, quick-fix way to satisfy impact-protection standards. But though the basic TR design was well over a decade old by 1969, this "manly" sports car was still selling pretty well despite its age—or maybe because of it. Time would eventually catch up with the TR6 but not before over 94,000 were sold, again mostly in the U.S.

# 5

## 1970-79: Winners and Losers

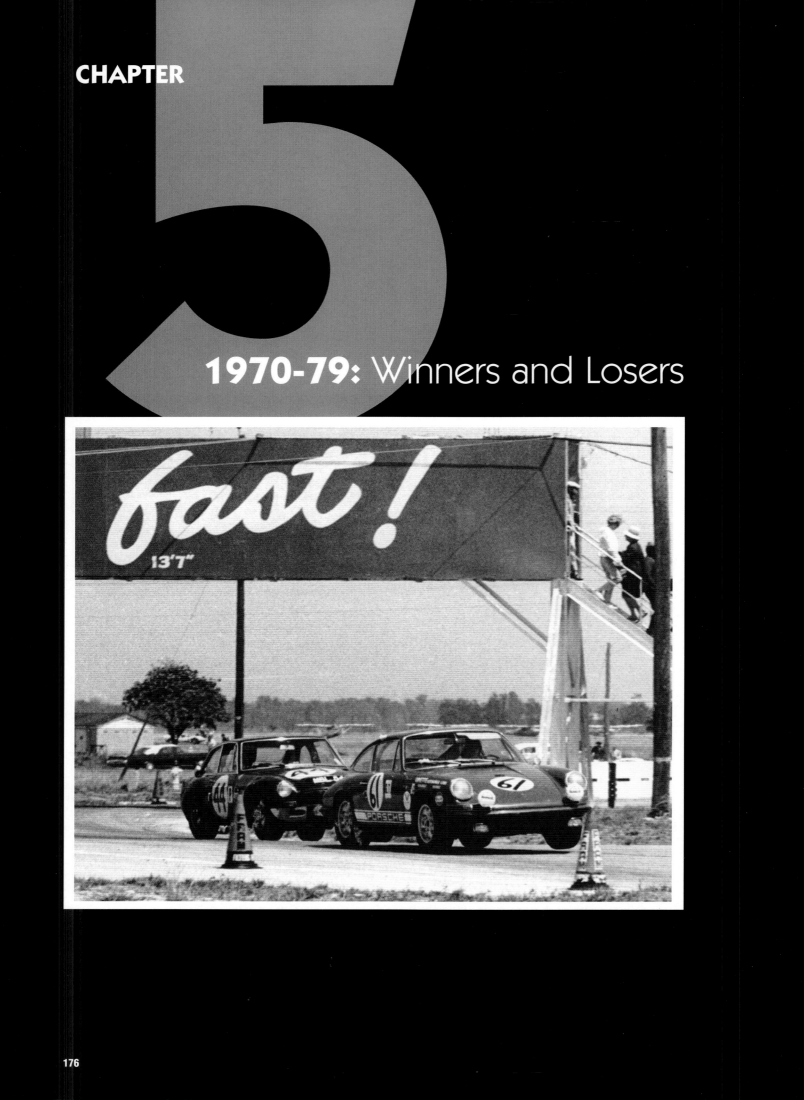

In May 2001, *New Yorker* magazine critic Louis Menand likened the 1920s to "a Pierce-Arrow driven by a man in a raccoon coat"; the Thirties to "a Model T with a mattress strapped to the roof, bound for California"; the Forties to "a black sedan, driven by a Negro chauffeur"; the Fifties to "a station wagon...with four kids in the back, and no seat belts"; the Sixties to "a Mustang with the top down...passing a pink VW mini-bus, headed for a sit-in";—and the 1970s to a "Pinto in a gas line. It's an unlovely decade, the nineteen-seventies; but there are those who care about it, and some of them write books." Menand was reviewing Bruce J. Shulman's just-released *The Seventies: The Great Shift in American Culture, Society and Politics*, with passing mention of David Frum's 2000 book, *How We Got Here: The 70s: The Decade That Brought You Modern Life—For Better or Worse*.

How times change. Conventional wisdom once decried the Seventies as a time when America turned from social idealism to self-absorbed navel-gazing, symbolized by tacky artifacts like leisure suits, disco, shag carpeting, and *The Gong Show*. Now experts of various stripes were saying the "Me Decade" wasn't so trivial after all.

It was undeniably eventful, even if the country may have wished otherwise. The activism unleashed in the Sixties led to more campus protests and new drives for greater equality by women, Latinos, and the gay/lesbian population. There were wrenching new events to absorb too: governmental corruption at the highest levels; impeachment proceedings against a once-popular president, who resigned before the gavel could fall; the ignominious withdrawal of U.S. forces from Vietnam after more than a decade of bitter controversy and thousands of deaths; new shooting wars in the Middle East; and an unprecedented world "energy crisis" that dramatically spotlighted America's hitherto unheralded dependence on foreign oil.

The halt in U.S. oil shipments by the Organization of Petroleum Exporting Countries was brief, lasting from October 1973 to the spring of '74, but its effects were immediate and profound. All over the land, drivers were forced to wait in long lines to pay record prices for gasoline—when they could get it—and public attitudes toward Detroit and the automobile itself began to shift. Buyers rushed from traditional gas-guzzlers to smaller, more economical cars like domestic Ford Pintos and Chevy Vegas, but also a rising tide of well made, well equipped, increasingly appealing Japanese-made Toyotas, Datsuns, and Hondas. But the entire U.S. car market suffered, and the U.S. economy with it. After climbing to 11.2 million units in calendar 1973, sales plunged over 20 percent to near 8.6 million in '74 and 8.5 million in '75. The market then rallied, but never surpassed its '73 high.

In response to the gas crunch, Congress mandated higher "corporate average fuel economy" (CAFE) for all automakers doing business in the U.S., starting with model-year 1978. But more government mandates were hardly what manaufacturers needed. Even Detroit was still struggling to reduce tailpipe emissions specified by the Clean Air Act of 1970. And there were more safety standards to meet, including bumpers able to survive 5-mph shunts without damage, required for 1973 (front) and '74 (rear).

Such sobering new realities took their toll on many fun-loving sports cars. To be sure, some great new models appeared in the Seventies: the terrific Datsun 240Z, the astounding Lamborghini Countach (whose very name roughly means "Good Lord!"), Ferrari's first midengine supercar, and the innovative Mazda RX-7. But even larger, more capable manufacturers often had trouble making each year's cars as clean and safe as Washington demanded, and smaller outfits like Lamborghini, Lotus, and Maserati could hardly afford to try. As a result, many sports cars lost power and added weight as time passed, becoming slower, clumsier, and usually uglier in the process. Other models simply weren't "federalized" for U.S. sale, because their makers lacked the wherewithal to do so. This left would-be U.S. owners to do without or to truck with "gray market" importers, some of whom were less than reputable.

Nowhere was the sad state of Seventies affairs more evident than in the American-market sports cars of British Leyland. BL had been formed in 1968 with the merger of British Motor Corporation and Standard-Triumph. It was thus home to all of England's native mass-market makes except GM-owned Vauxhall and British Ford, which meant that MG, Triumph, and Jaguar now lived under the same roof. But chronically hobbled by its enormous size and corrosive internal politics, BL took a curious let-'em-eat-cake approach to the vital U.S. market. For example, to meet 1973's "crash bumper" standard and another new rule for minimum bumper height, BL simply larded on black-rubber cowcatchers and jacked-up MG suspensions the requisite number of inches. "Sorry we spoiled the looks and handling, Old Bean. Blame your government, not us." Emissions control? Keep detuning until engines passed their smog checks, then substitute a larger, more tunable one with no more horsepower. Replace an elderly basic design? "Sorry again. Can't afford it right now." Even when BL did manage something new, it was often disappointing. The Triumph TR6 might have been nearly 20 years old by 1978, but it was an honest six-cylinder roadster of the traditional stripe. Its erstwhile replacement, the TR7, suffered by comparison as a four-cylinder coupe that looked like it belonged on TV's *Space: 1999*. And workmanship, never a strong suit of British cars, was worse than ever.

We don't mean to pick on the British. The Italians were just as nonplussed by the onslaught of "Fed regs," and the French didn't bother at all with genuine sports cars for the U.S. Even the invincible Germans and fast-rising Japanese had problems. But not all Seventies sports cars were unmitigated disasters. The Chevrolet Corvette, for example, never lost its style. Some performance was lost to clean-air necessity, but also because insurance companies had raised hot-car premiums to impossible heights early in the decade. Chevy was thus correct to morph the 'Vette from fiery muscle car to a more efficient, tight-handling gran turismo, especially once the energy crisis left behind permanently higher gas prices. The Porsche 911 also adapted to changing times without losing its essential character, and became even more exciting when the high-power Turbo version came along. Porsche's midengine 914 and later front-engine 924 might not have been everything people expected of the marque, but at least they were affordable and surprisingly practical new choices. The rotary-powered Mazda RX-7 was hailed on its 1978 debut as a "new 240Z" and thus a hopeful sign that sports cars did have a future after all.

That symbolism was put to the test when a second energy crisis hit in early 1979, triggered in part by the ouster of the Shah of Iran. It hit hard, especially in Detroit, which was soon hitting the brakes in the face of another market downturn, aggravated by increasing sales losses to "Japan, Inc." Thus ended one of the most turbulent decades for the U.S. economy since the Depression.

The Seventies might not have led to the American life we know in the early 21st century, but the events of those years definitely left the automotive world forever changed. Happily for our story, one thing could not be changed: Sports cars are forever too.

**1970** DeTomaso unveils midengine Pantera • Congress passes Clean Air Act mandating lower exhaust emissions • British Motor Corporation kills Austin-Healey marque • Datsun 240Z hits U.S. shores, wows critics at $3526 • Lamborghini trots out Jarama 400GT and midengine "baby Miura" Urraco • Porsche bows "budget" 914 with midships VW 4 cyl; 911-powered 914/6 arrives at year's end • Triumph bows Spitfire Mk IV, restyled GT6 Mk 3 **1971** Lincoln-Mercury dealers begin selling $10,000 DeTomaso Pantera • Jaguar replaces 6-cyl E-Types with overhauled V12 Series III models • Volvo's sporty coupe morphed into 1800 ES "sportwagon" **1972** Ferrari 365 GT4 2+2 debuts; it's almost a "family" car • Alfa Romeo suspends U.S. sales • Fiat announces targa-top X1/9, a petite "middie" • Donald Healey, U.S. sports-car baron Kjell Qvale bring out Jensen-Healey • Mercedes-Benz SL redesigned • Porsche 911 engines grow again, now to 2.4 liters; RS debuts for track only **1973** Gas prices soar, drivers line up in first U.S. energy crisis • Ferrari adds "junior" 2+2 with V8 Dino 308 GT4 • Front 5-mph "crash" bumpers required on most cars sold in U.S. • Alfa Romeo 1750 Giulias become 2000s with new injected 2-liter engine • Chevrolet Corvette gets handsome new nose • Revised Datsun 260Z adds 2+2 version • GT-like DeTomaso Longchamps debuts • Triumph adopts MG power for Spitfire 1500, drops GT6 **1974** Gas crunch ends • Rear 5-mph "crash" bumpers required on most cars sold in U.S.

Having received a bigger small-block V8 for '69, Chevrolet's Corvette entered the Seventies with a bigger block, punched out from 427 to 454 cubic inches. Two versions were listed, but only the 390-horsepower four-barrel LS5 unit saw genuine production. *Car and Driver* tested one 'Vette with an LS7 option featuring higher-compression aluminum cylinder heads, high-lift cams, and mechanical lifters, good for 460-465 bhp. Though the magazine reported a sizzling quarter-mile of 13.8 seconds at 108 mph, the LS7 was not readily available, and few if any other '70 Corvettes were so equipped. One reason had to do with an auto workers' strike that delayed initial Corvette sales to February 1970 and nearly halved model-year production to 17,316 units, the lowest total since 1962. Convertibles like this accounted for 6608 units, reflecting the accelerating drop in demand for droptop models through the American industry. Base prices that season were up $4849 for the convertible and $5192 for the T-top coupe.

**Above and below:** Corvette styling was little changed for 1970. Front parking lamps and dual exhausts went from round to rectangular, and "eggcrate" inserts appeared in the grille and front-fender vents. Not that much change was needed. After all, the "shark" generation was only in its third season. As before, the grille was literally just a "front," as the radiator drew in air from under the front bumper, making this a "bottom breather" design. **Right:** Most sports-car drivers like to go fast, and no one likes getting tickets. That's why CB radio and radar detectors became quite popular in the Seventies, helped by miniaturized electronics and ever-falling prices. This ad touts a "safety" benefit for one early-model radar detector, a likely code word for the real aim of such devices—helping leadfoot drivers preserve their licenses.

Chevy Corvette gains restyled tail, loses last big V8 options • DeTomaso Pantera departs U.S. • Ferrari replaces front-V12 Daytona with midships-boxer 365 GT4 BB • Fiat 124 Coupe dropped; Spider continues • Italy's Iso builds final Grifo coupes, exits car business • Gullwing V12 Lamborghini Countach starts production as "ultimate supercar" • Maserati's midengine siblings, the V8 Bora and V6 Merak, belatedly start U.S. sale • Maserati launches sleek front-V12 Khamsin, drops Indy and Ghibili • Improved Porsche 911s get discreet "crash" bumpers, 2.7-liter engines, sporty Carrera • Triumph Spitfire sprouts big, black "crash" bumpers **1975** Jensen GT coupe joins Jensen-Healey roadster • Chevrolet builds last Corvette convertible—for a while • Larger engine, fuel injection restore zip, drivability in refined Datsun 280Z • Ferrari unveils midengine 308 GTB ready for *Magnum P.I.* • Jaguar ousts sporting E-Type for new grand-luxe XJS coupe • MG Midget and MGB get saddled with big black bumpers **1976** Porsche breaks tradition as front-engine, water-cooled 924 replaces 914 • Ferrari 365 GT4 now a 400i with more power and 'gasp!' optional automatic transmission • Jensen-Healey, Jensen GT cease production by year's end • Lamborghini Urraco flips its lid to become the 2+2 Silhouette • Wedgy midengine Lotus Esprit replaces Europa • Maserati's mid-V6 GT renamed Merak SS • Porsche blows up a storm with potent 911-based Turbo Carrera • Triumph stirs controversy with new 4-cyl bubbletop wedge TR7 coupe

**Top and above:** The Datsun 240Z was one of America's most talked-about cars on its 1970 debut—and no wonder. Priced from just $3526, it offered the style and performance of sports cars costing thousands more, plus GT-like comfort and convenience. Riding a 90.7-inch wheelbase, the thoroughly modern Z boasted an overhead-cam 2.4-liter inline six with 151 horsepower, five-speed manual or optional three-speed automatic transmissions, all-around coil-spring/strut suspension, rack-and-pinion steering, and front-disc brakes. Some critics said it had the burly charm of the late Austin-Healey 3000, while others applauded the smooth hatchback coupe styling and well-equipped cockpit. Americans scrambled to buy 9977 Zs in 1970, nearly 27,000 in '71, and some 46,600 in 1972. Sales were equally strong worldwide. **Below:** The 240Z was quick to pile up victories in U.S. road racing, with factory-aided teams under Bob Sharp and Pete Brock vying for trophies. Driving a Brock Racing Enterprises Z like this, John Morton won SCCA's C-Production national championship in 1970 and again in '71.

**Above:** Despite a few questionable details, the 240Z still looks good after more than 30 years. Count Albrecht Goertz of BMW 507 fame contributed much to the basic design, which had elements recalling his earlier work for what became Toyota's 2000GT. Though not immune to rust, the unitized Z was far more solid than Datsun's MGB-like, body-on-frame roadsters of the Sixties. Shown here (and opposite) is one of about 50 factory-restored 240Zs offered to U.S. buyers in 1997-98 from $29,950—a long way from the original 1970 price. **Below:** If not Detroit muscular, the 240Z's straight six was very smooth and potent enough, helped by a modest 2300-pound curb weight and sensible gearing. *Road & Track* reported a respectable 8.7 seconds 0-60 mph, a standing quarter-mile of 17.1 seconds at 85 mph, and 122 mph all-out—plus 21 miles per gallon, more than acceptable all things considered. *R&T* concluded that first Z test by predicting the Datsun would "establish a market of its own, [forcing] other makers to come up with entirely new models to gain a share in it. The Japanese industry is no longer borrowing anything from other nations. In fact, a great struggle may be ahead just to prevent a complete reversal of that cliche."

" After conducting a nationwide search for a rust-free Z I found my car—right here in Chicago, the heart of the rust belt. The ad read simply, "1970 Datsun 240Z, $750 or best offer." What I found was a blue-over-black Z with 76,000 miles that was absolutely stock. A few small dents and a bit of surface rust marred the body, but the chassis looked to be as clean as the day it landed on these shores, and it ran like a top. I didn't haggle over the price. It served as my daily driver for one fun-filled summer, after which I put it away with 84,000 miles on the clock to preserve for future restoration. Fourteen years later, it still had 84,000 miles on it. By this point, it had become clear that its resurrection would have to come at the hands of someone with far more leisure time. Freeing a stuck carburetor float got it running while a quick brake bleed got it to stop, and that old Z went down the road as well as it had that glorious summer years ago. A tear welled in my eye as a young guy from Indiana towed it away. A young guy, I might add, who had been conducting a long search for a rust-free Z.... "

— Rick Cotta
Chicago

**1977** Porsche unveils luxury 928 coupe with front water-cooled V8 • Aston Martin V8 muscles up into 400-hp Vantage • Maserati Kyalami bows as Maserati-powered DeTomaso Longchamps **1978** CAFE everyone? U.S. fuel-economy standards take effect • BMW unveils Italian-bred midengine M1 • Aston Martin adds Volante convertible • Chevy Corvette turns 25, changes roofline, paces Indy 500 • Redesigned Datsun 280ZX adds bulk, luxury, gadgets • Mazda spins out a true rotary sports car with RX-7 • Porsche evolves 911 to 3.0-liter SC form, U.S. 928 sales begin **1979** Shah of Iran deposed; touches off Energy Crisis II • Lotus introduces Esprit Series 2 • Porsche 924 now available in Turbo form • Porsche Turbo, aka Turbo Carrera, boasts bigger engine, more power

Alejandro DeTomaso persuaded Ford to sell his new midengine Pantera through U.S. Lincoln-Mercury dealers for model-year '71. Featured were a new unitized structure engineered by Gianpaolo Dallara and built by Ghia with styling by American Tom Tjaarda. A Ford 351 V8 sent 310 horsepower through a five-speed transaxle. At an intial $10,000, the Pantera was surprisingly affordable for an "exoticar" yet no less fiery, with 5.4-second 0-60 mph acceleration and 130-mph top speed. Events conspired to kill the Pantera after 1974 and some 5600 U.S sales, but production would continue for other markets into the 1990s.

**Top and above:** Beginning regular sale in 1972, the Lamborghini P250 Urraco was a sort of "baby Miura," with a similar midengine layout and chassis features, but a single-cam 2.5-liter V8 instead of a twincam V12. The purposeful body design with 96.6-inch wheelbase was by Marcello Gandini and built by Bertone. To cope with the performance-sapping effects of multiplying U.S. regulations, a P300 was added in 1974 with big black-rubber bumpers, evident here, but also a 3.0-liter twincam V8 with 265 horsepower, up 45. Though fast and agile, the Urraco had practical drawbacks that turned buyers off, and fewer than 780 were built through early 1979. **Right:** Replacing Lamborghini's front-engine Islero in 1970, the Jarama 400 GT combined a 93.5-inch-wheelbase cut-down of the big Espada chassis with angular new Bertone body-work by Marcello Gandini. Somehow, though, the Jarama ended up much heavier than the Islero, so in 1973 its 350-bhp 4.0-liter V12 was tuned up to 365 for a replacement 400GTS model, which sported a thin, wide hood scoop. But the Jarama never really impressed critics or buyers, and it was dropped in 1978. Just 327 were built.

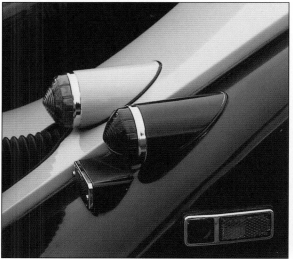

Britain's Morgan offered its first four-wheeler, the 4/4, in 1935. A slightly larger, more powerful sports car, the Plus 4, replaced it in 1950, but the 4/4 returned five years later as a lower-priced four-cylinder Morgan. Things haven't changed very much since. In fact, aside from engines and various equipment items, the 4/4 you can buy brand-new today won't look very different from this 1978 model, which we only recognize as a '78 from the helpful license plate. Like most every Morgan ever built, the body is a wood-frame steel-paneled affair in nostalgic Thirties roadster form. Equally little-changed over time is the simple ladder-type chassis with underslung rear axle, very stiff springs and shock absorbers, and a sliding-pillar front suspension first used in 1910 on the company's three-wheel car. Morgan has always relied on engines from other car companies, subject to availability and price. This 4/4 carries a 1600cc British Ford unit with 96 DIN horsepower, the sole choice from 1968 to 1982 and familiar in the U.S. in various Ford-built cars—and Formula Ford racers. As expected of a "cottage industry" make like Morgan, the 4/4 evolved in step with the Plus 4 and its 1968 replacement, the V8 Plus 8, which was soon followed by a four-seat 4/4. Morgan has since installed newer engines and even revived the Plus 4, but the cars themselves still seem as immutable as Gibraltar. But that's fine with Morgan's customers, who keep coming back year after year for this unique blend of "trad" sports-car character and modern componentry. No wonder there's still a years-long waiting list for these old-fashioned cars built the old-fashioned way.

American-market tastes loomed large in the redesigned Mercedes-Benz SL launched in 1971. Against the W113 series of the Sixties, the new R107 was longer and heavier. Wheelbase went to 96.7 inches, while curb weight ballooned to well around 3600 pounds, as almost all body panels were built of steel rather than aluminum. But the result was also a stronger, quieter, and more refined two-seat Mercedes, which was just what the market wanted. The added heft was also deemed necessary to meet looming U.S. crash-protection standards, but required a larger, torquier engine to compensate. The R107 thus bowed in Europe as the 350SL with a new 230-horsepower 3.5-liter overhead-cam V8. For easier compliance with U.S. emissions limits, Mercedes sent over a 450SL with a 4.5-liter V8 but no more power. Euro models also wore single-lens headlamps, shown here; the 450SL got a quartet of round sealed-beams that looked far less tidy. But despite such compromises, lack of true sports-car agility, and inevitably higher prices, the R107 sold like no SL before. The 450SL drew over 66,000 U.S. sales through 1980, after which the basic design solidered on with a new engine as the 380SL.

Branded a Porsche for its 1970 U.S. debut, the midengine 914 was actually a coproduction with Volkswagen, which supplied many components including a 1.7-liter air-cooled flat four. The two-seat targa-top coupe was quite practical for a "middie," with a roomy cockpit and a useful trunk at each end, but didn't have the expected race-car-like handling nor the acceleration expected of a Porsche. And engine access was tough. A stiff $3500 initial price also turned off critics and buyers. Worried about a sullied reputation, Porsche quickly cooked up the 914/6 with a beefed-up chassis and a 2.0-liter, 110-horsepower 911 flat-six, plus extra equipment including five-spoke 911 alloy wheels. Despite a much higher $6100 base price, the 914/6 was accepted as a "true" Porsche, able to clock 0-60 mph in under 9 seconds and top 120 mph. But with 911s priced only about $1000 higher, the 914/6 never caught on and vanished by late 1971 after just 3351 were built. The four-cylinder 914 continued with various yearly improvements through 1976, racking up total worldwide sales of 115,596.

**Above:** The 914 was always badged "VW-Porsche" for Europe. Even as it launched there in 1969, Porsche tried stuffing in a 300-horsepower 3.0-liter flat eight from its Type 908 racer. The resulting "914/8" could hit 155 mph and scale 0-60 in around 6 seconds. But Porsche concluded there was no market and gave up after building this one prototype, to which it affixed the proud Porsche crest. The car was later given to Dr. Ferry Porsche as a 60th birthday present. Porsche also eyed a 916 with modified bodywork and a 190-bhp version of the 911's latest 2.4-liter six, but built only 20 samples. Here, too, the reason was a likely lack of sales, especially as price was projected at a high $15,000-$16,000. **Left:** Skinny standard tires compromised the agility of four-cylinder 914s, as contemporary road tests pointed out. **Below:** Weekend racers were quick to realize the car's handling potential, thanks to competition parts available from Porsche and aftermarket companies. Porsche was then paired with VW-owned Audi in the U.S., and the "Porsche + Audi" dealer network often supported U.S. hotshoes competing with 914s, as shown here. This Porsche's most notable racing triumph came in 1970, with a GT class win and sixth overall at the LeMans 24 Hours.

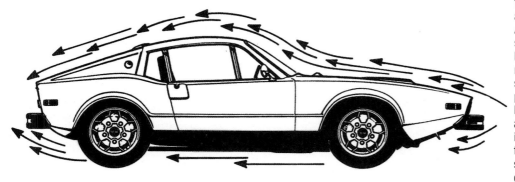

**Above and left:** Unveiled at the 1970 New York Auto Show, the Saab Sonett III built on the previous Sonett II with a 1.7-liter German Ford V4, a new nose and tail by Italian Sergio Coggiola, and an upgraded cockpit. The new styling improved aerodynamics, but added weight that the larger engine couldn't offset, so performance actually declined. Though offered mainly for the U.S., the Sonett III was dropped after 1974 due to the planned North American phaseout of the parent Saab 96 sedan. Production ended at 8351 units. **Below:** Triumph's Spitfire entered 1970 in new Mark IV guise with TR6-like rear-end styling and a much-improved rear suspension. A larger four-cylinder engine followed in 1973, mainly to preserve power against detuning for U.S. emissions limits. American-market models reflected this by being renamed Spitfire 1500, as shown here. U.S. safety standards mandated large, rubber bumper guards.

**Above:** The Triumph Spitfire remains a great low-cost way to go racing. About all you need do are tune up the engine, ditch the windshield, and bolt on a rollover bar and suitable rubber. Oh, and pass the test for your racing license. **Right and bottom:** U.S. Spitfires from 1973 used the same 1500cc engine as contemporary MG Midgets, both sports cars having by then come under the British Leyland banner. Post-'73 Spitfires also got "1500" decals for nose and trunklid, two-inch wider axle tracks, a more coherent dashboard, and reclining bucket seats. Fittingly, the revised rear-end styling, introduced with 1970's Mark IV update, was done by Giovanni Michelotti, who'd shaped the original Spitfire. Unfortunately, BL took an on-the-cheap approach to meeting U.S. safety and emissions standards in the Seventies, so Spitfire performance steadily declined, bottoming out in 1974 with just 57 horsepower and typical 0-60-mph times of close to 16 seconds. Even so, U.S. sales remained healthy enough to keep the Spitfire alive into 1980, when production economics and rising red ink forced BL to give up on traditional sports cars altogether. Ironically, the Spitfire would be a model for the popular Mazda Miata of the 1990s.

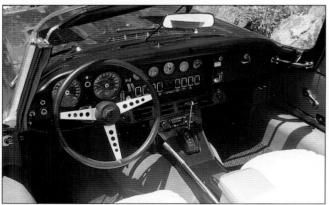

It may have resembled earlier E-Types at first glance, but the much-modified Series III of 1971 boasted V12 power, an artifact of Jaguar's supersecret "XJ13" racing-car project of the early Sixties. Replacing the venerable XK six cylinder, the V12 delivered 250 SAE net horsepower from 5.3 liters through four-speed manual or three-speed automatic transmissions. To accommodate the longer engine, the E-Type convertible was reengineered on the same extended chassis as the 2+2 coupe, though the open model was still basically a two-seater. All Series IIIs got a cross-hatch grille insert, reshaped tail, detail updates inside, wider wheels, and reinforcements to the unitized central structure and tubular front subframe. Though heavier than previous E-Types, the V12 would do0-60 mph in around 7 seconds and well over 130 mph—real Ferrari/Lamborghini stuff. Yet it was far more affordable than the Italians at around $7000 to start in the U.S. This Jaguar lasted into 1975, when production stopped at 15,287, about a fifth of all E-Types ever built.

**Top and above:** Jaguar's production V12 wouldn't fit in the two-seater E-Type coupe, so the Series III offered only the familiar higher-profile 2+2 style first seen for 1966. The new single-overhead-cam engine was a tight fit—and complex with its quartet of carburetors—but service access wasn't too bad with the E-Type's traditional lift-up hood/front fenders assembly. In U.S tune, the Series III could return only about 14.5 miles per gallon, a failing highlighted by the unpredecented world energy crisis and gas shortages that hit in late 1973. But that's not why the E-Type expired in early '75. Quite simply, the basic design was looking dated by then. Indeed, one U.S. magazine termed the Series III "a magnificent engine in an outclassed body." Then, too, Jaguar had become part of the increasingly troubled British Leyland combine, and was working hard on a replacement sports-tourer designed for the latest U.S. crash standards. But in a last hurrah, a team of race-prepped V12 roadsters running under the Group 44 banner captured the national SCCA B-Production championship in 1975, recalling Jaguar's rise to the pinnacle of world racing in the Fifties. **Right:** The Series III E-Type bowed with a choice of 12 exterior colors, including that traditional enthusiasts' favorite, British Racing Green.

AZURE BLUE     FERN GREY     BRITISH RACING GREEN

DARK BLUE     GREENSAND     OLD ENGLISH WHITE

PALE PRIMROSE     SABLE     SIGNAL RED

SILVER GREY     REGENCY RED     TURQUOISE

COLOR COORDINATED INTERIOR TRIM AVAILABLE.

**Top and above:** Fans of the late Austin-Healey took note of 1972's new Jensen-Healey, a sedate-looking two-seat convertible built by a small, struggling British outfit heretofore known for fast Chrysler-powered GTs. Jensen had just been bought by San Francisco sports-car baron Kjell Qvale, and the legendary Donald Healey was Jensen president. Together they cooked up a medium-price sports car with a 2.0-liter Lotus-sourced twincam four-cylinder engine, a unitized structure with 92-inch wheelbase, and chassis components borrowed from a variety of mass-market British cars. Despite a modest 140 U.S. horsepower and conventional live-axle rear suspension, the J-H was decently quick and very agile, but engine woes, a near-$5000 price, and strong competition prevented sales from reaching what Jensen needed for financial recovery. **Left:** By mid-1975, Donald Healey had left the J-H venture and Qvale had added a 2+2 hatchback coupe titled simply Jensen GT. But the new model didn't help, and it expired along with the convertible in 1976. Jensen itself soon expired, though it was later revived several times by various would-be auto moguls.

Maserati swelled the ranks of midengine production sports cars with the 1971 Bora. One of the first projects for designer Giorgetto Giugiaro's new Ital Design studio, the unibody two-seat fastback arrived with a 4.7-liter version of Maserati's familiar racing-derived twincam V8, which sent 310 horsepower to the rear wheels via a manual five-speed transaxle. Striding a 102.2-inch wheelbase, the Bora used classic double-wishbone suspension and rack-and-pinion steering, but also disc brakes with high-pressure hydraulics by Citroën of France, which had recently taken over Maserati and furnished the needed funds for the new model. The hydraulics were also used for power-adjustable pedals, which combined with a tilt/telescope steering wheel for an unusually accommodating Italian cockpit. Tightening emissions limits delayed U.S. sales until 1974, when a substitute 320-bhp 4.9-liter engine solved the problem. Though capable of 160 mph and 0-60 in just 6.5 seconds, the Bora was a civilized supercar, but predictably pricey and rare. Just 571 were built through 1980. Interim changes were few.

**Top and above:** Though the little Austin-Healey Sprite departed after 1971, the sister MG Midget solidered on until '74, when a revised Mark IV appeared with rounded rear wheel arches, plus triple windshield wipers and other changes dictated by blossoming U.S. regulations. Besides an accessory luggage rack, this example wears five-spoke "Rostyle" steel wheels, then a popular alternative to costlier alloy rims. **Left:** The Midget returned to flat-top rear wheel arches for '75, but the big news was a 1500cc four-cylinder engine to replace the previous 1275, which was being strangled by detuning to meet U.S. emissions limits. Also new were a jacked-up suspension and big black rubber bumpers to be literally in line with Washington's latest crash-protection edicts. Alas, the bumpers and other added equipment only increased weight, while the larger engine could only manage 50-62 horsepower in U.S. trim, about the same as before. Such halfhearted measures largely reflected growing financial trouble at parent British Leyland and an elderly basic design that was increasingly difficult to update. BL ladled on jazzy decals and "free extras" to keep buyers interested. And for a time it succeeded. Midget sales remained relatively healthy, even in the vital American market. But this wasn't enough help for beleagured BL, which reluctantly dropped the Midget after 1979. Over 86,000 Mark IV/1500s were sold, most in America.

**Above:** The Fiat 124 Sport spider would survive the Seventies with relatively little styling damage, though emissions-prompted detuning reduced U.S.-model performance as time passed. Here, a Euro-market model circa 1972. **Left:** Fiat pitched an "Italian connection" in period U.S. advertising. **Below:** Fiat took a 1290cc four-cylinder engine from its front-drive 128 sedan and plunked it amidships in a petite two-seat targa-top coupe. Presto! The X1/9. Sent to the U.S. for model-year '75, the X1/9 wasn't as quick as it looked—about on par with a concurrent MGB—but it was very nimble and fun to drive. Pretty affordable, too, at around $4600 to start. Early "federalized" models like this wore tacked-on rubber bumper pads.

**Top and above:** The Maserati Merak resembled the mid-V8 Bora, but carried a new Maserati-designed 3.0-liter twincam V6 with 180 horsepower in U.S. tune. This allowed a $5000 lighter price—about $22,000. Add-on "flying buttress" members mimicked the Bora's rear roof profile without glass inserts, and a flat decklid replaced a lift-up hatch. Parent Citroën used the V6 for its far-out period SM coupe, while the Merak used the SM dashboard. U.S. sales began in late 1974, shortly before Alejandro DeTomaso took over Maserati. One result of that was the improved 1976 Merak SS, shown here, with discreet chin spoiler, wider wheels and tires, Bora five-speed transaxle, and conventional non-Citroën brakes and dashboard. A good performer even in emissions-strangled U.S. form, the Merak would run through 1983 and modest production of 1699 units. **Left:** Maserati had trouble meeting U.S. regulations in the Seventies, so sales were spotty in these years. This ad from 1979 pairs the Merak with Maserati's then-new second-series Quattroporte ("four door") sedan.

**Top:** The Porsche 911 kept evolving for 1972, with an air-cooled flat-six stroked to near 2.4 liters, plus a one-year-only external flap, behind the right door, for the engine-oil filler. The familiar trio of T, E, and S models now claimed respective U.S. horsepower of 157, 185, and 210. **Above left and right:** Built for Group 4 GT racing and reviving an historic Porsche name, the 1973 Carrera RS boasted a new 230-bhp 2.7-liter flat six, beefed-up chassis, and lightweight coupe bodywork with broader fender flares, bold bodyside graphics, and distinctive "ducktail" rear spoiler. Porsche ran off 1636 RS 2.7s, mainly for Europe, where the model was street legal. A few came to America, but a "dirty" engine meant owners couldn't drive them except on a racetrack. **Right:** For 1973, U.S. 911s wore large front bumper guards to meet that year's new rule for 5-mph front crash protection. They're visible on the S Targa here. Posing with it is a 911E, which got new-design alloy wheels. At midyear, base T models got standard fuel injection like other 911s, which improved drivability and bumped horsepower to 137 SAE net.

The Lamborghini Miura had been improving in stages since its 1966 debut. The last and fastest iteration of the iconic mid-V12 coupe was the P400SV, appearing in 1971. Against the previous Miura S, it packed 15 extra horsepower—385 total—thanks to more changes in cam timing and carburetors, plus bigger valves. Other alterations included a larger fuel tank, more effective engine oiling, vented brake rotors (versus solid), and revised rear suspension geometry that raised ride height slightly but improved handling in concert with another upsizing of wheels and tires. The cockpit wasn't ignored either, as switchgear, instruments, and trim were either upgraded, remodeled, or both. The wild Marcello Gandini styling still looked great even after six years and wisely wasn't changed much. However, the SV did get visibly wider rear flanks (to accommodate the broader tires), a discreet ID badge on the tail, and layback headlamps without the surrounding "eyelash" trim that had caused a few giggles on earlier Miuras. With top speed up to 175 mph and acceleration to match, the SV was faster than a Ferrari Daytona and most any other street-legal machine. But Lamborghini was readying an even more outrageous supercar, so the Miura said goodbye in January 1973 when the last SV was sold. Ironically, an unprecedented world energy crisis hit just nine months later, that, at the time, seemed to spell the end for all high-power "exoticars." Fortunately, that pessimistic view would prove to be quite inaccurate.

**Below:** This view highlights the 1971-72 SV's more muscular rear flanks and the rear-window slats used on all Miuras. The latter became became something of a Seventies styling cliché for various production cars and as a popular bolt-on accessory for aftermarket companies. **Above left:** Another design feature common to all Miuras was a functional louvered engine air scoop nestled behind each door window. **Left:** This basic alloy wheel design also persisted throughout the Miura's lifespan, but rim widths progressively increased. **Above:** Raising the Miura's rear-hinged rear "clip" revealed Lamborghini's beautifully finished crosswise-mounted V12 with individual throttle butterflies.

199

Ferrari finally answered the Lamborghini Miura in 1974 with its own midengine supercar, the 365 GT4 BB. The initials stood for Berlinetta Boxer and signaled a new 4.4-liter horizontally opposed 12-cylinder engine with twin overhead camshafts on each cylinder bank and a rousing 344 DIN horsepower. Such engines are called "boxer" because their pistons pump side to side like the arms of two people sparring. Bodywork, again by Pininfarina, melded steel main panels with aluminum doors, engine lid, and nose cover. Underneath was a complex chassis framework of rectangular and square tubing, plus the expected all-around coil-spring/double-wishbone suspension and four-wheel disc brakes. Though rather heavy at 3420 pounds, the BB decisively raised the bar for high performance, as expected of the successor to the fabled front-V12 Daytona. *Road & Track* ran its BB to 175 mph all out, "the fastest road car we've ever tested." Acceleration was equally vivid, with 0-60 mph in 7.2 seconds, the standing quarter-mile in 15.5 at 102.5 mph. Ferrari built around 400 BBs, then upped the ante in 1976 with the 512 BB. With an enlarged 5.0-liter engine and some 360 bhp, *R&T*'s test car clocked 0-60 in just 5.5 seconds and was estimated to reach no less than 188 mph. Modest styling changes carried on for the fuel-injected 512 BBi of 1981, but it claimed "only" 340 bhp due to stricter emissions tuning. Amazingly, these fleet *cavallinos* would soon be overshadowed by even faster Ferraris.

Though it replaced the Dino 246 in 1973, the 308 GT4 was quite a different junior Ferrari. For starters, it was a 2+2 on a 100.4-inch wheelbase, up eight inches from that of the previous two-seaters, and the only body style was a coupe; no targa-top here. What's more, styling was by Bertone, making this the first production Ferrari in nearly 20 years not shaped by Pininfarina. But the biggest departure was the new twincam V8 replacing a V6 in a similar midengine chassis. Sized at 3.0 liters, the V8 was variously advertised with 205 or 240 horsepower in U.S. tune, 255 for Europe. Regardless, performance was in the Ferrari tradition, with 0-60 mph available in a swift 6.4 seconds and a top speed of over 150 mph. Perhaps because of its relatively sedate styling, this Dino isn't highly regarded among *Ferraristi*, though it sold well enough despite few improvements over a six-year lifespan. For many, the most important of those came in 1976, when Maranello inexplicably reversed itself and made a Dino an "official" Ferrari by adding prancing-horse badges to the nose, wheel hubs, and steering wheel. But the GT4's real significance is in introducing the engine that would serve a new generation of roadgoing Ferraris destined for far higher success.

**Opposite page, top:** Washington mandated stronger "5-mph" front bumpers for 1973. Unlike most cars that year, the Chevrolet Corvette complied with style, thanks to a smart new body-color nose. But in another sign of fast-changing times, engines were down to a pair of small-block V8s and one big-block. Performance was down, too, exaggerated by the industry's recent switch from SAE gross to more realistic SAE net horsepower quotes. Still, Corvette was one of the few real excitement machines left on the U.S. market. No wonder model-year sales were better than ever at 34,464. **This page:** Despite a sudden energy crisis and long lines at gas pumps, Corvette sales hit 37,502 for '74, when a restyled "5-mph" tail made news. The total was 38,465 for 1975, but only 4629 were convertibles like this. Accordingly, the droptop "shark" did not return, a victim of changing buyer tastes and steadily falling demand. Engines that year comprised 350 V8s with 165 or 205 bhp. **Opposite page, center:** Power finally went up again for the otherwise little-changed '76 'Vette, though only to 165 standard, 210 optional. Against all odds, though, sales kept on climbing, totaling 46,558 for the model year. **Opposite page, bottom:** The '77 edition was no longer a Stingray, and changes were again of the detail sort, yet sales set another new record at 49,213, amazing for a now-decade-old design. But that's no doubt because the 'Vette had evolved by popular request from thirsty, unruly hot rod to a relatively efficient, comfortable *gran turismo*, still very agile and with unique style and presence.

"One year before I had my license my father brought home the tomato orange '75 Corvette. It was the first year to completely lose the chrome, but the back bubble glass had yet to become a fixture. It had a big metal spoke steering wheel and an 8-track player; it was the last of the old guard. I would often slowly back it down the driveway when my dad was at work and dared a couple trips around the block.

One Saturday, while still on my learner's permit, my father offered me the keys. Thus far, I had only (legally) driven his '74 Beetle. After cautiously maneuvering out of our neighborhood I eased onto the main two lane. Dad took a noticeable breath and told me to "punch it." I looked over to see if it was indeed my father in the passenger seat. I slammed my right foot to the floor and felt the blast of wind through the T-tops. The nervous parades around the block would never suffice again."

– David Piluski
Cary, Illinois

"By conventional standards, the Lotus 7 (and the later Caterham) isn't even a whole car. There just isn't enough of it, but nobody ever forgets their first ride in a 7! Invariably the owner is at the wheel and even more invariably trying to impress you, and there you are: trapped in a seat that feels no more substantial than a lawn chair as the idiot screams around corners at speeds that would have any other car flying off into the scenery. You're hanging on for dear life—wind and noise blasting your face—as he whips in and out of heavy traffic with the hub nuts of heavy trucks flashing past at eye level... When he finally pulls it over, you're breathless. Shaking a little. Impressed, terrified, and angry all at the same time. And then the idiot lets you drive. And all of a sudden you get it. This 7 is so low, so light, so nimble, and so lively that you just can't help yourself. Now it's the owner's turn to hang on."

– **Burt Levy**
Oak Park, Illinois

Often likened to a "four-wheel motorcycle," the no-frills Lotus Seven roadster evolved through four series from 1957 to '73, after which Lotus dealer Caterham Cars, near London, took over production, marketing, and further development. Like the Lotus originals, Caterham's Super Seven combines a complex but strong multitube chassis with a ground-hugging, cycle-fender body made mostly of aluminum and measuring just 132 inches long on an 88.6-inch wheelbase. This ultralight platform—curb weights run from just 1140 to 1400 pounds—has supported all manner of chassis components and four-cylinder powertrains over the decades, most borrowed from contemporary mass-market British cars. But no matter the pieces used, the Seven is still celebrated as a classic dual-purpose sports car with unrivaled agilty and giant-killer acceleration. Most Caterham Super Sevens have been built with 1.3- to 2.0-liter engines and horsepower ranging from 72 to 175. As late as 2003, the company offered a 165-bhp Superlight R300 version that would sprint from 0 to 60 mph in just 4.7 seconds and top 130 mph despite the vintage "aerodynamics." Sevens of all ages have long been favored by weekend-racing Americans, but they've not always been easy to obtain or certify for road use in the U.S., owing to the safety and emissions standards that began blossoming in the Seventies. As of this writing, however, Caterham's U.S. branch will be happy to put you in the driver's seat.

Wheeler-dealer Malcolm Bricklin decided America would go for a "safety" sports car, but his Bricklin SV-1 was here in '74 and gone in '75. A strong rear-drive chassis-mounted Ford 351 or AMC 360 V8s, while the fastback coupe body with gullwing doors was made of a novel color-impregnated acrylic backed by fiberglass. But though it did well in crash tests, the Bricklin was heavy, thirsty, cramped, none too nimble, and not well built. It wasn't cheap either. No wonder fewer than 3000 were built.

" Jeff just gave me a dull wave, or maybe it was a sign slightly less cordial. I was supposed to be scrubbing the bay floors, and he figured I was screwing around instead. What I was doing was driving back and forth in front of the cashier's window in a cry for help. I was trapped. I had opened the gullwing door of the Bricklin easily enough, but once seated, I was unable to raise the massive flap. Clearly the struts that helped support the door had failed, and I was their hostage. I couldn't honk; the car was in for an electrical system short that had claimed the horn. Then it hit me, I would pull up to the full-serve island and yell to Jeff when the next customer drove up. Finally, when he was close enough, I screamed, "I can't get out." Jeff nonchalantly pulled up the door and asked, "Why didn't you say so?" A regular visitor to the station, the semi-exotic Bricklin had been a welcome biweekly distraction from the regular crowd of Cutlasses and Fairmonts. But peeking under the hood to find a mass-market AMC engine, and subsequently being jailed in its suede belly had seriously sullied the car's mystique for me. Now if only the guy with Pantera would drive by. "

— Tom Appel
Palatine, Illinois

**Above:** Datsun's popular 240Z was updated in 1973 to become the 260Z. The new name reflected an inline six enlarged to 2.6 liters to offset performance losses from tightening U.S. emissions standards. SAE net horsepower rose by 10 to 139, but was partly negated by weighty new "crash" bumpers that also dulled handling. The following year, parent Nissan added a 260Z 2+2 on a 102.6-inch wheelbase. Most critics thought it less lovely than the two-seater, as this pairing may suggest. With U.S. sales starting to soften, Nissan added more displacement and fuel injection for America-only 280Zs that bowed in March 1975 with 168 bhp. With that, two-seater performance returned to near 1970 levels, though handling didn't. By this point, the Z was offered with automatic transmission and air conditioning, both obligatory for the U.S. Clearly, the sportiest Datsun was fast moving toward GT land, and would get there with the replacement 280ZX of 1978. **Below:** Though less impressive than early Zs on the street, the 260/280Z won SCCA national C-Production championships in 1974-76. This 280Z ran in 1978's new Showroom Stock-A class, which was won by neophyte driver Dale Fazekas.

A "cutaway" view of the 260Z highlights the engineering and packaging of the original Datsun Z-Car. Note the simple but effective all-independent suspension with lower wishbones and coil-over struts. Note, too, that the powertrain is placed so that most of its weight is behind the front-axle centerline—the so-called "front/midengine" layout that tends to balance fore/aft weight distribution and optimize handling. Also visible here are the prominent U.S.-model bumpers backed by long tubes designed to crumple in low-speed impacts.

# YUTAKA KATAYAMA
## From Mr. K, the car called Z

In 1951, Yutaka Katayama founded the first postwar sports-car club in Japan. In 1958, he led a team of the Nissan Motor Company's Datsun cars to an unprecedented victory in a grueling Australian endurance rally. In the 1960s, working with limited resources against incredible odds, he laid the foundation for Nissan's successful advance into the U.S. auto market. Also, he's always loved to fly kites. The man that many hail as the "Father of the Z" is both personable and irrepressible, whimsical and tenacious. His keen understanding of the American market played a key role in the introduction of the revolutionary Datsun 240Z.

Katayama was born in Japan in 1909 to upper-class parents. His family's wealth provided him a privileged upbringing, enabling him to indulge his passion for driving and to travel abroad. His love of cars drew him to employment with Nissan, but he clashed with the bureaucracy there almost from the start. The young advertising executive's individualism did not sit well with his superiors, and in early 1960 he was "reassigned" to America and tasked with overseeing Nissan's fledgling import operations in California.

For most of his cloistered colleagues, such an assignment would have been a nightmare. For Katayama, it was paradise. He quickly took to American culture and the freedom it offered. He worked tirelessly, often personally delivering vehicles to his handpicked dealers and sometimes going door to door in Japanese neighborhoods to sell Datsun trucks. The exuberance and worldliness that soured his working rela-

tionships in Japan served him well in sunny California. His outgoing nature quickly won him American friends, who referred to him simply as "Mr. K." An avid landscape painter, he would pick his favorite piece and put it on his Christmas card for the year. Eventually, his card list was over 10,000 names long. Mr. K thrilled to American sporting events, loved to hike and fish, and could never quite kick his habit of speeding. He would pretend he couldn't speak English when pulled over, but cops caught on quickly. Soon, he was on a first name basis with police...and had a sizable stack of citations.

Throughout his tenure in California, Katayama was constantly pushing the executives and engineers back in Toyko for bigger-engined, sportier cars to lure American auto buyers. The Datsun 240Z was the car Mr. K had always wanted Nissan to build, and he was overjoyed when it finally came in 1970. In the Z, Nissan had finally produced a car that matched his own spirit—sturdy, passionate, energetic, and accessible.

By 1977, Nissan's place in the U.S. market was secure, but Katayama was still on shaky ground with Nissan management, who hadn't forgotten his insubordination over the years. He was called back to Japan, informed he had retired, and given a lesser advertising job. In 1998, he was inducted into the Automotive Hall of Fame in Dearborn, Michigan, a rare honor for a Japanese auto executive. With the revival of the original Z concept in the 2002 Nissan 350Z, Mr. K, still vivacious in his nineties, enjoyed a new swell of admiration and credit for his pioneering role in crafting the legacy of the original Z.

Unveiled as a concept in 1971, the midengine Lamborghini Countach was no less astonishing when sales began in '74. Replacing the Miura, the new LP400 transferred the familiar 5.0-liter twincam V12 to a waist-high Bertone-designed coupe with "scissor" doors and 98.4-inch wheelbase. It was cramped, stiff-riding, and tough to see out of, but who cared? The Countach was Batmobile cool and bat-outta-hell quick, capable of 175 mph and 0-60 in well under 7 seconds. In 1978 came the LP400S with flared fenders, ultrawide wheels and tires, front spoiler, and refinements to suspension and cockpit. It wasn't any faster, but it was somewhat easier to drive in traffic—if you had to. Alas, few Americans got the chance, and then mainly through "gray market" channels, as Lamborghini's mounting financial troubles prevented it from meeting all U.S. standards, thus largely precluding factory sales. That only made the Countach even more the dream ride for "bad boys" with connections and over $50,000 to burn.

Typical of Porsche, the 1974-model 911s kept pace with U.S. regulations, gaining artfully designed "crash" bumpers and a cleaner new 2.7-liter version of the familiar air-cooled flat six. Models were shuffled to base, S, and a new American-spec Carrera with the show but not the go of the earlier European RS. Only the S and Carrera were offered for 1975-77, little-changed except for added standard equipment—and inflation-fuel prices that reached beyond $14,000. Even so, sales remained brisk.

**Above:** America missed out on the Rover-powered MGB GT V8, which could do 125 mph but drew only 2591 sales in 1973-76. **Left and below left:** Instead, the MGB roadster halfheartedly met U.S. regulations from 1975 with an elevated suspension, debatable big "crash" bumpers, and just 62 emissions-strangled horsepower. Age, new competition, and rising prices conspired to end production for all markets in late 1980. **Below:** U.S. ads for early Seventies MGBs played on the public's longtime fondness for the marque since the first spindly, GI-imported TCs of the late Forties.

MG. The sports car America loved first.

Right-hand drive, sweeping fenders, folding windscreen, cut-down doors and 19-inch wire wheels.

Room enough for two. And fun enough to breed a generation of sports car enthusiasts.

That was the MG-TC. Behind its wheel, thousands of Americans first discovered the joy of downshifting through a curve and the quickness of sports car handling.

Today that car has evolved to the MGB. Still pure sports car. Still most at home on twisting ribbons of almost forgotten scenic route where cars go to be driven, not scorched off the line in a brute display of acceleration.

As Motor Trend reported in October, '71:

"You can find them any day on any piece of twisting pike...leaving the bigger 'now' cars in their wake."

Yet today's MGB is equally at home on six-lane expressway. With direct rack-and-pinion steering, 10.5-inch front disc brakes, race-

seasoned suspension, 4-speed close-ratio gearbox and a high performance 1798 c.c. overhead valve engine—all the world is its road.

Even in the fiercely competitive world of racing, MGB excels in its class. It's the reigning SCCA National Champion in E Production.

MGB also sports reclining bucket seats, full carpeting, leather wrapped steering wheel, oil cooler and full sports car instrumentation including tachometer and trip odometer.

What about you? Do you want to discover or re-discover the sheer joy of sports motoring?

If so, scour the want ads for a vintage MG-TC. Or see an MGB at your MG dealer.

For his name and for information about overseas delivery, dial (800) 631-1972. In New Jersey, dial (800) 962-2803. Calls are toll free.

BRITISH LEYLAND MOTORS INC., LEONIA, N.J. 07605

**Top:** The true successor to the Dino 246, the midengine Ferrari 308 GTB bowed in 1975 as a fixed-roof two-seat coupe on a 92.1-inch wheelbase. This targa-top GTS version followed in late 1977. Both featured Ferrari's new 3.0-liter twincam V8, here rated at 205 horsepower, and curvy, well-formed styling by the masterful house of Pininfarina. Long upper-bodyside scoops fed cool air to the engine. Unlike the 2+2 GT4, these 308s were an instant success with press and public alike, and they'd only get better in the 1980s.
**Right:** Actor Tom Selleck stormed around Hawaii in a 308 GTS—red, naturally—in his weekly role as a private detective on *Magnum P.I.*, which likely helped spur U.S. demand for Ferrari's latest midengine two-seater. It might also have inspired some questionable driving, especially the opening title scene showing the car in a fairly lurid tailslide.

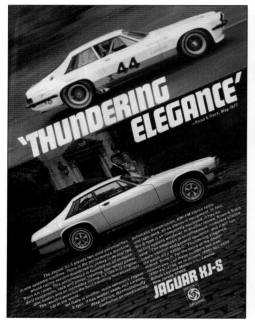

**Top:** Based on Jaguar's XJ sedan, the new 1976 XJS was a 2+2 luxury coupe with a 102-inch wheelbase and a newly fuel-injected V12 with 244 horses. But though smooth, quiet, and quick, it was no sports car. **Above:** Even so, Group 44's race-prepped XJS won the SCCA Trans-Am series in 1978. **Right and above right:** Storming onto U.S. roads for '76, the Porsche 911 Turbo coupe packed 234 emission-legal bhp from a new forced-fed 3.0-liter flat six, good for just 4.9 seconds 0-60 mph, 13.5 seconds in the quarter-mile, and 156 mph flat out. A big "whale tail" rear spoiler and bulging bodywork made it easy to spot. The name was just Porsche Turbo for 1978, when a 253-bhp 3.3-liter engine improved drivability, but not velocity. Then again, this was the fastest roadgoing Porsche yet and thus a genuine "gotta-have" the world over.

Seeking a more viable "budget" model, Porsche replaced the midengine 914 with the front-engine 924, which launched in America for 1977, two years after its European debut. Porsche had originally designed it to be a Volkswagen, but took it back after VW begged off, though Porsche tapped VW-owned Audi to handle assembly. Riding a 94.5-inch wheelbase, the 924 broke more new ground for Germany's premier sports-car builder with a water-cooled engine, an overhead-cam VW/Audi 2.0 liter four cylinder with 95 horsepower in initial U.S. tune. A thin propshaft connected to a manual four-speed rear transaxle, a layout that helped balance fore/aft weight distribution. A modern all-independent suspension also aided handling, which most reviewers judged excellent. Also new for Porsche was a hatchback coupe body style, whose big curved rear window lifted for easy luggage access. Despite its mixed parentage, the 924 was more readily accepted as a Porsche than the 914, so it proved more popular. Still, critics carped about engine noise and tepid acceleration, especially with optional automatic transmission. Porsche responded in 1978 with a manual five-speed option, then a 143-bhp 924 Turbo that cut 0-60 mph by some 4 seconds to around 7.7. And Porsche itself built the Turbo, which suggested even better 924s were on the way—as indeed they were.

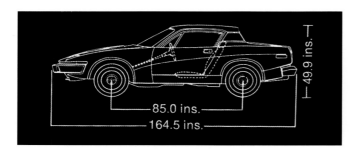

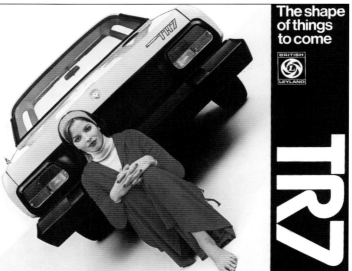

The shape of things to come

BRITISH LEYLAND

TR7

While phasing out the Spitfire and TR6, Triumph issued a new sports car unlike any it had built before. Dubbed TR7, it came to the U.S. in 1976 as a unibody coupe with a 2.0-liter overhead-cam four-cylinder engine and 86-90 horsepower. The engine was from the parts bins of parent British Leyland. So were the standard front-disc/rear-drum brakes, all-coil suspension with front struts and a live axle on radius arms, and the manual four-speed and optional five-speed overdrive gearboxes. A three-speed automatic was available as an American-market must. Despite riding a three-inch-shorter wheelbase, the TR7 was about as long as the TR6 and somewhat wider, so cockpit and luggage space were uncommonly good for a two-seater. Styling wasn't so good. Originating with an off-hand sketch by BL designer Harris Mann, it sought to emulate the "flying wedge" look of contemporary Italian exotics, but didn't go over with most buyers, notwithstanding ad claims to the contrary. A convertible arrived in 1979 looking somewhat nicer, but consistently subpar workmanship and BL's increasingly publicized troubles hampered TR7 sales, especially in the vital U.S. market, and the addition of V8-powered TR8 models didn't help. As a result, Triumph was forced to abandon sports cars in late 1981.

" Oh, no! They've done it on this side too! "

— Giorgetto Giugiaro
Italian Master Stylist upon seeing the TR7's bodyside crease

**Above:** Though dogged by many problems, the Triumph TR7 drew over 112,000 worldwide sales in six years. We doubt many were made on the basis of styling. **Left and below:** Unveiled in early 1976, the Lamborghini Silhouette was a semiconvertible based on the midengine Urraco coupe with flared, squared wheel arches and "five-hole" wheels. Everything else was the same. Cash-short Lamborghini hoped the new model would boost sales, but couldn't afford to certify it for the U.S. market, where it might have sold best. This left would-be American buyers to deal with the questionable "gray market" or a few private companies that would "federalize" a Euro model—for a price. But it didn't matter anyway. Lamborghini couldn't build many cars of any kind in this period, managing a mere 50 or so Silhouettes through 1977. After that, the marque would be absent from the U.S. until 1983.

Lotus moved upmarket with its mid-Seventies replacement for the midengine Europa. A wedgy, sharp-edged two-seat coupe penned by Giorgetto Giugiaro, the Esprit followed Lotus tradition with a fiberglass body atop a steel "backbone" chassis with coil-spring/double-wishbone suspension. The engine, however, was a new Lotus-developed 2.0-liter twincam four with 140 horsepower in initial U.S. tune. A planned Esprit Turbo launched overseas in 1980 with a force-fed 2.2 liter, stiffer chassis, revised suspension, and "aero" lower-body addenda. It came to America several years later with 205 bhp, which gave a Ferrari-like 0-60 mph of 6.6 seconds and nearly 150 mph all out. Regular or Turbo, the Esprit has always been one of the world's best handling cars, and would prove to have enduring appeal. Despite on-again/off-again U.S. sales, it would be Lotus' chief money-earner into the early twenty-first century.

Unveiled in late 1978, the M1 was BMW's first midengine production car, though it was conceived at least five years before as a Porsche 911-beater in production-class racing. BMW lacked experience with "middies," so it contracted chassis development to Lamborghini and body design to Giorgetto Giugiaro's Ital Design. The result was a handsome, if not beautiful, two-seat coupe with a fiberglass skin and a complex multitube chassis. BMW developed a special version of its trademark inline six-cylinder engine, a 3.5 liter with dual overhead cams, four valves per cylinder, and a strong 277 DIN horsepower, delivered through a manual five-speed transaxle. Suspension was naturally all-independent. Wheels were uncommonly large 16-inchers wearing suitably wide, grippy tires. A few 470-bhp racing M1s were built for Europe's 1979-80 "Procar" support series, and a handful of 3.2-liter turbocharged racers had no less than 850 bhp. But BMW had lost interest, so the M1 was discontinued in 1981 after total production of 450 units. Today it's a highly sought-after collector car—and one of the quickest, able to do 0-60 mph in 5.5 seconds and at least 160 mph all out.

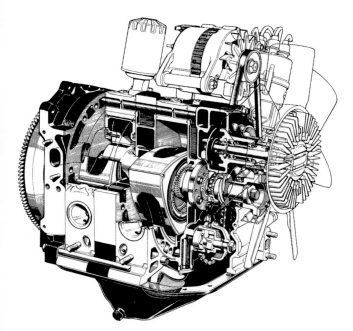

Hitting U.S. streets as a late 1978 model, the Mazda RX-7 was a new symbol for the growing success and influence of Japanese automakers. The small two-seat coupe combined conventional engineering with a most unconventional engine: a compact Wankel rotary type producing 100 horsepower from a nominal 1.2-liter displacement. At around 2500 pounds in U.S. guise, the RX-7 could run 0-60 mph in 9.7 seconds with standard five-speed manual gearbox, and was great fun on twisty back roads. "An enthusiast's dream come true," said one critic. Even better, it was well built, well equipped, and initially bargain priced at around $7000. The RX-7 would continue for six years with no basic design change, but got styling tweaks, added features, and, for 1984, an upmarket GSL-SE model, shown here, with a 135-bhp 1.3-liter rotary.

" I bought my first sports car in 1979, a new Mazda RX-7 that I found to be incredibly responsive and a blast to drive. There was a real cult around the car, given its unique engine and the neat pop-up headlights that served as a wink to a fellow owner. I was starting my own ad agency, and felt that it not only gave me a good "look" with clients, but also provided an incredible incentive to succeed, because I didn't want to lose the car! Alas, as with all good things, I ultimately parted with it in 1985—but only because my first child was born and my wife rebelled at having to curl up in the hatch area while my daughter got the front seat. If I could have added a rear seat, I might still be driving it today. "

– Dennis Collins
Arlington Heights, Illinois

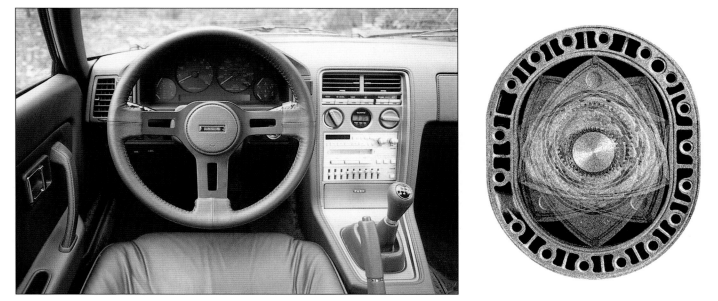

**Above:** Among the RX-7's many virtues was an orderly, well-furnished cockpit, though space was at a premium for six-footers. **Above right:** Instead of pistons, the RX-7's Wankel engine used a roughly triangular rotor spinning within a specially shaped housing to provide the normal four-stroke cycle. The RX-7's two-rotor unit used a pair of these assemblies. German engineer Felix Wankel devised this concept in the 1950s, and others experimented with it, but only Mazda was still perfecting and producing this type of engine in the late 1970s. **Upper center:** The RX-7 was a fast success on the racetrack and showroom alike. During the Eighties, they would dominate the small-displacement GTU class of the International Motor Sports Association, winning the national trophy each year except 1988. The RX-7 also fared well in SCCA competition and international rallying. **Lower center:** The RX-7 claimed near-ideal sports-car weight distribution thanks to a light, compact engine mounted well back in a well-sorted chassis. **Below:** If not stunning or original, RX-7 styling was at least clean and tidy. Always sold as a hatchback coupe with a 95.3-inch wheelbase, Mazda's first genuine sports car saw only detail appearance changes, mostly to body trim and wheel design. This '82 was photographed along the Chicago lakeshore as part of the editors' original new-model road test. We loved it. Though popular worldwide, the RX-7 was especially hot in America, racking up over 144,000 calendar-year sales in 1978-79.

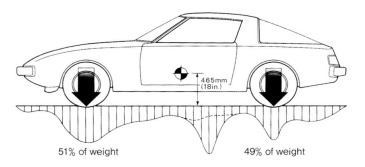

465mm (18in.)

51% of weight        49% of weight

The Silver Anniversary Corvette.

25 years of men, machines, and memories.

**Right and below:** For 1978, America's sports car celebrated its 25th birthday with a fastback roofline, numerous minor changes, and a limited-edition Silver Anniversary option package. Horsepower continued recovering from its middecade nadir, with the hallowed small-block tuned up for 185 bhp standard and 220 optional. Despite all this, year-to-year Corvette sales declined for the first time in a long while, easing to just under 48,000 for the model run.

**Above:** A highlight of Corvette's 25th birthday year was being selected as pace car for the fabled Indianapolis 500. Chevrolet shared the honor with 'Vette fans by running off 6502 Pace Car Replicas like this. Each left the factory with special two-tone paint, glass roof panels (a new option for other '78s), racy spoilers front and rear, wider tires, and unique high-back seats. A set of body decals was also included for owners to apply if they wanted the full race-day effect. Despite a stiff base price of $13,653, the Pace Car Replica was an easy sell—so much so that some fast-buck artists tried to make a killing with counterfeit Replicas, which caused Chevy no little grief.

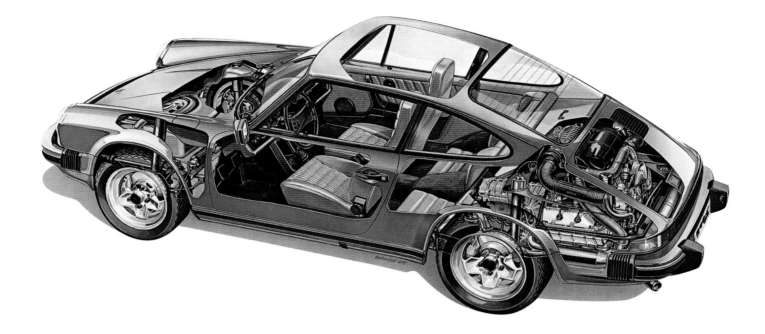

Besides a 3.3-liter 911 Turbo, the 1978 Porsche lineup included a freshened 911SC coupe and Targa with many features of the previous Carrera, including wider rear wheels, tires, and fenders. One new wrinkle was a normally aspirated 3.0-liter flat six with 172 SAE net horsepower, plus a broader torque spread that reduced the need to shift so much at low speeds. A stronger crankshaft improved durability, and adoption of catalytic converters helped satisfy prevailing U.S. emissions standards. The one downside was record prices, now near $17,000 minimum, reflecting at least of a decade of inflation. The '79s cost even more—over $20,000 to start—and could really soar with special options like the plaid upholstery on the Targa shown here. By now, some pundits were starting to think that regulations would soon catch up with the 911, but Porsche would keep defying conventional wisdom by keeping its evergreen rear-engine sports car bang up to date for years to come.

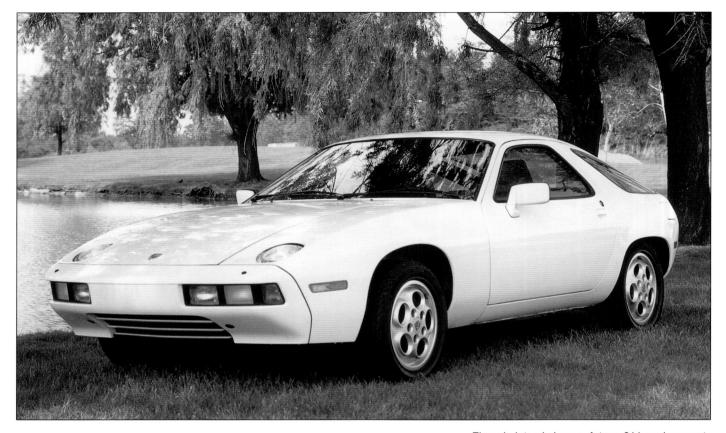

**Weight distribution**

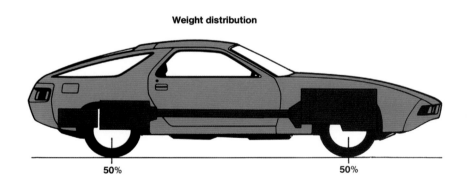

50%          50%

Though intended as a future 911 replacement, the Porsche 928 ended up a posh, high-speed GT coupe. A sleek 2+2 hatchback body semed shrink-wrapped around a front-mounted water-cooled V8—a first for a production Porsche—and a 924-like rear transaxle that helped balance weight fore to aft. Bowing in the U.S. for 1978, the 928 sent 219 horsepower through five-speed manual or optional three-speed automatic transmissions. Despite weighing a hefty 1.5 tons, it could scale 0-60 mph in 7-8 seconds, the quarter-mile in some 15-16 seconds at 90 mph, and breeze on to 140 plus. Four-wheel independent suspension and big disc brakes provided handling and stopping power to match. Styling, by American Tony Lapine, featured slick body-color bumpers and Lamborghini Miura-style "reclining" headlamps. Despite lofty pricing—initially $26,000—the 928 was a solid success in its own right and would evolve into the mid-1990s, but would never take over from the evergreen 911.

"Call it the German Enigma Machine. My 928 was a ton of good and a ton of bad. I never got entirely over the bad. The beast was fast: 100 mph seemed like nothing. The 928 had a feeling of solidity and heft. A V8 burble made it sound like a Hemi-Cuda, but it would rip through traffic without the high-rev downshifts you'd need in a 911. Just punch it and go. But one day the punch stopped: timing belt failure. Then strange power losses occurred. The dealer replaced parts until the car ran again, but never did find out what went wrong. The final kick came the day after I sold the thing, when the new owner called. "A red light came on, and now there's oil all over my garage floor." We went to the Porsche dealer, who looked at the front of the oil-splattered engine and said, "Oh, they all do that eventually. But we have the parts in stock." It cost another $1600, but I was finally free of the car, losing more in depreciation than my six prior cars combined."

— Robert H. Gurr
Los Angeles

# 6

## 1980-89: New Challenges, New Ideas

If "a Pinto in a gas line" represents the Seventies, as Louis Menand wrote, what motoring metaphor for the 1980s? A BMW cruising Wall Street might be apt.

Wall Street and its ways became increasingly important to Eighties America, not least because of a popular new pro-business president. Ronald Reagan swept into office at decade's dawn promising less government and lower taxes to leave more money in the public pocket. But while many taxes and programs were indeed cut, military spending was vastly increased. This combined with aggressive new foreign competition in many industries to produce record deficits and unemployment. By 1983, some 12 million Americans were out of work, the most since 1941. "Supply-side" economic measures were supposed to help all, but only the rich seemed to get richer. Among them was the horde of go-getting thirtysomethings that came to symbolize the Eighties, the so-called Young Urban Professionals or "Yuppies." They were the Baby Boomers who had railed against all things "Establishment" in the Sixties. Now they themselves were in charge, and determined to live the high life. An MBA degree was the price of admission. Conspicuous consumption came back in style, especially when it involved high-status brand names. Bigger was again better in the corporate world, as new "leveraged buyout" tactics improbably allowed small companies to swallow much bigger ones. Never mind the long-term cost in dollars or jobs. How did the stock do today? A period film provided a perfect mantra for such dealings: "Greed is good." Not coincidentally, perhaps, the film was *Wall Street*.

Though not everyone prospered in the "Reagan Revolution," the actor-turned-governor-turned-president scored another landslide election victory in 1984. By that time, the economy was rebounding from the early-decade doldrums brought on by the second energy crisis. U.S. calendar-year car sales, which had bottomed out in 1982 at just over 7.9 million, went back above 10.3 million in '84, the best since pre-recession 1979. The total was 11.4 million in 1986, the best year ever. Even more impressive was America's fast-growing appetite for light trucks, led by the minivan, which was pioneered for 1984 by Chrysler Corporation and pretty much saved that company from going under. Buyers were also becoming entranced with something called the sport-utility vehicle—SUV. With that, total car/truck sales reached a record 16 million in banner year 1986. Though car sales eased through decade's end, truck sales kept rising, a trend that did not go unnoticed in Detroit.

But Motown struggled against another trend: the steady, seemingly unstoppable sales growth of Japanese-made cars, which only accelerated once North American "transplant" factories began turning out Honda Accords, Toyota Camrys, and other popular models. Ironically, these plants hired many workers that had been laid off by the Big Three in do-or-die cutbacks prompted as much by the sour early-Eighties market as Japanese competition. But try as it might with X-cars, K-cars, and other import-fighters, American automakers kept losing ground. By 1989, Japanese-brand models accounted for a third of total U.S. car sales—and each of the Big Three was selling cars produced by a Japanese "affiliate." Well, if you can't beat 'em, join 'em.

The U.S. sports-car scene mirrored the general fall and rise of the nation's economy and new-vehicle market. The decade began on a sad note when the MGB and Triumph TRs followed the Midget and Spitfire to the heavenly parking lot. For the first time since World War II, Americans had no new British-built roadsters to buy. It hardly seemed possible. The

Alfa Romeo Spider rolled on against all odds but increasingly looked a relic of another age—which, of course it was. So, too, the Fiat X1/9 and 124 Spider, only they wouldn't last the decade, running through 1988 and 1985, respectively. Before the end, Fiat handed over marketing and some design functions to the coachbuilders, who applied their own names—and little else—for the upgraded but short-lived Bertone X1/9 and Pininfarina Spider 2000.

Among Italian exotics, DeTomaso was still frozen out by its inability to meet U.S. regulations, while grim economic realities forced Maserati to abandon its high-power GTs for lower-priced sporty sedans blatantly patterned on the popular BMW 3-Series. Ferrari, by happy contrast, pushed excitement to new heights with the burly flat-12 Testarossa, the racy 288 GTO with mid-mounted V8, and, to celebrate the marque's 40th birthday, the super-rare competition-inspired F40.

To no one's surprise, the Porsche 911 and related Turbo sailed through the Eighties with thoughtful yearly improvements that kept the now-classic rear-engine sports car forever young. The posh 928 grand tourer steered a similar course. What did surprise was the 944, a faster, more agile, and much better-built "entry-level" Porsche based on the 924. Almost a brand-new car, the 944 was a revelation right out of the box, and became even more so when higher-performance S and Turbo models came along.

Chevrolet provided more good news with the 1983 release of the first clean-sheet Corvette in 20 years. Its only link with the past was a hallowed small-block V8, and even that was fully updated. Though less flamboyant than the "shark" it replaced, the "C4" was a more practical, sophisticated Corvette just right for its time. The same could be said for the popular Datsun/Nissan Z and Mazda RX-7, which also began new design generations that emphasized comfort and convenience without spoiling the sports-car fun.

The Eighties also produced its share of interesting newcomers, some from unexpected quarters. The Pontiac Fiero and Toyota MR2 followed earlier "parts bin" models by using high-volume drivetrains in a unique two-seat package with mid-engine mystique. Each had its own distinct character, but both were fun, affordable, and easy to live with. Cadillac raised eyebrows with the swank Allante convertible for 1987, and Buick did likewise the following year with its own two-seater, the Reatta. As spinoffs of larger front-drive models, neither could be serious driver's cars, though they were enjoyable luxury tourers. Another sporty image-builder, the 1989 Chrysler's TC by Maserati, suffered from much more humble roots, though it, too, seemed a good idea at the time. And then there's the DeLorean DMC-12, which embodied so many not-so-good ideas as to strain belief. History has long since recorded the rear-engine coupe with the stainless-steel body panels and gullwing doors as an exercise in personal hubris. It was thus almost fated to fail, which it did in spectacular, headline-grabbing fashion. Today, the DeLorean is thought of as either a campy prop from the *Back to the Future* movies or a symbol of most everything wrong with the Eighties.

Of course, every era has its contradictions. And for all the ups and downs, the 1980s not only left us some very capable, rewarding sports cars, it paved the way for even better things. Though the Acura/Honda NSX, Dodge Viper, Mazda Miata, and others would await the Nineties, they were conceived in the tough, winner-take-all environment of the Eighties. Considering how good they would be, maybe greed wasn't so bad, after all.

**1980** MG abandons sports cars, departs U.S. • Third postwar regime takes charge at Aston Martin Lagonda, Ltd. • Ferrari Mondial 8 bows with 308GT4 powerteam in larger, new-style 2+2 • Lotus adds 150-mph 2.2-liter Turbo Esprit • Triumph introduces TR7 convertible and V8 TR8 models **1981** Alfa Romeo Sprint Veloce swaps 4-cyl for V6 power to become GTV-6 • DeLorean DMC-12 gullwing coupe arrives after 7-year gestation • DeTomas Pantera returns to U.S. as "private" import after seven years • Ferrari production models swap carburetors for fuel injection • New, smaller V8 turns Mercedes' 2-seater into a 380SL • Triumph gives up on sports cars, says cheerio to U.S. market **1982** Death claims Lotus founder Colin Chapman • Alfa Romeo Spider gets electronic injection, stiffer structure, improved build quality • Chevrolet Corvette ends "shark" era with special Collector Edition model • DeLorean ends production amid poor sales, financial scandals • Jaguar returns to international endurance racing with U.S.-bred V12 XJR-5 • Ferrari V8 powers up with four valves per cylinder • Revised Lamborghini Countach LP5000 V12 enlarged to 5.0 liters • Porsche 924 dropped from U.S. • Porsche 944 bows as faster, restyled 924 with Porsche power, premium fittings **1983** Minor styling tweaks freshen Alfa Romeo Spider • Chevrolet bows all-new "C4" Corvette as early '84 entry • Lotus returns to U.S. market with Turbo Esprit, revised non-turbo Esprit S3 • After four years in Europe, Porsche 928S bows in U.S. with bigger V8, upgraded chassis

Pininfarina's basic design for Alfa Romeo's two-seat roadster was strong enough to survive more than two decades. It bowed in the mid-Sixties as the Duetto with covered headlamps and a tapered rump and finished in the early Nineties with slightly more power and only slightly altered nose and tail styling. In between, it became a classic. The twincam four grew from 1.6 to 1.8 and finally 2.0 liters in 1972. Output drifted between 115 horsepower and 150 as fuel-delivery and emissions hardware evolved. Bumpers went from chrome to mid-Seventies black plastic to body color by 1990. The stern wore a black spoiler from '83 to '89, then reverted to a more original-style, squared-off look. The arms-out-legs-in driving stance was a constant. In 1985, Alfa named the base Spider the Graduate, to recall Dustin Hoffman's movie wheels. Pictured is an '86 Spider Veloce. At $16,995, it bridged the $13,995 Graduate and $19,600 Quadrifoglio. All had a five-speed manual and all-disc brakes. Quadrifoglio got 15-inch wheels, the others 14s. These Alfas spent most of their final years eclipsed by RX-7s and Nissan Zs on price and performance but never on character.

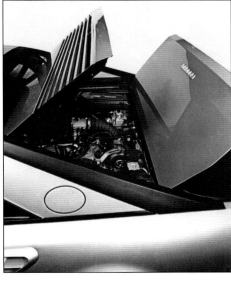

Ferrari's initial midengine 2+2 was the 308 GT4 unveiled in 1972. That was the first non-Pininfarina-styled Ferrari in 20 years, and its wedgy Bertone lines never really resonated. To replace it, Ferrari returned to Pininfarina for the more visually appealing successor unveiled in 1980 as the Mondial 8. **Right**: The transverse-mounted 205-horsepower 3.0-liter V8 was borrowed from the two-seat 308GTB. So was the chassis, though stretched in wheelbase from 92.1 inches to 104.2 to fit small rear seats. The Mondial 8 did 0-60 mph in 9.4 seconds. Quattrovalvole four-valve heads and new engine electronics for '82 gave 230 bhp and cut more than a second from that time. Mondial's real pleasure lay in its balance and refinement, and even its modicum of utility. To some testers, it was the sweetest-driving Ferrari of its day.

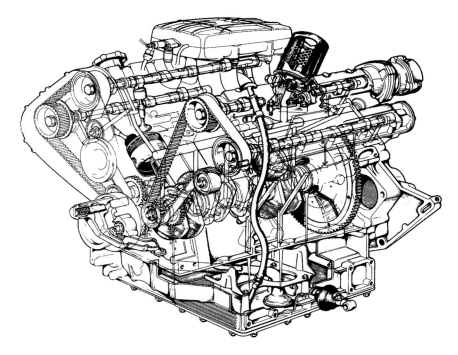

**1984** Chevy Corvette goes from 205 to 230 hp with new "Tuned Port Injection" • All-new V6-powered Nissan 300ZX replaces Datsun 280ZX • Chrysler Corporation takes a stake in Maserati • Ferrari starts building a new "288" GTO with twin-turbo midships V8 • Mazda RX-7 adds GSL-SE version with larger, more potent rotary engine • Pontiac Fiero 2M4 bows as low-cost "parts bin" sports car, paces Indy 500 **1985** Buick unveils futuristic, mid-engine Wildcat sports-car concept • Ferrari replaces BB with stunning mid-V12 Testarossa • Ferrari ups displacement, tweaks styling for revised 328GTB/GTS • Lamborghini Countach renamed 5000 Quattrovalvole for new 4-valve 5.2 V12 • Pontiac Fiero adds lively V6 GT with uprated chassis, "go fast" cosmetics • Porsche 928 improves performance with new twincam 5.0 V8 **1986** Aston Martin adds high-power Vantage V8 Volante droptop, limited-production Zagato coupe • Chevy Corvette convertible returns, paces Indy 500 • Mazda launches redesigned RX-7 with 2+2 and first-time Turbo models • Mercedes issues U.S.-exclusive 560SL with more power, improved dynamics • Pontiac Fiero GT adopts "flying buttress" roofline, German 5-speed gearbox **1987** Aston Martin taken over by Ford Motor Company, adds V8 Volante Zagato • Cadillac challenges Mercedes' SL with Pininfarina-built Allante • Chevy Corvette horsepower goes to 345 • Chrysler Corporation buys controlling interest in Lamborghini • Ferrari 288 GTO ends production at just 200 units; a few come to America

British Leyland tried to salvage its underachieving TR design in 1980 by installing the small V8 for which the car was originally designed. Replacing the TR7's 2.0-liter four-cylinder with a 3.5-liter V8 from corporate cousin Rover created the TR8. This was the aluminum overhead-valve V8 Rover had acquired from General Motors, where it began life in early Sixties Buicks and Oldsmobiles. Most TR8s had two single-barrel carburetors and were rated at 133 horsepower at 5500 rpm and 165 pound-feet at 3200. Emissions-sensitive California cars bowed with Bosch L-Jetronic fuel injection, which had little effect on power. A five-speed manual or three-speed automatic were gearbox choices. Upgrades to the TR8 included firmer damping, standard power steering, and nicer trim. U.S. price was $11,500, and five-speed TR8s were good for 0-60 in 8.5 seconds and a top speed of 133 mph. Most TR8s used the convertible body style introduced for 1979. Arguably prettier than the coupes, the ragtops were also far less rigid—enough that parking on shallow inclines could prevent opening the doors. That was symptomatic of the quality problems that dogged these cars. TR8 production lasted just two years, with 2308 of the 2497 built coming to the U.S. Just 202 were coupes.

The DeLorean DMC-12 was not so much an automobile as a notorious confluence of the Eighties' worst impulses. The rear-engine two-seater was the brainchild of former Pontiac and Chevrolet chief John Z. DeLorean, whose image inspired middle-age swingers everywhere. Developed by Lotus of England with a French-sourced 130-horse-power V6 and built in Northern Ireland, its pedigree was suspect from the start. Materials and design at least sounded exotic, though the stainless-steel body panels—intentionally left unpainted—and gullwing doors served mostly to divert attention from the $25,000 car's mediocre performance and subpar assembly quality. Allegations of shady financing dogged the project from its beginning, and in 1982, DeLorean himself was indicted on drug charges. He was later cleared of allegations that he bilked some investors, including the British government. DeLorean Motor Company went bankrupt in 1982 after building about 8500 DMC-12s. The final 1200 were sold at some $6000 off list by a Columbus, Ohio, liquidator.

Your eyes skim the sleek, sensuous stainless steel body, and all your senses tell you, "I've got to have it!"

The counterbalanced gull-wing doors rise effortlessly, beckoning you inside.

The soft leather seat in the cockpit fits you like it was made for your body.

You turn the key. The light alloy V-6 comes to life instantly.

The De Lorean. Surely one of the most awaited automobiles in automotive history.

It all began with one man's vision of the perfect personal luxury car. Built for long life, it employs the latest space-age materials.

Of course, everyone stares as you drive by. Sure, they're a little envious. That's expected. After all, you're the one Living The Dream. Start living it today at a dealer near you.

A dealer commitment as unique as the car itself. There are 345 De Lorean dealers located throughout the United States. Each one is a stockholder in the De Lorean Motor Company. This commitment results in a unique relationship which will provide De Lorean owners with a superb standard of service.

For the dealer nearest you, call toll free 800-447-4700, in Ill., 800-322-4400.

**THE DE LOREAN. LIVE THE DREAM.**

Ferrari commemorates four decades, announces fiery F40 • Porsche 924 returns to U.S. as upgraded S model with base 944 engine • Porsche's new 944S bridges price/performance gap between base and Turbo • Revised Porsche 928 S3 offers still more power, smoother styling • New twin-turbo, all-wheel-drive Porsche 959 offers 190 mph for $230,000 but isn't U.S. legal **1988** Death claims Italian sports-car legend Enzo Ferrari • Buick springs surprise with 2-seat Reatta, a semi-sporting luxury coupe • Chevy Corvette offers 35th Anniversary model, wins third straight SCCA class championship • Ford Motor Company buys controlling interest in Jaguar • Jaguar scores first win at LeMans in 31 years with high-tech XJR-9 racer • Lotus Esprit revamped with softer styling, nicer cockpit • Mazda introduces first RX-7 convertible • Pontiac Fiero dropped amid persistent teething troubles, sluggish sales • Porsche 944 lineup adds premium $48K Turbo S with 5.5-sec 0-60 sizzle **1989** New-look Aston Martin Virage replaces venerable V8 series • Composite-body BMW Z1 roadster starts Europe-only run • Chevy Corvette convertible revives optional lift-off hardtop • Chrysler's TC by Maserati bows as upscale 2-seat K-car, Italian-style • Dodge wows U.S. auto shows with Viper sports-car concept • Fiat drops Bertone-built X1/9 after near-20-year run • Porsche issues 2.7-liter base 944, 3.0-liter 944S2, belated S2 Cabrio • Porsche 911 line adds nostalgic Speedster, all-wheel-drive Carrera 4

Lamborghini's search for a car that could compete on price and performance with the likes of the Ferrari 328 and Porsche 928 and 911 Turbo led in 1982 to the Jalpa. As an update of the 1976-78 Silhouette, Jalpa was another targa-top two seater, but had less angular styling, a new interior, and a larger V8. Mounted transversely behind the seats and working through a gated five-speed manual, the quad-cam 3.5 liter made 255 horsepower at 7000 rpm. That was good for 0-60 mph in 7.3 seconds and the quarter-mile in 15.4 at 92 mph. Razor-sharp steering and a suspension that gave excellent control over virtually any surface were high points of the Jalpa, which listed for $58,000 in 1983 and for $65,000 in its final year, 1988. Lamborghini built 410 Jalpas, a decent number for a low-volume boutique manufacturer but not nearly enough to threaten the more-established brands.

"After parting with a black 1979 Corvette that he really never fell in love with, my father brought home a red '82. It was the summer of '84, and I was 18. My history of "aggressive" driving, bent axles, and over revved engines was already well established, and the odds of me driving the new car seemed slim. The "Cross-Fire Injection" logos on the front quarters both baffled and intrigued, but the engine made good noise and the tires could be spun free of the pavement almost at will. The brakes were undersized and would rattle and creak as the hot metal cooled in the garage after I "borrowed" the car. Dad's gone now but his 'Vette is in the garage, covered—a tribute to the man who loved it. Becoming a classic? Hard to say, but driving it isn't the same without worrying about getting caught."

– David Piluski
Cary, Illinois

The 1982 Collectors' Edition was Chevrolet's acknowledgement that a new-generation Corvette was just around the corner. It had special silver and black paint, opening rear glass, and was the first 'Vette to list for over $20,000; 6759 were built. All '82s previewed the next-generation engine, which dropped the L81 code for L83. The 350-cid V8 was unchanged, but its four-barrel carburetor was replaced by a hybrid carb/fuel-injection system Chevy called Cross-fire Injection. Horsepower increased by 10 to 200. Unfortunately, an automatic was the only transmission for '82, but it now had four speeds instead of three. Total model-year output fell from 40,696 in '81 to just 25,407 as buyers awaited the redesigned Corvette, due, they believed, for 1983.

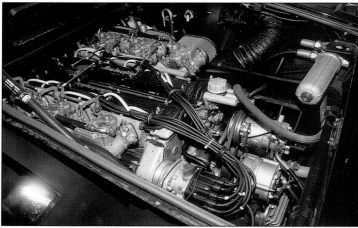

Lamborghini's relatively svelt original Countach, the LP 400 of 1974, got fiberglass fender arches for 1978. But it took the LP 5000 S of 1982 for Countach to hit its stride as a supercar shocker. It's pictured here in all its flared and spoilered glory. The mid-mounted V12 was enlarged for the occassion, fighting tightening emissions standards by growing from 3.9 liters to 4.8, though horsepower was unchanged at 375. If the car was no faster (5.7 seconds 0-60, 150 mph top speed), it certainly was more impudent. The tail wing was actually an option, but seemed to fit most every Countach buyer's attitude. In reality, it contributed only weight and aerodynamic drag and thousands to the price tag. The cabin was always quite businesslike, if hardly practical. Only the lower portion of the side window rolled down, and rear visibility was so bad that to back up, many drivers sat on the sill of the open scissor door and, looking rearward over the fender scoops, reached in to work the wheel and pedals. Countach was further sullied in this period by grotesque rubber bumper blocks fitted to satisfy U.S. crash regulations. By the time the LP 5000 S was retired in 1985, Lambo had built 323 of them.

**Right:** It was clear by 1985 that simply enlarging Countach's engine would not regain performance lost to smog hardware. So that year, Lamborghini fit four-valve heads to the V12 and boosted displacement from 4.9 to 5.2 liters. In a Countach rebadged LP 5000 Quattrovalvole, the 48-valve V12 made 455 horsepower at 7000 rpm in Euro tune, 420 in fuel-injected U.S. trim. Zero-60 times fell to 5.2 seconds, top speed rose to 173, and running updates to chassis, suspension, steering, and even air conditioning, made for the most civilized Countach yet. List was $138,800 and 610 were sold through 1988. **Below:** Lamborghini marked its 25th year as an automaker in 1988 with the Anniversary Edition Countach. The 5.2 V12 was unchanged, but the body got rocker-panel strakes and air intakes that were more gracefully integrated with the rear fenders. Composite plastics replaced aluminum for these and other exterior components. Some of this was the influence of Chrysler Corporation, which had purchased Lamborghini in 1987 for $30 million. Its intent was a more livable supercar, and, to that end, the Anniversary Edition also benefitted from more comfortable seats and added sound insulation. None of this detracted from performance, which the factory listed as 4.7 seconds 0-60, 12.9 in the quarter-mile, and a top speed of 183. This was the final Countach, and critics said it was the best since the original if not the finest of all. For certain, it was the best-selling Countach ever, with 650 built through the end of production in 1990.

A whipsaw economy and fuel-price flux compelled Eighties enthusiasts to expand their definition of a "sports car." **Above:** For some, Honda's CRX was a keen blend of economy and fun. It bowed for 1984, and, at 76 horsepower, just 1720 pounds, and $6865, was surprisingly entertaining. The shapelier 1988-92 generation of the Civic-derived two-seat hatchback had up to 108 bhp and sharp front-drive handling. **Left:** Fiat's X1/9 looked more the sports car but also rearranged components from an economy sedan. Its mid-mounted four-cylinder never made over 85 bhp, so the car wasn't as fast as it looked, but it was affordable and sinfully tossable. The two-tone version bears the badge of its Bertone coachbuilder, which distributed the X1/9 after Fiat bailed from the U.S. in 1984.

From a heritage of championship race car design...

...Fiat X1/9: one of the 10 best cars for the eighties.

Nothing moves you like a Fiat Sportsca

Pontiac's Fiero was another corporate kit car in the pseudo sports-car mold. GM brass approved it for 1984 as an economy product, but Pontiac was happy to suggest it was something more. The muddled marketing dogged the car's development and ultimately doomed it. Components cribbed from workaday sedans mounted in a steel space frame sheathed with plastic body panels. Weight was 2500 pounds. Fiero debuted at under $10,000 and was initially a hot seller. The 2M4 badge meant two-seat, midengine, four cylinder. Early versions had 92 horsepower. A 150-bhp V6 pepped things up for '85. **Right:** The fast-back GT version bowed for '86 and benefitted from ongoing gearbox and suspension upgrades. Never allowed to be a gas sipper or a road ripper, Fiero was shelved in 1988, its true potential never realized.

Zuffenhausen's first foray into the water-cooled front-engine realm was a commercial success, but the Volkswagen/Audi/Porsche amalgam that was the 924 never really established itself as a true Porsche. Its successor was an altogether superior car and a bonafide Porsche. The 944 was introduced for 1983 and used a single-overhead-cam 2.5-liter four-cylinder that was essentially half of the V8 from the mighty 928. Initial U.S. horsepower was 143 at 5500 rpm, and Porsche kept it under control with strong all-disc brakes and a suitably beefed-up chassis. The arresting new body had blistered fenders and undeniable presence. Base price was $18,450 with the standard four-speed manual transmission; a three-speed automatic was also available. Leather upholstery was a $950 option. The 2778-pound coupe had two small rear seats and decent luggage space beneath its glass hatch. It did 0-60 mph in 8.7 seconds and topped out at 132 mpg. A 49/51 weight balance was the real key to this Porsche's nature, and the 944 distinguished itself as among the very best-handling cars of the Eighties. "The 944 is great because it responds crisply and decisively to every command, and it builds up to its limit in perfectly linear fashion," said *Car and Driver*.

944 Weight distribution

49,2%                    50,8%

It was far from the all-out fastest sports car on the market, but the 944's range of attributes was hard to beat. *Road & Track,* in fact, picked it in a 1983 comparison test over the new '84 Corvette, the Ferrari 308 GTBi Quattrovalvole, and even the 928S. "...The 944 won simply by having so few weak points..." while being fun to drive and proving itself a useful, fine-handling, well built all-around car," said *R&T*. Porsche's way is to start with just such an outstanding core design, then develop its power and performance in a seemingly unrelenting march of upgrades big and small. For 1987 the 944 took a small step to 158 horsepower, and Porsche took a big step by launching the 944 Turbo (see page 250). That created a huge price gap over the base 944. The solution was the 944S. It topped the 2.5 with a twincam, 16-valve head for 188 horsepower, a fatter torque curve, and a 142-mph top speed. Also added was an antilock brake system. Then, for '89, the base 944 traded its 2.5 liter for a new eight-valve 162-bhp 2.7. That cut 0-60 times by more than a second, to 7.5. "Now," said *R&T,* the 944 "hustles with greater alacrity, in any gear, at any time...It simply has more flexibility and is more fun to drive." To no one's surprise, development like that was just another rung on the 944 ladder.

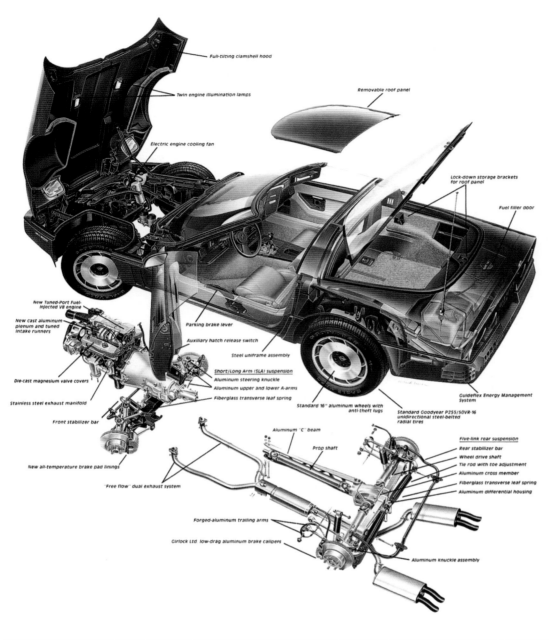

Full-tilting clamshell hood

Twin engine illumination lamps

Removable roof panel

Electric engine cooling fan

Lock-down storage brackets for roof panel

Fuel filler door

New Tuned-Port Fuel-Injected V8 engine

New cast aluminum plenum and tuned intake runners

Die-cast magnesium valve covers

Stainless steel exhaust manifold

Front stabilizer bar

New all-temperature brake pad linings

'Free flow' dual exhaust system

Parking brake lever

Auxiliary hatch release switch

Steel uniframe assembly

Short/Long Arm (SLA) suspension
Aluminum steering knuckle
Aluminum upper and lower A-arms
Fiberglass transverse leaf spring

Standard 16" aluminum wheels with anti-theft lugs

Standard Goodyear P255/50VR-16 unidirectional steel-belted radial tires

Guideflex Energy Management System

Aluminum 'C' beam

Prop shaft

Five-link rear suspension
Rear stabilizer bar
Wheel drive shaft
Tie rod with toe adjustment
Aluminum cross member
Fiberglass transverse leaf spring
Aluminum differential housing

Forged-aluminum trailing arms

Girlock Ltd. low-drag aluminum brake calipers

Aluminum knuckle assembly

There was no 1983 Corvette—Chevy couldn't overcome fuel-economy and emissions complications or factory snafus. So the fourth-generation bowed as an '84 model. Shedding nearly nine inches of length and 250 pounds, it had improved handling and fuel economy. Styling was more aerodynamic and featured a clamshell-opening hood and lift-up rear glass. A fiberglass skin remained, but the car was no longer body-on-frame, using instead a rigid new aluminum backbone chassis and steel substructure. The cabin was wider and more comfortable, befitting a car that started at $21,800. New digital gauges were gimmicky, but a bigger problems was the harsh ride, which was softened for '85. The C4 was designed from the start with a convertible in mind, and, for '86, Chevy introduced the first factory-built Corvette ragtop since 1975. Antilock brakes also were added as standard equipment on all '86s. By '88, sales had declined to 22,789 as base prices nipped at $30,000 for the coupe and $35,000 for the ragtop. Throughout the Eighties, Corvette engineers strove to improve handling with a series of ever-more-sophisticated suspension options. By '89, 17-inch wheels were standard and the driver-adjustable FX3 suspension was available. Still, as decade's end neared, Corvette needed an image boost.

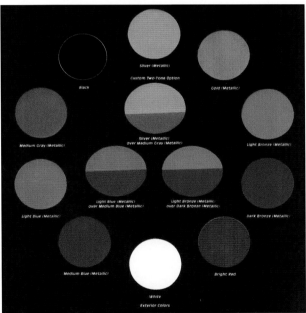

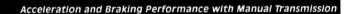

**Acceleration and Braking Performance with Manual Transmission**

| MPH | 0 | 60 | 100 | 0 |
|---|---|---|---|---|
| SECONDS | 0 | 5.7 | 15.2 | 20.2 |

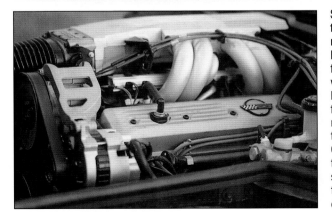

Starting in '84, Corvette's 350-cid V8 was referred to as a 5.7 liter. **Left:** For '85, tuned aluminum intake runners signaled a change from Cross-fire injection to more-advanced tuned-port injection. Accordingly, the L83 5.7 was renamed the L98 and boasted an increase of 25 horsepower, to 230. Acceleration dropped a full second, to 5.7 0-60 mph and 14.1 at 97 mph in the quarter-mile. Top speed was an honest 150, and gas mileage increased about 11 percent. For '86, the L98 switched from cast-iron to aluminum cylinder heads to shed 125 pounds, for the first sub-3000 pound 'Vette in about 20 years. Horsepower continued to rise in increments and was at 245 by the end of the Eighties. Through most of the decade, Corvette offered a four-speed automatic transmission or a "4+3 Overdrive" manual. This was a normal four-speed with button-activated electronic overdrive in second, third, and fourth. It was dumped for '89 for a better-shifting six-speed manual that had a gas-saving forced one-to-four shift at light throttle. The 26,412 'Vettes built for 1989 would be the highest total for the next eight years. But subdued sales didn't mean a lack of excitement (see page 260).

## DAVE McLELLAN
### Carried the Torch

To most car guys, landing a job under father-of-the-Corvette legend Zora Arkus-Duntov would be the opportunity of a lifetime. But for Dave McLellan the job was only temporary, as he would soon replace Duntov and take personal responsibility for the next generation Corvette. McLellan's dream job took a nightmarish turn however, as corporate, economic, and environmental forces conspired to threaten the project's success. Dave McLellan was a 15-year General Motors veteran when he was assigned the job of staff engineer under Corvette legend Zora Arkus-Duntov. Prior to that, McLellan had been involved in other GM performance car projects, most notably the first-generation Camaro. In 1975, six months after joining the Corvette team, McLellan stepped into the retiring Duntov's shoes as Chief Engineer of Corvette.

When McLellan took the helm, Corvette's future was uncertain. The current 'Vette was starting to look dated, and a host of prototypes had been devised as possible future Corvettes—both mid- and front-engine designs. McLellan's first Corvette freshening resulted in the well-received 1978 hatchback coupe, but the basic platform was in need of a major update and McLellan faced challenges Duntov never imagined.

Though an American icon, Corvette had become bloated. Waves of horsepower-choking EPA regulations had tamed its V8 heart, while luxury and safety equipment had taken their toll on the car's once trim figure. McLellan's goal was to pay due homage to the 'Vette's storied past, while bringing the car and its systems up to the state-of-the-art. GM had also made it clear that the low-volume sports car had to be financially self-sufficient.

McLellan demanded an aerodynamic design because of its effect on fuel economy and top speed—and because the press had latched onto aerodynamics as a measure of a car's technical fortitude. McLellan cited customer research and cost concerns as the primary reasons to stick with a front-engine design, and work began in earnest on a radical update of the basic Corvette structure.

Working with styling chief Jerry Palmer, McLellan and his team designed the fourth generation (1984) Corvette—the first 140 mph 'Vette in more than a decade. McLellan's changes included substituting a unitized steel frame for the separate frame and "bird cage" underbody structure. His team introduced such high-tech options as antilock brakes, traction control, keyless entry, run-flat tires, and airbags into the Corvette, many of which were GM firsts.

Despite criticisms of its bone-crushing ride, the 1984 Corvette was an undeniable success with critics and the driving public. More than 50,000 new Corvettes found buyers, doubling the previous model year's sales—despite a hefty price increase.

As a finale, McLellan led the development of the venerable ZR1, the "King of the Hill" Corvette. McLellan described his main objective for ZR1: "Create a car that is second to none in acceleration—nothing less than the fastest production car in the world."

While the ZR1 may have fallen shy of total sports car domination, its astonishing performance and modest price compared to like-performance exotics made it a darling of the motoring media.

McLellan retired from GM in 1992, having stayed long enough to bask in the glow of his accomplishment; his new Corvette was a modern and worthy successor to Duntov's iconic masterpiece. Fighting battles Duntov never imagined, McLellan carried the Corvette torch forward, bringing Chevy's flagship to a new generation of drivers.

**Above:** Fiat's evergreen 124 Spider reached its ultimate form by 1981 as the Spider 2000, with a fuel-injected 120-horsepower 2.0-liter four cylinder. Fiat fled the American market in 1984 but transferred Spider production and marketing to the coachbuilder, which sold an upgraded edition, the Pininfarina Azzurra, for another year or so in the U.S. **Right and below:** Nissan redesigned its Z car for 1984, with a 3.0-liter V6 replacing the 280ZX's 2.8-liter inline-six to create the 300ZX. It was trimmer, quicker, and had better handling than its predecessor. The look was classic Eighties, inside and out, with a wedgy body and available digital instrumentation that was "high tech" but hard to decipher. Pictured is the two-seat model; the 2+2 version had a slightly different roofline. Horsepower was 160 in the base 300ZX, which started at $15,799, and 200 in the Turbo, which included driver-adjustable shock absorbers in its $18,199 base price. Both came with a five-speed manual and three- or four-speed automatic. At sales of 52,936, the 300ZX was America's most-popular sports car in '84. This design was freshened for '86, and again in '87. Its final model year was 1989.

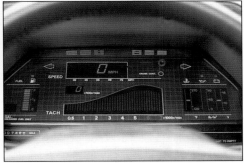

In 1984, Enzo Ferrari revived a hallowed old name for his new road/racing car: GTO. Pininfarina's styling themes were familiar and the car used Ferrari's production steel-tube chassis, but its structure was a new mix of fiberglass, aluminum honeycomb, and carbon, Kevlar, and Nomex composites. It was officially the 288 Gran Turismo Omologato. "288" denoted the 2.8-liter twin-turbo V8, which made 395 horsepower at 7000 rpm in road trim, some 600 bhp in racing form. "GTO" made it a GT homologated, or approved, for track competition. As such, it required a cabin suited for two, plus street-legal instrumentation, lights, ground clearance, mirrors, and windshield wipers. Handling was its forte, though even in road spec, it did 0-60 in 5.0 seconds, the quarter-mile in 13.1 at 112 mph. Unfortunately, the international racing series for which it was designed, Group B, dissolved before the GTO had a chance to compete. It cost $83,400, and 200 were built through '87.

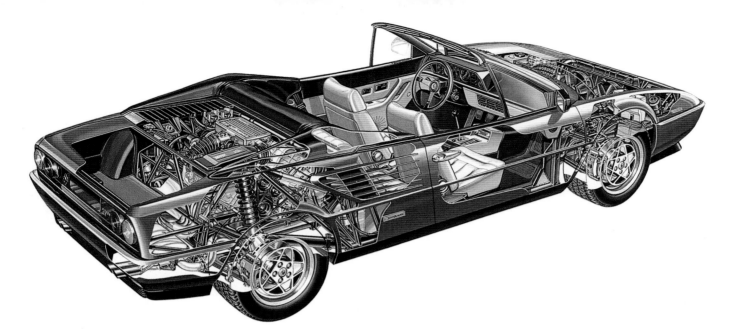

Ferrari created the world's first midengine four-seat convertible with the Mondial cabriolet. Introduced in 1983, it was also the first fully open roadgoing Ferrari since the 1969 Daytona Spider. Like the closed Mondial, the cabrio was based on Ferrari's two-seat 308 platform, but unlike the targa-top 308GTS, the drop-top 2+2 was a true convertible. Large rear-fender vents continued to feed the transverse V8, which in 1985 was increased from 3.0 liters to 3.2. That rebadged these cars the 3.2 Mondial. They had 260 horsepower at 7000 rpm, a five-speed manual transmission, weighed about 3640 pounds, and did 0-60 mph in 7.1 seconds, topping out at around 150 mph. Finishing with the 300-hp 3.4-liter Mondial t of 1989, the Mondial proved one of Ferrari's most viable lines. Not only did it sell in relatively strong numbers, but it inspired enough confidence in Ferrari to serve as the platform on which the company debuted such features as fuel injection, power steering, antilock brakes, and a transverse transmission.

“I still recall my 1991 C4 cabriolet as one of the most incredible cars I have ever been in. What I also remember is the cost of all that German engineering prowess. Though the car's performance exceeded my expectations, keeping it on the road was pricey. In my care the Blaupunkt audio system flaked out, and a popped gear in the roof assembly was a costly nightmare to fix. Oh, and the first tune-up, consisting of 12 quarts of oil, 12 sparkplugs, and precision timing was a $300+ shocker—but the driving was worth every deutsche mark. I've heard boats called "holes in the water that you throw money into"—and while my 911 C4 was expensive to maintain—all it took was one warm, sunny day with a winding road in front of me to bring on true road rapture.”

– Dennis Collins
Arlington Heights, Illinois

**Above:** As the Eighties began, Porsche's mainstay in its classic rear-engine lineup continued to be the 911SC. Offered in coupe and targa body styles, its venerable 3.0-liter flat-six made 172 horsepower and furnished a 140-mph top speed. Such amenities as air conditioning and power front windows were now standard. And Porsche continued to tame the rear-drive chassis' tailhappy tendencies. It also brought back the Carrera name for '84 and, along with it, a bump to 3.2 liters and 200 bhp. That took nearly a second off acceleration times, which dropped to 5.3 seconds 0-60 mph and 13.9 at 100 mph in the quarter-mile. Top speed stretched to 146 mph. Larger brakes were part of the ongoing roadability upgrades, but transmission choices were still limited to the five-speed manual. In these rear-drive models, the 3.2 would go to 214 bhp for '87, where it finished the decade in this basic bodywork or in a variety of bespoilered and slant-nose sheetmetal options.

**Above:** Turbocharged 911s took a hiatus for the late-Seventies gas crunch but were back in the U.S. for 1986 in all their whale-tail glory. At $48,000 and in coupe body only, these were the costliest rear-engine Porsches. Their turbo 3.3-liter flat-six had 282 horsepower, they weighed about 3100 pounds, and did 5.0 seconds 0-60, 13.4 at 103 in the quarter-mile, and topped out around 167 mph. By decade's end, the 911 Turbo was available as a coupe, targa, and, for $85,060, a cabriolet. That cabrio body had bowed for 1983 as Porsche's first factory-built convertible since the 956. It had a manual top that folded compactly enough to retain the rear seats. **Right:** The 911 Carrera ended the Eighties with subtle appearance revisions for '89 that belied bigger changes to chassis and suspension. **Below:** Centerpiece of the '89 revamp was introduction of an all-wheel-drive system under the Carrera 4 label. Launched on coupes, it spread quickly to the other body styles and normally sent 69 percent of the power to the rear wheels, redistributed as needed to maintain optimal traction. Carrera 4s used a 247-bhp 3.6-liter six and were the first 911s with power steering.

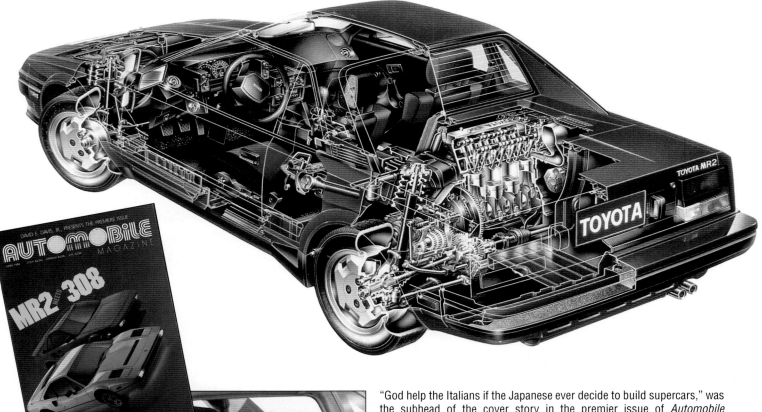

"God help the Italians if the Japanese ever decide to build supercars," was the subhead of the cover story in the premier issue of *Automobile Magazine*. Toyota's new sports car—Japan's first midengine production automobile—was in fact spirited enough, if not fast enough, to beg comparison with Ferrari's midengine V8 of the day. MR2, for "Mid/Rear engine 2-seat," came to the U.S. for 1986. It didn't act like a mix of off-the-shelf Toyota parts, but it was: transverse four-cylinder engine and transaxle from the Corolla mounted behind the two-place cockpit. The same car's front strut suspension and disc brakes were used at both ends. The steering didn't need power assist, given the 44/56 split of the tidy 2396-pound curb weight. Styling was spunky if not svelte, but the car was eminently tossable, had a 112-horsepower 1.6 liter that loved to rev, wrist-flick shift action, and Toyota reliability. Top speed was 121 mph, 0-60 was 8.1 seconds, base price was $10,999. A supercharged version '88 had 145 bhp and did a seven-second 0-60. The original "Mr. Two" ran through 1990.

Ever-tightening emissions regulations were the bane of performance manufacturers in the 1980s, and Ferrari's mainstay V8 sports cars coped by adopting fuel injection in 1980 and four-valve heads in '82, then increasing displacement to 3.2 liters from 3.0 in 1985. That got the 308 GTB and 308 GTS rechristened the 328 GTB and 328 GTS. GTB denoted the Berlinetta, or closed model. GTS designated the open "spyder," or, in this case, a lift-off center roof panel that stowed behind the seats. Despite less structural rigidity on bumpy roads than the GTB, the GTS was quite popular in the U.S, even at some $64,400 in 1986. Its smooth V8 had 260 hp at 7000 rpm, 213 pound-feet at 5500, and made intoxicating noises. Working through a machine-tool-precise five-speed manual, it was good for 0-60 mph in 5.6 seconds, the quarter-mile in 14.2 at 97 mph, and a top speed of 153. It required some expertise on a twisty road, seeing that 58 percent of its 3090-pound curb weight was on the rear wheels. But get it right and no '80s sports-car experience was more satisfying.

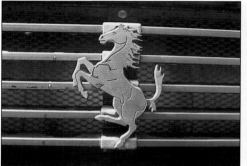

Supercars are the bad boys of the sports-car world, menacing with size, shape, and sheer speed. One-upped in this war of intimidation by Lamborghini's ever-more-unnerving Countach, Ferrari replaced its Boxer for 1984 and evoked what few rivals could: a racing heritage. Ferrari's winning Testa Rossa sports-racers of the 1950s were named for the crimson color of their camshaft covers—literally, red head. This roadgoing Testarossa was linked to those storied machines by red-crackle-finish cylinder heads. It followed the Boxer formula with a mid-mounted 5.0-liter horizontally opposed 12-cylinder. But this engine had four valves per cylinder and 380 horsepower at 5750 rpm in U.S. trim. Torque was 354 pound-feet at 4500. Just as impressive was the fabulous new Pininfarina styling. It was a low wedge, larger yet lighter than the Boxer, and, at an imposing 77.8 inches, only the Countach was wider. The earliest examples used a single, outrigger rearview mirror on the windshield pillar that lent an avant-garde touch. For the U.S. list price of about $115,000, the Testarossa owner got sumptuous leather upholstery and more passenger and cargo space than in the Countach, though some complained the seats were too broad to hold tight during fast cornering. The wide doorsills collected mud in wet weather, and quick gear changes could be frustrated by Ferrari's tradition-bound gated shift plate. Luckily, the flat-12's broad powerband and the well-spaced gear ratios meant shifting could often be treated as an amusement, not a requirement.

Cooling Testarossa's big flat-12 was critical, and a pair of radiators was located ahead of the rear wheels instead of in the nose. This helped eliminate the circulation of liquids that could overheat the cabin. The size and shape of the inlets also influenced aerodynamics, and Pininfarina had to fit them with horizontal ribs to meet European intake-size limits. The strakes became a copied styling cue. Testarossa weighed 3660 pounds distributed 40/60. It did 0-60 mph in 5.3 seconds, the quarter mile in 13.6 at 105, and reached 178 mph. It got 12 mpg. Its suspension was communicative and surprisingly compliant, its steering informed with slight kickback—a Ferrari characteristic. It was an Eighties icon not revised until 1992, as the 512TR. That version had 421 bhp and a top speed of 187 mph, plus a stiffer chassis and larger, wider tires. A 1994 facelift eliminated the retractable headlamps and brought 440 bhp. But Ferrari called that iteration the 512M, relegating its red head once again to the pages of history.

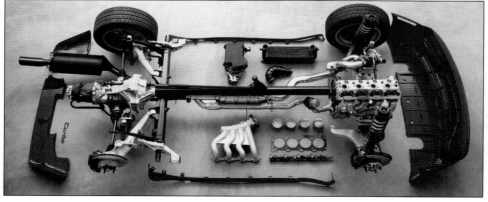

**Above and left:** Introducing the 944 Turbo for 1986, Porsche took an encompassing approach, adding not only a water-cooled KKK turbocharger to the 2.5-liter four but altering its internals with such details as ceramic exhaust-port inserts and adding aero-enhancing fascias. The 217-horsepower 944 Turbo did 0-60 in 6.0 seconds and hit 155 mph. By '89, it had 247 bhp. **Top:** Inserted between the $35,969 162-bhp 944 and the $47,600 944 Turbo for '89 was the 944S2. It looked like the turbo but had a 208-bhp twincam 3.0-liter four, did 0-60 in 6.2 seconds, and came as the $45,285 coupe or this $52,650 cabriolet.

**Right:** For 1983 U.S. versions of Porsche's big, brawny, 928 got their first notable change since the car's 1978 intro. The basic formula of a rock-solid, pricey, posh 2+2 GT with a liquid-cooled front engine and slightly overbearing styling was unchanged. But the 218-horsepower 4.5-liter V8 grew to 4.7 liters and 234 bhp, the optional automatic transmission gained a ratio to become a four speed, and the car was renamed the 928S. Five-speed versions shed about one second 0-60 mph, to under 7.0, and gained six mph overall, to 146. Automatics were at 8.5 and 143. Base price rose $3500, to $43,000. A bump to 5.0 liters and a doubling of camshafts to four and valves to 32 for '85 brought an additional 54 bhp for 0-60 under 6 seconds and 154 mph flat out.

**Above:** Aero trim additions, including a free-floating tail spoiler, signaled 1987's arrival of the 928S4. The 5.0 V8 climbed to 316 bhp, 0-60 fell to the mid-5s, top speed reached 170, and price hit $58,900. This put the 928 in true supercar territory, where it would remain through its 1995 retirement. Highlights along the way included a 1990 shove to 326 bhp. The final development was 1993's 345-bhp 5.4-liter GTS. Escalating prices—well over $73,000 by the late-Eighties—helped doom it, even though most testers said it was probably worth what Porsche charged. Basically, the 928's legacy is of a great sports car that couldn't fit into the even-greater Porsche mystique.

Its styling was criticized as a derivative blend of Porsche 944 and Chevrolet Camaro. But the second-generation RX-7 that debuted for 1986 was a thoroughly developed extension of the original and imitated no other car in its use of the compact, smooth-running rotary engine. Size hardly changed from the 1978-85 version, but the new RX-7 was some 240 pounds heavier (about 2625 pounds in base form) and added a 2+2 model, which had the same dimensions as the two-seater. Rack and pinion steering ousted recirculating ball and featured variable electronic assist. Front suspension was improved, and the old live rear axle was discarded for a new independent setup with disc brakes instead of drums. The rotary had electronic fuel injection and displaced 1.3 liters. In base form, it had 146 horsepower at 6500 rpm and 138 pound-feet of torque at 3500. The Turbo II version (Mazda had offered a first-generation "Turbo I" in Japan) had 182 bhp at 6500 and 183 pound-feet at 3500. This was good for 0-60 mph of 9.7 seconds and a top speed of 125 mph for the base model, 8.5 and some 135 mph for the turbo. Both came with a five-speed manual transmission, with automatic available with the naturally aspirated engine. The ride was choppy and the cabin tight for taller people, but the RX-7 was grippy, stable, and solid. It sold well, too, with prices starting at just $11,995 and around $20,000 for the Turbo.

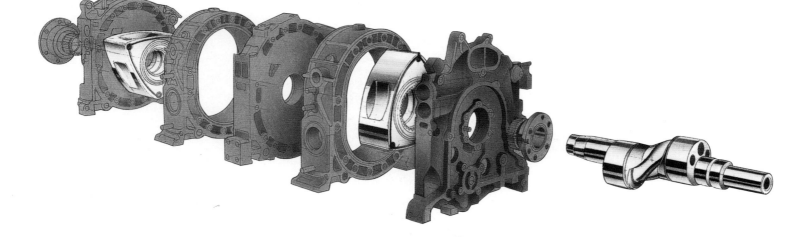

**Above:** A deeper chin spoiler and a working hood scoop were functional RX-7 Turbo features.. As on all RX-7s, small windows in the headlamp covers allowed use of flash-to-pass with the lights off. Antilock brakes arrived for 1987 as a $1300 option on the Turbo and top-trim GLX base model. **Right:** The cockpit blended period squared-off shapes with gauges and a three-spoke steering wheel that would complement a sports car of any day. **Below:** Mazda released its first factory-built RX-7 convertible for 1988. It listed for $20,500, or $22,900 with an option package that added leather upholstery and an audio system with a compact disc player and stereo speakers in each headrest. The top was a unique two-section design. The portion above the seats was a rigid fiberglass-compound panel that could be stored in the trunk to create a targa-roof arrangement. The soft rear section folded conventionally. The ragtop also introduced a wind-blocking plastic panel that fit vertically behind the seats to quell high-speed turbulence. As much cruiser as combatant, this generation RX-7 was right for the Eighties. But by its retirement after 1992, the world was again ready for a Mazda rotary sports car in its purest form.

The name commemorated Ferrari's 40th year as an automaker and was the last Ferrari built while Enzo Ferrari was alive. It took the great man back to his automotive roots. This was no grand touring machine, but a sports car shorn of amenities and packed with power. The chassis used carbon fiber and Kevlar, and the lightweight plastic body was shaped to provide aerodynamic downforce at the car's 196-mph top speed. Fuel was stored in two rubber-celled tanks, and fire-resistant Nomex served as the upholstery. Pull cords opened the doors, and there was no carpeting. Antilock brakes were not offered, the F40 relying instead on huge discs and the driver's ability. Lifting the louvered tail section revealed a 2.9-liter twincam V8 with dual turbos and 478 horsepower, enough to shoot the 3018-pound car from 0-60 mph in 3.8 seconds. A conventional five-speed manual was the transmission. The F40 cost $470,000, and each of the 1000 built was a collector piece. It was unveiled in July 1987. Enzo Ferrari died on August 14, 1988.

**Above:** Lotus's late-Eighties Esprit update replaced Giugiaro's doorstop styling with rounded contours by Britisher Peter Stevens. The 2.2-liter four-cylinder remained. In 264-horsepower turbo form, the fine-handling exotic did 0-60 mph in about six seconds and topped out around 160 mph. **Below:** Operating on the fringes of credibility was Vector Aeromotive Corporation, which raised $20 million in 1988 to build a Ferrari-beating midengine supercar but was suspiciously broke within a few years after producing fewer than 30 automobiles. The W2 Twin Turbo pictured here is typical of the variations on a theme Vector periodically unveiled to keep press and public baited. It purported to use military aircraft technology and had an aluminum honeycomb structure, composite body, and a twin-turbo 5.7-liter V8 of a claimed 600 bhp. Subsequent owners did produce a V12 Vector, but neither car nor company would last.

The Porsche 959 was a towering technological achievement that combined levels of acceleration, top speed, and all-around control rivaled by precious few automobiles in history. Built as a racing car, its Group B competition series disbanded before it could run, and the world was left with a roadgoing sports car of fabled reputation. Porsche's engineering obsession was unreined for this one and though the car looked something like the 911 coupe on which its was based, the 959 was far different in function and design. It had all-wheel drive, unholy power, and a body ducted, spoilered, and widened to suit its stratospheric needs. Production was limited to just 230 during the mid-Eighties. A competition version, the 961, proved itself by winning the punishing Paris-Dakar Rally in 1984 and '86. Production versions were offered in 1987 and '88 in "Comfort" and lighter "Sport" form. The 959 was too specialized to be sold in the U.S., and though a handful came stateside, most stayed in Europe where transaction prices routinely topped the $230,000 retail price. The ultimate Porsche to many, it was, in the words of renowned racer and writer Paul Frere, "a new dimension in motoring."

Flanking the 959's steel central body were functional aerodynamic panels of lightweight Kevlar and other advanced materials. The engine was a flat-six but used water-cooled heads, two turbochargers, and other advanced features to get 450 horsepower from just 2.8 liters. A six-speed manual was the sole transmission. Weight was 3088 pounds, top speed 190 mph, and 0-60 mph came in just 3.7 seconds. A multiplate clutch acted as a front differential, and torque apportioning was computer-governed or followed one of four driver-selected programs, from locked front and rear to 20/80 in full acceleration. Suspension departed from the 911 with double wishbones and computer-controlled coil-over shocks with soft, firm, and automatic damping modes, plus three ride heights. Some of these elements made their way into subsequent Porsches, but the 959 stands apart as a signal achievement.

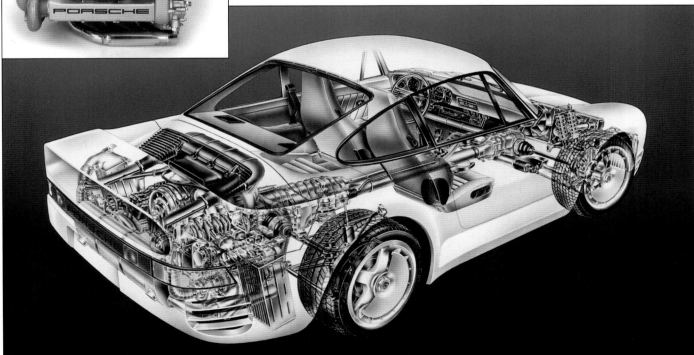

**Above:** Porsche's U.S. sales slipped from over 30,000 in 1986, to just 9479 for '89. There was management dissension back in Germany and increased competition. One balm was a limited-edition 911 model guaranteed to generate corporate profit. Thus, the Speedster of 1989. The name and packaging recalled the beloved 356 Speedster of the Fifties. Here was another open Porsche with a cut-down windshield for a chopped-racer look. Unlike the original, this one had power glass side windows instead of snap-in plastic curtains and lots of amenities, though its roof was a simpler, unlined version of the one on the 911 Cabriolet. The 911 Speedster was based on the non-Turbo 911s, though all but 169 of the 2100 built wore the optional Turbo Look package. Base price was $65,480, most went out the showroom at around $75,000, and the cars appreciated to as much as $90,000 within three years. **Left and below:** The formula worked so well, Porsche revived it for 1993, again with a distinctive flip-up double-hump rigid tonneau. The base price was $66,400.

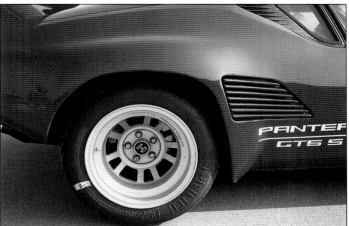

**Above and right:** A trickle of federalized DeTomaso Panteras made it to the U.S. in the Eighties. Outrageously bespoilered and flared, their image was of a poor-man's Countach. The GT5 of 1980 started it by sticking wheel arches, gapping air dam, and big rear wing onto Pantera's clean original body. Its 1985 successor, the GT5-S, pictured here, integrated those elements for a marginally less tacked-on look. It had a 350-horsepower 5.7-liter Ford V8 and did 5.4 seconds 0-60 mph, 13.6 at 105 in the quarter-mile. **Below:** A belabored gestation that deferred its launch to the last moments of the decade was just one burden for Lotus's revived Elan. It looked fine, with exotic-worthy composite bodywork over a stout backbone platform. And Lotus chassis expertise meant the 2450-pound roadster was one of the best-handling front-wheel-drive cars ever, delivering 0.9g despite a 66/34 weight split. Even power was OK: The 165-bhp turbo version did 6.7 seconds 0-60 and hit 130 mph. But the engine was a coarse Isuzu 1.6-liter four, not a good pedigree given a base price inflated by delays and overruns to a sales-sapping $39,040. U.S. sales totaled just 470 over two years.

Rumors about it had circulated for years, and by late 1989 it was ready: the ZR1. Actually a $27,000 option for the $32,000 1990 Corvette coupe, the ZR1 extended the Corvette credo of world-class performance at middle-class prices to a new level. Fans called it King of the Hill, and some paid $100,000 for the first examples off the assembly line—then put them in storage. The ZR1's Ferrari-like performance helped give GM a needed image boost, though its only visual distinction from other 'Vettes was squared-off taillamps set into a wider, convex tail, a design needed to accommodate its wider rear tires. The FX3 adjustable suspension with touring, sport, and performance settings was standard. **Below:** The ZR1 arrived with a revamped interior that introduced a driver-side airbag, a design common to all '90 Corvettes. A showcase of powertrain technology, the ZR1 would be offered through 1995, and a total of 6939 were produced.

After considering a variety of homegrown turbo powerplants, Chevy got Britain's Lotus to design a sophisticated naturally aspirated V8. Dubbed the LT5 and built by Mercury Marine in Oklahoma, the all-alloy dohc 32-valve 5.7 had 375 horsepower and came with a console-mounted "valet key" that cut power to about 210 bhp. It propelled the 3500-pound coupe from 0-60 mph in 4.5 seconds, through the quarter-mile in 12.4 at 111 mph, and to a top speed of 175. Plus it averaged 17 mpg city/26 highway. A six-speed manual was the only available transmission. Horsepower would rise to 405 for 1993. ZR1 showed America could produce world-class performance and helped propel the sports car into a new golden age.

# 7

## 1990-99: A Revival Revs Up

The Nineties ushered in a "A New World Order" beset by intractable old problems. Ominously, the decade began with war. In August 1990, Iraqi forces occupied neighboring Kuwait, gateway to the oil fields of Saudi Arabia so vital to Western economies. President George Bush led formation of an international military coalition to liberate tiny Kuwait, accomplished in early 1991 with a 100-hour blitzkrieg, "Operation Desert Storm." It was an impressive show of military might and political cooperation, but it left Iraqi dictator Saddam Hussein to fight another day.

Soon afterward, the Soviet Union dissolved, ending the Cold War and leaving America the world's only superpower. Communism had already crumbled in Poland, Czechoslovakia, and even East Germany, where the hated Berlin Wall was torn down in 1989. But as democracy spread, it exposed bitter ethnic rivalries suppressed for decades, and brutal civil wars soon erupted in Bosnia, Serbia, Kosovo, and other regions on newly redrawn maps. Looming in the background were grave concerns about Soviet-era nuclear weapons, no longer under central control and apparently vulnerable to terrorists and rogue regimes bent on imposing their own new order.

Old battles dragged on. The Israeli-Palestinian conflict defied peacemaking efforts while producing more bloodshed and terrorism, some of which began to touch American interests. At home, the "War on Drugs" seemed no more winnable than it had in the Eighties. So, too, the fight against AIDS, the deadly disease first identified in 1981 that had become a global epidemic, yet stubbornly eluded a cure. Americans were increasingly divided on issues ranging from taxes to abortion rights. The 1987 Wall Street crash, the worst since '29, triggered an unwanted U.S. recession and an economic meltdown in Japan, South Korea, and other Asian nations, which were very slow to recover. The U.S. turnaround took long enough that Bill Clinton was able to defeat President Bush in 1992.

By mid-decade, though, America was into a record-long run of prosperity in a "service economy" fueled by new technology and a huge upsurge of investment in the stock market and promising "start-up" ventures. Consumer spending, corporate profits, and the Dow Jones Average rose in lockstep, and to unheard-of heights. Millions of people were soon earning trillions of dollars—at least on paper. With all this, car and truck sales grew steadily except for dips in 1991 and '98. To the delight of manufacturers, high-margin luxury models outstripped other segments in sales growth.

Another key Nineties trend was the strong public shift from passenger cars to light trucks—minivans, traditional pickups, and especially sport-utility vehicles. Big or small, pricey or cheap, SUVs sold like crazy, and manufacturers raced to get them onto dealer lots. By 1999, light trucks as a whole were pulling in almost as many sales as passenger cars—8.2 million to 8.75 million—and were poised to take the lead.

So sports cars were history, right? Far from it. Rising affluence stoked demand for sporty rides, and manufacturers were learning how to produce "niche" models that could make money with relatively modest sales. As a result, the Nineties produced an unusual number of new sports cars, most every one an enthusiast's delight.

The most commercially important—arguably the most charming—was the Mazda Miata. A 1990 debut, it picked up where the British had left off as a small, affordable roadster of the beloved traditional stripe. The Miata reminded some of the early Lotus Elan. Collectible Automobile® magazine more aptly termed it "a Triumph Spitfire that works." And in fact, Mazda used a Spitfire to help gauge the market. Pert, agile, and fast enough, the Miata offered workmanship and reliability no British two-seater ever knew and was priced right. Though filling such an obvious market gap might seem a no-brainer now, the Miata was a brave decision at the time, because no one knew for sure whether it would sell. But sell it did, year after year, helped by steady technical improvements and a stream of "limited edition" specials.

At the opposite end the 1990 market was another Japanese newcomer, the NSX. Sleek and low, this midengine coupe was a technological showcase for Honda and a flagship for the company's new upscale U.S. Acura line. A pioneering lightweight aluminum structure and a high-tech twincam V6 made for vivid acceleration and decent fuel economy. The NSX could sound like a Formula One car and almost handled like one, yet could easily double as a daily driver—a truly "practical exotic." Though always rare and very costly, the NSX carved out a solid niche to last over 10 years without basic change.

After a decade of drift and bloat, the Nissan Z returned to its spiritual roots for 1990 with a new 300ZX. It was all business from striking exterior to taut chassis to strong V6, and the high-power Turbo version delivered Corvette-like go. Sunworshippers cheered the '93 addition of the first factory-built Z convertible. Unfortunately, a weakening dollar/yen exchange would price the Z out of its market by 1996, and Nissan ended U.S. exports to ponder next steps. The same fate awaited two other Japanese gems, the Toyota MR2 and Mazda RX-7. And more's the pity. A 1991 redesign made "Mister Two" look like a sort of baby Ferrari, while the rotary-powered RX-7 became a turbocharged canyon-carver in a 1993 makeover with the same "back to basics" emphasis as the latest Nissan Z.

"Basic" certainly described the Dodge Viper RT/10. So did "fearsome." New for '92, the Viper was conceived as a modern Shelby Cobra, and Chrysler wisely called on 'Ol Shel to make sure it was done right. It was. Raw and visceral, the Viper was short on comforts but long on thrills, packing a massive V10 that could wrinkle asphalt. A coupe version added for '97 quickly proved a winner in international racing. Interestingly, Shelby went off to do his own "new Cobra," but the car business had changed a lot since the Sixties, and his Olds V8-powered Series I was dogged by problems on its 1999 launch.

Old reliable Porsche suffered a near-death experience in the early Nineties as sales plunged along with world economies. But it came back strong late in the decade after shedding front-engine models and betting the farm on a new mid-engine roadster, the Boxster, which proved an immediate success. Soon afterward came another new 911. This one was completely redesigned from road to roof, yet had all the expected character intact. Ferrari twice updated its smaller cars in the Nineties but revived the grand spirit of the front-V12 Daytona for rapid, rakish new senior models, the 456GT and 550 Maranello. Lamborghini returned to the U.S. market with the Diablo, an even more wicked Countach that would run the full 10 years.

Last but not least, the Chevrolet Corvette. Bracketed by the high-power "King of the Hill" ZR-1 and an all-new "C5" generation, the 1990s were vintage 'Vette years. Other sports cars might be faster down the road or through a curve, but none could match the Corvette's enduring charisma and all-American persona. To quote an old ad for a very different car, the 'Vette was still "unique in all the world," and rightly so.

All in all, sports-car life was livelier in 1990s America than it had been in quite some time. And the party was just beginning.

**1990** Chrysler confirms production Viper • Buick Reatta convertible makes belated debut • High-tech mid-V6 Honda NSX comes to U.S. as new flagship Acura • Chevrolet unleashes burly "King of the Hill" Corvette ZR-1 • Chrysler's TC by Maserati dropped at year's end • Ferrari delivers first F40s after three-year delay • Ferrari 328 gives way to 328 tb/ts with new looks, more performance • Lamborghini Countach morphs into larger, devilishly fast Diablo • Lotus pins hopes on new Elan with front-wheel drive • Maserati departs U.S. market • Mazda's new "retro" Miata revives the affordable sports car, scores sales hit • Nissan unveils sleeker, more sophisticated 300ZX and ZX Turbo • Porsche drops base and Turbo 944s, adds long-delayed S2 cabriolet • Porsche bows reengineered "964-series" 911 Carrera 2 coupe, cabrio **1991** Dodge Viper prototype paces Indy 500 • First new Bugatti since '56 bows with quad-turbo mid-V12 EB110 GT • Buick drops Reatta after four years of lackluster sales • Chevy Corvettes get subtle facelift, much-revised LT1 V8 with extra 50 hp • Dodge debuts burly V6 Stealth 2+2 coupes built and engineered by Mitsubishi • Lotus drops Elan amid new corporate troubles • Mercedes redesigns luxury 2-seater as 6-cyl 320SL, V8 500SL • Mitsubishi bows 3000GT coupes topped by twin-turbo, all-wheel-drive VR-4 • Toyota MR2 redesigned with more room, Ferrari style—and tricky handling • Porsche 911 Turbo returns to U.S. with more power

**Above:** The mid-engined Acura NSX, Japan's first exotic supercar, debuted in 1990. The first NSXs carried a hefty $62,000 sticker price, but eager buyers shelled out almost twice that for early examples. **Above left:** Its 3.0-liter dohc V6 put out 270 bhp and could push the NSX to 5.3-second 0-60 times and a top speed of 165 mph. Extensive use of aluminum kept curb weight to a minimum; the first NSXs weighed just under 3000 pounds. **Below left:** The cockpit boasted excellent ergonomics and a host of "driver-friendly" features. However, the surgical precision of the NSX left many enthusiasts cold. After the initial rush, sales declined against idiosyncratic rivals like Ferrari and Porsche. Acura's mid-engined marvel seemed almost too polite and refined for the company it kept. **Below:** The open-top NSX-T introduced for 1995 rejuvenated interest and soon accounted for 95 percent of production. The roof panel could be stowed underneath the hatched rear window with no loss of luggage space. NSX sales struggled to top 1000 annually.

**Above and below:** The long-awaited replacement for the Ferrari 328 came in 1990 with the introduction of the 348, Ferrari's first unit-body car. The new model was similar in concept to its 328 predecessor, but featured new rounded Testarossa-like Pininfarina styling riding a four-inch longer wheelbase and measuring 6.5 inches wider. As on the Testarossa, the dramatic straked side scoops were functional: The left side's fed a coolant radiator, and the right's led to a smaller coolant radiator-plus-oil cooler. Both full roof berlinetta (GTB) and targa-roofed spyder versions (GTS) were offered. The 3.4-liter V8 was rated at 296 bhp at 7200 rpm and could push the 348 to 5.6-second 0-60 mph times and a top speed of 165-170 mph. The 348's main technical difference from the 308/328 was a gearbox turned from longitudinal to transverse and mounted beneath an engine resituated "north-south" (instead of east-west as on the 308/328). **Left:** The 348's interior was fully redesigned and competitively ergonomic. Furnishings were plush for a Ferrari, with no-cost air conditioning, electric windows and mirrors, and a central locking system.

**1992** Dodge delivers first Viper RT/10 roadster • Chevrolet produces one-millionth Corvette • Aston Martin unveils Virage Volante convertible • Bugatti announces upgraded EB110S with 620 hp, 213-mph top speed • Fast safety: Corvettes add standard traction control • Lamborghini adds all-wheel-drive Diablo VT • Porsche updates its 4-cyl line one last time to create the 968 • Porsche adds limited-run 911 America cabrio, $180,000 Turbo S coupe • Subaru introduces speedy SVX touring coupe **1993** Porsche previews its future with midengine Boxster concept • DeTomaso Automobili shows midengine Guara coupe • Death claims Ferrucio Lamborghini • Bugatti baron Romano Artioli takes over Britain's Lotus from GM • Cadillac Allante premieres high-tech Northstar V8 • Chevrolet boosts ZR-1 Corvette to 405 hp, offers 40th Anniversary Package • Revised Lotus Esprit Series 4 boasts more speed, freshened styling • Mercedes adds flagship 600SL with V12 power • Nissan offers first factory-built 300ZX convertible • Porsche 928 evolves to final GTS form with 5.4-liter V8 • Porsche again drops 911 Turbo, adds racy, de-frilled RS America coupe • Toyota challenges Corvette with racy, new-generation 2+2 Supra **1994** Chrysler sells Lamborghini to Indonesia's MegaTech • Dodge Viper now at full production, adds factory A/C option • Dodge Stealth/Mitsubishi 3000GT get styling tweaks; turbo models add 20 hp • BMW-powered McLaren F1 hits the road as the world's fastest car • Lamborghini turns 30, issues rear-drive Diablo SE30 with 525 hp

**Above:** True to tradition, Lamborghini's supercar for the nineties was named for a fighting bull, but Diablo is another word for devil. Indeed, it certainly had enough power to feel possessed. Lamborghini engineers succeeded in the formidable task of creating a new car that one-upped the Countach while retaining its heritage and meeting modern-day safety and emissions standards. The Diablo was the only Lamborghini developed under Chrysler, which furnished computer-design expertise and also softened the lines of designer Marcello Gandini's original styling. The 492-bhp, 5.7-liter V12's performance was appropriately ferocious, with 4.5-second 0-60 times and a 202-mph top speed. **Below:** By 1996, the Diablo line had expanded to include the all-wheel-drive VT roadster, the lightweight SV with flashy body side graphics, and the race-ready SVR.

Genuine landmarks are rare in the world of automobiles, but the Mazda MX-5 Miata was one. Mazda showed enormous insight and sensitivity to the sports car ethic when it designed a two-seater roadster free of unnecessary weight or features or even power. The Miata was a timeless idea reinterpreted for the nineties, a beautiful marriage of the classic British/Italian two-seater spirit with Japanese reliability and workmanship. It rode a short 89.2-inch wheelbase, measured 155.4 inches overall, and weighed in at 2182 pounds. The 1.6-liter four cranked out 116 bhp at 5600 rpm and 100 pound-feet of torque at 5500 rpm. The independent suspension used coil springs and double wishbones all around. There was a disc brake at each corner and rack-and-pinion steering. The structure was impressively rigid thanks to computer-aided design and an aluminum powertrain truss. The top lowered in one easy motion, the ride was firm but not harsh, and the exhaust note appropriately snarly. Power steering and windows, a CD player, and cruise control could run up the $13,800 base price, but these weren't needed to enjoy the car. The Miata seemed to have achieved a rare blend of modest but fully usable power, accessible cornering limits, and all-around good cheer.

" I've owned my Miata for five years. I purchased it used with only 18,000 miles. Initially, I was disappointed with its performance. When I noted my chagrin to a fellow Miata owner, he volunteered to go for a ride with me. It only took a block for him to identify the problem: the driver. I didn't realize that I could (or should) take the engine as high as 7000 RPM. Once the "operator error" was solved, I fell in love with the car. The MX-5 is fun to drive and in 30,000 miles has been virtually maintenance-free. I have considered replacing the Miata with a used BMW Z3 or a Honda S2000, but I fear these cars will only be marginally nicer than my reliable and sporty red MX-5. "

– Mike Nikolich
Lake Barrington, Illinois

Porsche 911 Turbo/Turbo S return, along with new non-turbo Speedster **1995** Chevy builds final ZR-1 Corvette • Corvette is again Indy 500 pace car • Lotus launches spartan midengine Elise roadster—but not for U.S. • Shapely Aston Martin DB7 coupe bows in Europe with 335-hp supercharged-6 • Audi hints at a sports car with 2-seat TT concept coupe that looks showroom ready • Reborn Bugatti company files for bankruptcy • Dodge Viper gets numerous improvements, plus even more muscle • Ferrari 348 evolves into thoroughly improved F355 coupe • Honda/Acura adds targa-roof NSX-T model • Racing McLaren GTR wins LeMans 24 Hours • Mitsubishi 3000GT lineup adds jazzy Spyder hardtop-convertible • Cycle-fender Ford V8-powered Panoz Roadster in production in Georgia • Porsche 911 renewed in much-improved "993 series" • Mazda RX-7, Toyota MR2 leave U.S. at year's end after sales fall due to stiff prices **1996** Struggling DeTomaso Automobili shows Bigua targa-coupe concept • Dodge adds racing-minded Viper GTS coupe as early '97 model • Aston Martin bows DB7 in U.S.; improved Virage bows as the V8 Coupe • BMW launches upscale "retro roadster" with new U.S.-built Z3 • Chevy ends C4 Corvette with Collector Edition, high-power GS specials • Final season for Dodge Stealth, a victim of sluggish sales • Ferrari adds F355 Spider, returns to front-V12 models with all-new 456 GT • Lamborghini adds targa-top Diablo VT Roadster; racier SV coupe replaces SE30

**Opposite, top and center:** Debuting in 1994, the Miata's $1500 R Package was aimed at weekend "club racers." It delivered a track-oriented sport suspension with uprated sway bars, rear springs, and special Bilstein shock absorbers, plus unique alloy wheels, Torsen differential, lower body skirting, and bold nose-to-tail racing stripes. **Opposite, bottom:** The limited-production 1994 Miata M Edition included a leather interior with Nardi wood shifter and brake handle. **Right:** Later Miatas received minor tweaks, but Mazda wisely kept the car's overall character intact. An automatic transmission was available shortly after launch, and anti-lock brakes were options for '91. The engine grew to 1.8 liters and 128 bhp for '94, and to 133 bhp for '95. This 1993 model sports the lift-off hard-top, a $1500 option.

# TOM MATANO
## Form and Function

The Mazda stylist was at work on what would become the 1993 RX-7. He looked to a Ferrari 275 GTB for inspiration. But the 1960s Pininfarina masterpiece would not reveal what made it a timeless design, how it seemed to breathe. Then Tom Matano rolled the Ferrari from his studio into an open-air courtyard.

"Its shape seemed to reach dynamic tension," he said, "as if the atmospheric pressure was equalized, allowing the car to assume its natural shape." The phenomena underscored that good design, lasting design, requires balanced tension. And good design, Matano said, "has a power within that is not diminished by the strength of nature."

That perspective helped guide Matano as he participated in creating some of the best sporting-car shapes of the late 20th Century. His third generation RX-7 emerged stretched tight over an athlete's muscle. He helped draw the first-generation Miata and led the crew that designed the second generation; both were evergreen forms that balanced function and charm. Before that, at BMW, he worked on initial themes for the 1992 and 1999 3-Series, whose taut proportions influenced an era of sports sedans and coupes. Even his designs for the Mazda 929, Millenia, and MX-6 were studies in slack-free equilibrium.

It was not a perspective much in demand at his first design job, with General Motors in the mid-1970s, where assignments included the baroque 1978 Oldsmobile Toronado—though his waterfall grille for the '76 Cutlass had a certain fortitude.

Tom Matano was born in Nagasaki, Japan, in 1947. He grew up in Tokyo, amid uncommon prosperity for postwar Japan. His family's involvement in commercial shipping and fishing allowed it foreign goods, the rarest of privileges, and Matano traced his interest in design to a boyhood fascination with such exotic imports as vacuum cleaners, Parker pens, and most of all, his uncle's 1957 Cadillac. A relative's cargo ship brought him to America in 1969, and he toured the country by Greyhound. In Los Angeles, he was entranced by the Art Center College of Design.

Matano harbored a love of design but was deficient at architectural drawing and feared losing face by failing engineering school in Japan. He had drawn cars to amuse himself and showed enough talent to get into the Art Center, from which he earned a degree in transportation design. He joined GM design in 1974, then worked in the studios of Volvo, Holden, and BMW. He went to Mazda in 1983, rising through its North American ranks. As Chief Designer, product planning and research, he laid out a development building so the facility itself functioned as a design tool, an achievement he called the most rewarding of his career—along with that third-generation RX-7.

Matano returned to his homeland in 1999, and by 2000, was managing Mazda's worldwide design group. In 2002, he left Hiroshima for San Francisco to assume directorship of the Academy of Art College School of Industrial Design. Nurturing young designers lent a natural conclusion to his professional career, Matano said, and besides, it helped assuage a bit of an inferiority complex at not completing engineering school in Japan.

Symmetry, even in that.

Lotus Esprit gets twin-turbo 350-hp V8, genuine supercar fire at last • Lotus sold to Malaysian mass-market carmaker Proton • Nissan cancels 300ZX's U.S. visa in the face of insurmountable market forces • Panoz introduces lighter, faster A.I.V. Roadster • Porsche 911 line adds new glass-roof Targa, all-wheel-drive Turbo, Carrera 4S **1997** All-new C5 Chevy Corvette hatchback coupe starts sale • Aston Martin Virage Volante replaced by updated V8 Volante • BMW adds 6-cyl Z3 and high-performance M3 version • Bugatti reborn again as VW Group acquires facilities, name rights • Dodge Viper goes to 450 hp; racing GTS-R takes world GT2 and GT crowns • Ferrari 456-based 550 Maranello comes to U.S.; 2 seats, 200 mph for $200,000 • Ferrari takes control of struggling Maserati • Honda/Acura NSX offers enlarged V6 teamed with new 6-speed manual gearbox • Mitsubishi 3000GT, Subaru SVX take final bows • Mercedes SLK bows as "junior SL" with retracting metal hardtop • Plymouth rolls out a different sort of sports car with Prowler "retro hot rod" • Toyota Supra phased out of U.S. market **1998** Audi debuts production TT coupe in Europe • Bugatti shows EB118 concept coupe with unique 555-hp W18 engine • Chevrolet adds C5 Corvette convertible, provides another Indy 500 pace car • Chevrolet announces Corvette C5-R racer for '99 international enduros • Chrysler Corporation and Daimler-Benz "merge" into DaimlerChrysler • DeTomaso signs San Francisco's Qvale Group to handle future-model production, marketing

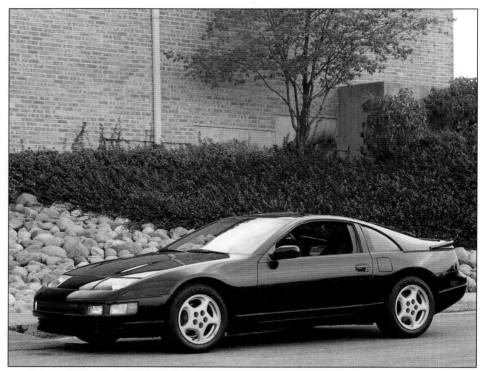

The 1990 Nissan 300ZX was recognized as a new sports car benchmark upon its introduction. A 222-bhp base model debuted first, followed months later by a 300-bhp twin turbo version (shown). All used an iron-block, aluminum-head 3.0-liter V6 with state-of-the-art dual cams and variable valve timing. To each cylinder bank the Turbo added an oil-cooled turbocharger and an intercooler for lag-free thrust right to the 7000-rpm rev limiter. The 300ZX convertible bowed as an early 1993 model. Escalating yen values soon pushed 300ZX base prices over $42,000, and sales fell off accordingly. Nissan dropped the US market 300ZX after the 1996 model year.

## DIMENSIONS/WEIGHT DISTRIBUTION

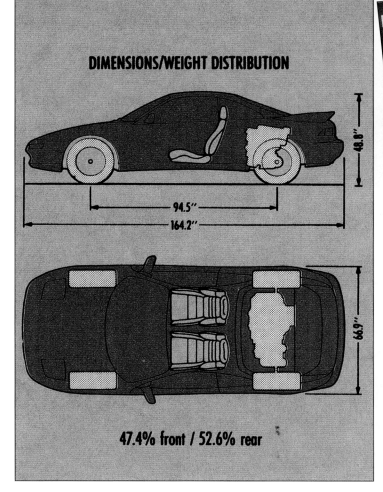

94.5"

164.2"

48.8"

66.9"

47.4% front / 52.6% rear

THE 1993 TOYOTA MR2. IF IT WERE ANY SLOWER, IT WOULD BE A FERRARI.

*I love what you do for me!* TOYOTA

**Top and left:** The redesigned 1991 MR2 gained new "baby Ferrari" styling, larger dimensions, and more power over the 1985-1989 first-generation models. The new model boasted 3.2 inches more wheelbase for extra cockpit space, 8.7 inches more body length for a roomier rear trunk, and curb weight increased more than 400 pounds. The base MR2 got a twin-cam 2.2 with 130 bhp, up 13 percent, and a revvy new Turbo version packed a 2.0-liter inter-cooled engine with 200 bhp, up 38 percent. Turbo MR2s, such as the 1992 model shown at top, came with a standard T-top roof. Tendencies toward sudden oversteer prompted Toyota to add wider tires, stronger brakes, and significant suspension revisions to 1993 models. **Above:** A playful 1993 ad, complete with faux "internal memos," took a tongue-in-cheek potshot at Ferrari, but Toyota wasn't laughing for long. Despite its combination of exotic-car credentials with Toyota reliability and build quality, the MR2's tenure in the marketplace was short-lived. Escalating yen values ruined its "budget exotic" appeal: Base prices in 1991 were a reasonable $14,898 for the standard model and $18,228 for the Turbo. But by 1995, they had ballooned to $24,000 and near $30,000. This in a nervous economy and amid insurers hostile to two-seaters. U.S. sales that topped 14,000 in calendar year '91 shriveled to 387 for 1995. There was no '96 model.

Dodge Viper GTS-R wins class at LeMans, repeats as world GT/GT2 champ • Jaguar evokes E-Type days with posh new XK8 2+2s • Lamborghini welcomes Audi as latest owner; Diablo gains 38 hp to 530 **1999** Mercedes and UK's McLaren team up on exotic Vision SLR concept • Chevy Corvette C5-Rs come home 10-11 at LeMans 24 Hours • Mercedes-McLaren SLR gets production go-ahead for 2004 • Bugatti stuns with concept EB118/3 Chiron, a 180-mph W18 supercar • Bugatti stuns again with racy mid-engine EB 18/4 Veyron • DeTomaso Automobili marks 40 years, unveils "New Pantera" concept • Aston Martin offers its first production V12 in updated DB7 Vantage • Audi TT starts U.S. sale with front drive, 180 hp; Quattro model added in summer • BMW Z3 loses base 4-cyl Roadster, adds 6-cyl hatchback coupes • Chevrolet Corvette adds "hardtop" model aimed at serious drivers • Dodge Viper GTS-R takes American LeMans series, another class win at LeMans, third GT/GT2 crown; "club racers" welcome ACR option • Ferrari 348 steps aside for all-new 400-hp 360 Modena • Honda's Acura NSX offers lighter, quicker, sharper Alex Zanardi Edition • Lamborghini Diablos get mild facelift, revised cockpit • Mazda Miata offers carefully evolved styling, stiffer structure, improved chassis • Panoz winds down Roadster production, reveals 2-seat Esperante convertible • Production Boxster arrives as new "volume" Porsche • Porsche bows water-cooled "996-series" as first clean-sheet 911 since original

Mercedes' top-line SL two-seat convertible bowed for 1991 in straight-six-powered 300SL and V8-powered 500SL iterations. All were equipped with an innovative roll-over bar designed to deploy in 0.3 second if sensors detected an impending rollover. With their two-ton curb weights and a lengthy list of posh standard features such as headlamp washers and heated power mirrors, SLs were more luxury tourer than genuine sports car. Even so, stability and roadholding satisfied, and V8 models were musclecar-quick: 1998 500SLs did 0-60 mph in six seconds. The 1993 Mercedes-Benz 500SL shown here packed a 5.0-liter, 315-bhp V8 and standard traction control. But the big news for '93 was the addition of the 600SL, a flagship model that came with a 389-bhp V12 and a $119,500 window sticker. For those who could afford their royal sticker prices, the 1991-2002 SL series offered a tantalizing mix of Teutonic build quality, coddling features, and exquisite performance.

**Above and below:** Announced for 1992, the 968 followed Porsche tradition by keeping the best of its predecessor and improving the rest. A descendant of the 944, the 968 was the last and finest of its breed. There was no Turbo version this time, just a well-equipped coupe and cabriolet, again with all-independent suspension and rear transaxle. Lay-back headlamps in a reshaped nose provided distinction from the 944 and a family kinship with the big 928. Superb road manners, enticing styling, and a surprisingly strong 3.0-liter four-cylinder engine won it deserved credibility. Even with dual cams and a new-variable-valve-timing system, a jumbo four seemed a bit unsophisticated for Porsche. But it was highly effective. The engine boasted more torque than any non-turbo 3.0-liter of its day, and the 968 was among the fastest four-cylinder Porsches, with 0-60 times of well under six seconds. **Right:** The purposeful 968 cockpit possessed Porsche's characteristic aura of overall quality and engineering precision that couldn't be quantified by test numbers. Worldwide 968 production from '92-'95 totaled 19,120.

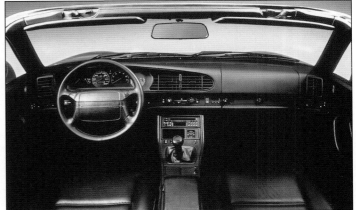

**Opposite above:** Chrysler revived the spirit of the hallowed 1960s Shelby Cobra 427SC with the milestone Dodge Viper RT/10. After a show-stopping concept debut at the 1989 Detroit Auto Show and a whirlwind development cycle, production Vipers were ready for the 1992 model year. A true roadster, Viper was an unapologetic celebration of American brute horsepower unencumbered by high-tech gadgetry or creature comforts. **Opposite below:** The plastic composite body and space-frame chassis were new design technologies to Chrysler, while the all-independent suspension, 13-inch brake discs, and 17-inch steamroller tires were logical applications. **Above:** Chrysler turned to Lamborghini, its Italian subsidiary at the time, for an aluminum adaptation of the Dodge Ram pick-up's 8.0-liter V10. The 488 cubic-inch monster was rated at 400 bhp at 4600 rpm and 450 pound-feet of torque at 3600 rpm. A Borg-Warner six-speed manual was the only transmission. **Top right:** The Viper's outrageous bodywork payed obvious homage to the Cobra. **Upper right:** Quality problems with the huge clamshell hood assembly limited 1992 model year output to only 162 cars. **Lower right:** An attractive cloisonne-style badge adorned both nose and decklid. The wheel center caps and horn button carried the same smirking snake logo. **Bottom right:** In lieu of roll-up windows, pre-1997 Vipers utilized cumbersome snap-in side curtains. Likewise, a flimsy canvas top required assembly before use. With both in place, the cockpit quickly turned into a sauna. **Below:** The Viper was 2.6 inches wider than a Corvette of the same vintage. The V10's ferocious torque necessitated extra-meaty tires—the sticky Michelin XGT-Z radials were a whopping 13 inches wide at the rear.

On the road, everything about the Viper seemed exaggerated, from the gasps elicited by its bawdy bodywork to the endless-torque acceleration, to unpredictable handling at the limit. Side exhausts honored the Cobra but created flesh-singeing door sills and emitted a muted rasp. With no antilock brakes, no electronic suspension, no traction control, and no airbags, driving skill was a prerequisite for getting the most out of a Viper. Civility was near the bottom of the priority list; brute force was at the top. Viper was never as refined as its supercar counterparts, but because it cost a mere fraction of a Lamborghini Diablo or a Ferrari F40, few buyers complained. In fact, a rabid cult following sprang up instantly around the car, with active national clubs, aftermarket accessory manufacturers, and performance tuning specialists.

## TEAM VIPER
### Modern Mavericks

On March 28, 1989, just 12 weeks after the concept Viper's smash debut, Chrysler management approved the formation of Team Viper.

From the more than 200 employees who volunteered for the team, 20 self-proclaimed car nuts were selected from throughout the company. Their immediate task was to determine how quickly Viper could be built and at what cost.

Early on, a Viper Technical Policy Committee (TPC) was formed, with the concept's "four fathers" as its nucleus: Chrysler President Bob Lutz, Vice President Francois Castaing, Vice President of Vehicle Engineering Thomas C. Gale, and performance consultant Carroll Shelby.

Unusual for a bureaucracy the size of Chrysler, Team Viper was given complete autonomy in the creation of the car but was required to meet with the TPC every few months to assess progress and review program direction.

Moving this level of decision-making down the management stream was unheard-of at Chrysler or any other Detroit automaker. But it was nothing compared to the ambitious goals Team Viper had set for itself. Within three months, Team Viper, headed by veteran engineer Roy H. Sjoberg, reported to the TPC that they could not only deliver a road-ready Viper, but could do so in just three years and for only $50 million— a pittance even for then-struggling

Chrysler—and an incredibly low sum for the development for an all new car.

"My ulterior motive," Sjoberg later confessed, "was to be so cheap that everyone would leave us alone—to set such an impossible task that bureaucracy, which would normally get in the way, would say 'I am not going to go near that.' And stay away—until they realized this thing was going to be a success. Then we got more bureaucracy than we wanted." Sjoberg added, "I had the advantage of Bob Lutz who gave us only two charters: 'be ethical and moral—and don't worry about the procedure manual.'"

"The real secret," recalled Lutz "was keeping the program small and the car simple. Had the traditional planning people gotten involved, the program risked growing to huge proportions. So we gave responsibility to the team. There was an initial shock. Guys would say, 'I've done this little piece of the steering system, you mean now I'm responsible for the whole system?' and we'd say 'Right!' It was the realization that the group in this room would have to do the whole car."

Viper's successful launch in 1992 depended heavily on a concept deeply ingrained in sports car lore, the maverick believer. While no single Ferrari, Porsche, Maserati, or Chapman fought singly for Viper's creation, a team of determined spirits managed to battle the odds as a unit, mustering the same entrepreneurial spirit as their pioneering predecessors. In this case, the unlikely hero was not a passionate individual, but 200 people willing to work outside the corporate box, fulfilling a dream instead of a marketing plan.

Mazda's third-generation 1993 RX-7 restored the rotary rocket as a pure sports car. About all it had in common with the 1986-1992 series were rear drive and a front-mounted, turbocharged Mazda Wankel engine displacing 1.3 liters. But now there were two turbochargers acting in sequence; one provided boost at low- to medium-engine speeds, the other spooled up for high-rpm assaults. A four-wheel double-wishbone suspension and low profile 16×8 tires supplied near telepathic handling, but the ride was unforgiving. A $1000 "R-1" package added Z-rated tires, dual oil coolers, front and rear spoilers, a stiffening brace between the front shock towers, and markedly firmer suspension damping. The purposeful cockpit, though cramped, was a model of efficient design. But for all its stripped-down character, the RX-7 carried a hefty price tag for its day: $31,300 for starters, over twice the price of a Miata. Yen-friendly exchange rates soon pushed the base price up even more, and already lukewarm sales sank further. With unsold '95s still clogging dealer lots, Mazda stopped importing the car for '96.

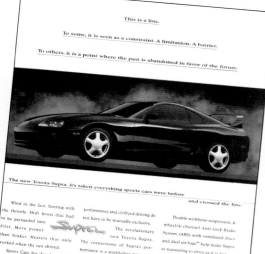

The second-generation Toyota Supra bowed in 1993, just as the market for high-buck Japanese sports cars began to collapse. Its 3.0-liter inline six made 220 bhp in base form and 320 in the Turbo, which used one turbocharger for low-rpm boost, kicked in a second above 4500 rpm, and then ran both to make an impressive 106.8 bhp per liter. The Turbo's performance capabilities were world-class: 0-60 came in 5 seconds flat, on the way to a 154-mph top speed. An excellent suspension and resolute ABS disc brakes made for near-faultless control in most any maneuver. An ostentatious rear spoiler was a $420 option said to provide 66 lbs of downforce at 60 mph. Sport Roof models featured a removable aluminum roof panel. Some critics felt the Supra's over-all design lacked the passion-inspiring lines of many European rivals. Sales dragged at 2000-3000 units a year in a fickle sports car market, and the car was dropped for 1999.

Drawing on multiple Formula 1, CanAm, and Indianapolis victories, England's McLaren organization set about creating its first road car in 1989. Revealed to the public in 1992, the McLaren F1 was on the road by 1994 and in the winner's circle at LeMans in 1995. With its no-holds-barred engineering, the F1 redefined the term "supercar." Scissor-type doors provided access to a leather interior with an unusual "1+2" layout: a form-fitting driver seat was centrally located, with a passenger seat slightly aft on both sides. A BMW-designed 6.1-liter V12 was mounted amidships and packed 627 bhp. A carbon-fiber body/chassis structure made for an unprecedented power-to-weight ratio of under four lbs per horsepower. Price and performance were equally stratospheric: $810,000, 0-60 in 3.2 seconds, 11.1-second quarter-mile times, and a 231-mph top speed. Ninety-five mph was possible in second gear. When production ceased in 1997, only 100 cars, including GTR and LeMans competition versions, had been built.

Introduced in Europe in 1995 and the U.S. in 1996, the DB7 was the first Aston Martin developed under Ford Motor Company, which took control of Aston in 1987. Aston Martin wisely revived the DB name, which had been dropped in 1972, for this model. Ford money helped develop, test, and certify the car, but the DB7 was designed by Aston to be an Aston. Available in both coupe and Volante convertible versions, the voluptuous body was styled by Aston's Ian Callum, formerly of Ford's Ghia studio, with subtle nods to DBs of the past. A refined dohc inline-six put out 335 bhp with the help of an Eaton supercharger and propelled the DB7 to 5.5-second 0-60 times and a 165-mph top speed when equipped with the standard five-speed manual transmission. Sumptuous interiors featured Connolly hide upholstery, deep-pile carpet, and burr walnut dashboard and console trim. Production of under 700 cars per year guaranteed exclusivity, as did the $125,000 sticker price. A topline DB7 Vantage was introduced for 1999. Its 6.0-liter V12 put out 420 bhp and was good for top speeds of over 180 mph. Although underwritten by Ford, these cars represented the summit of British automaking.

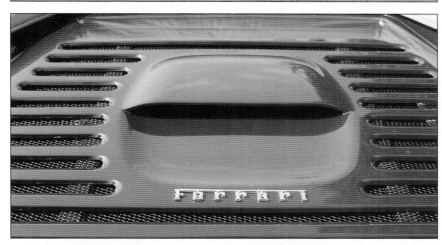

**Above left:** While specialty cars such as the F50 captured headlines, Ferrari was busy developing "volume" models that by any measure were among the marque's best autos ever. The 1995 Ferrari 355 debuted in solid-roof berlinetta form, and was joined in '96 by targa-roof GTS and ragtop Spyder body styles. **Above:** The distinctive Ferrari shiftgate looks at home even next to modern climate-control knobs. It would be joined by an optional Formula-1-inspired paddle shifter in 1998. Two steering-wheel mounted paddles (one for upshifts, one for downshifts) controlled the gearbox and also worked the clutch. **Left:** The 355's vented decklid covered a lusty, high-revving 3.5-liter V8 that made 107 bhp per liter. **Below:** Launching the Spyder version gave Ferrari the world's first mid-engine convertible with a power top. Lucky drivers got the sun and the moon and a real Ferrari.

**Above:** A smoother nose and tidier bumpers marked the new 993-series 911s that arrived for model-year 1995. The product of a $300 million design effort, they were three inches wider than 964 Carreras, but also 20 percent stiffer, to the benefit of handling. The second-generation all-wheel-drive Carrera 4 (shown) got a new viscous clutch that reapportioned power (up to 39 percent) to the front wheels only when traction demanded. It worked better than the original C4's computer-controlled system and weighed half as much. The '95 C4 debuted at $72,000, did 0-60 in 4.9 seconds, and hit 161 mph. All 1995 911s featured a much-improved double-wishbone rear suspension, uprated brakes, quicker-ratio steering, and a traction-control system called Automatic Brake Differential (ABD). **Left:** After an 18-month-long furlough, the mighty 911 Turbo returned in late 1995 as a new 993-series model with 400 horsepower via twin "hair dryers," along with the C4's all-wheel drive as standard. A "phantom" look at the business end of the 993 Turbo highlights the large twin intercoolers for feeding two smaller turbos instead of one large unit, a change that made power delivery much more progressive and controllable. Porsche's worldwide sales continued moving up in '95, when calendar-year U.S. orders totaled 5771. Most were 911s.

**Above:** The 993 Carreras were the most tractable and forgiving 911s ever, yet no less thrilling to drive. Wider track, larger brakes, and Porsche's new Automatic Brake Differential made for safer handling, while a new six-speed manual transmission and an improved "Tiptronic S" automatic option made life easier in daily commuting. The Tiptronic could be used as a fully automatic transmission, plus it allowed changing gears manually by flicking a console shift lever or pushing switches on the steering wheel. **Left:** The new Carreras carried over the previous generation's pop-up engine lid, but the new unit was larger and reshaped. The cover rose automatically above 50 mph to increase aerodynamic downforce at the rear, thus improving high-speed stability. The diminutive trunk gained 20 percent more storage volume over previous 911s and housed the battery and spare tire. Ellipsoid headlights were integrated into the fenders with no separate trim ring. The headlights could be removed for bulb service by releasing a lever inside the front trunk. **Below:** A reshaped whale tail complimented still-wider rear fenders on the 993 Turbo. Like the previous Turbo, it had an all-aluminum two-valve 3.6, but now there was higher compression, smarter engine-management electronics, and an extra gear. Performance was unprecedented, with 0.95g cornering and 3.7-second 0-60 times. In its day, nothing short of a Ferrari F50, which cost about five times as much, or the McLaren F1, at eight times the price, could touch the 911 Turbo.

Inspired in part by the success of the Mazda Miata, European automakers staged a roadster revival in the mid-1990s. First to market was the 1996 BMW Z3. With its naturally aspirated four-cylinder engine, manual gearbox, and do-it-yourself folding top, it was more conventional than the Mercedes-Benz SLK or Porsche Boxster. Comparisons to the Miata were natural and showed the BMW to be seven inches longer in wheelbase, three inches longer overall, and nearly 400 lbs. heavier. BMW said the decorative front fender vents "can be interpreted as a small stylistic tribute to the BMW 507 roadster." Some were disappointed with the 138-bhp Z3's relatively ordinary acceleration and sedan exhaust note. But responsive handling, fine ride, and pleasant accommodations were not to be taken lightly. A far-more-powerful six-cylinder version waited in the wings, but the four-cylinder Z3 offered modern drivers a taste of the days when going fast in a sports car required some skill.

Chevrolet was not about to let the 1984-1996 C4 Corvette pass into history without commemorating the occasion with a special edition. In fact, two "ready-made collectible" versions were offered, a silver-hued Collector Edition and the Grand Sport edition shown here. Named for the legendary Corvette racers of the 60s, the 1996 Grand Sport package came in coupe ($3250) or convertible ($2880) form, with manual transmission only. The tack-on fender flares and extra-wide rear tires were exclusive to the GS coupe; otherwise, only paint and trim differentiated Grand Sports from regular '96 'Vettes. Black-finished wheels gave a sinister competition look, and a white dorsal stripe and red "hash marks" on the driver's side fender paid homage to original Grand Sport paint schemes. Standard on the Grand Sport and optional on manual-transmission-equipped '96 'Vettes was a revised 5.7-liter small-block V8 called the LT4. Though it gained 30 bhp, the LT4's performance numbers improved little over the previous LT1. The C4 'Vette's swan song was mildly disappointing, but an all-new model was in the works for 1997.

**Above:** Just as the Dodge Viper RT/10 roadster payed tribute to the Shelby Cobra roadster, the Viper GTS coupe was a Nineties paean to the Shelby Cobra Daytona Coupe. The vehicle shown is Dodge's 1995 concept car, but production versions that followed for the 1996 model year were virtually identical in appearance, right down to the "skunk" stripes and competition-look aluminum fuel-filler cap. **Below:** The coupe body style added a sliver of civility to the Viper's brutish nature, with standard driver- and passenger-side airbags, air-conditioning, power windows, electric door-latches, a security system, adjustable pedals, and a six-disc CD changer. Despite the added features, the GTS coupe was actually 70 pounds lighter than the RT/10 roadster, and faster too. *Road & Track* spurred a 1996 GTS on to a 4.4-second 0-60 sprint and a 12.8-second quarter-mile run. Skidpad and slalom numbers were a tick better than the roadster's as well. **Left:** Production 1996 GTS engines were rated at 450 bhp, 35 more than their roadster counterparts. A new aluminum engine block, improved heads, a lumpier camshaft, and a less restrictive exhaust were responsible for the gain; roadster models received the same upgrades in 1997. In 1999, an ACR (American Club Racer) package was added for those who wanted to race their Vipers on weekends. The $10,000 package included racing tires and suspension, five-point seat-belt harness, ACR nameplates and graphics, and deleted the air-conditioning, radio, and fog lights. Antilock brakes were not available until the 2001 model year, when Dodge introduced them as a standard feature. First-generation Vipers would reign until the 2003 model year, when they were replaced with a redesigned roadster with even more horsepower. Total 1992-2002 Viper production was over 14,000.

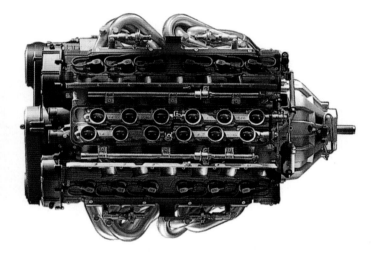

**Top:** The handsome 1995 456GT 2+2 coupe revived the classic front engine, V12 Ferrari layout. The 2+2 format added roominess and comfort while sacrificing little in the way of performance: The 0-60 sprint took a hair over 5 seconds, and top speed exceeded 185 mph. A GTA variant came with a 4-speed automatic in place of the GT's manual unit. **Left:** Based on a shortened 456GT platform, the 550 Maranello bowed for 1997. Ferrari engineers spent 4860 hours of wind-tunnel development time fine-tuning its aerodynamics, paying special attention to underbody and front-end streamlining. Their efforts resulted in a drag coefficient of 0.33. The refined aerodynamics and a 50/50 weight distribution ensured stable handling—even at maximum speed. **Above:** Exhibiting typical Ferrari beauty, The Maranello's 5.5 liter, 48-valve V12 turned out 485 bhp at 7000 rpm and 419 pound-feet of torque at 5000 rpm. **Below:** The Maranello's styling was less outrageous than the Testarossa it replaced, but its performance raised the bar. The factory claimed a 199-mph top speed and 0-60 mph took only 4.3 seconds. Around Ferrari's Fiorano test track, the Maranello was a full 3.2 seconds quicker than the Testarossa. In spite of its blistering performance, the Maranello was still spacious and comfortable for a supercar.

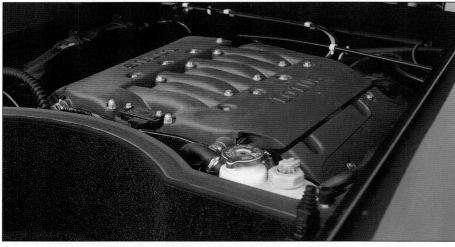

Like Porsche with the 911, Lotus refined and fortified the Esprit over the years. The evergreen Esprit evolved from a naturally aspirated sports car with as little as 140 bhp to a turbocharged one with as much as 300. In 1996 Lotus replaced the turbo four with the line's first V8 engine. The 350-hp twin-turbo 3.5 kept the Esprit's performance solidly into the supercar realm, with 4.5-second 0-60 times and a top speed of 178 mph. The Esprit's radical "door-stop" styling, aided by a 1987 freshening, still turned heads, but by the mid-nineties the overall design was showing its 20-year-old roots. Trundling along in traffic could be a real chore, due to the Esprit's noisy, claustrophobic cockpit, near-zero rear visibility, and weak torque below 3000 rpm. But out on a twisty, uncluttered road, screaming up near its 6900 rpm redline, it delivered joyous performance. High-speed handling was exemplary, with body-roll-free cornering and stable braking. Part of the Esprit's appeal was sheer rarity; its yearly production was always miniscule. Only 260 1996 models were built.

New Jaguars don't appear that often, so the introduction of the 1997 XK8 was a big event. Introduced in both coupe and convertible form, the XK8 was the first XK Jaguar since the beloved E-type (aka XKE) died 21 years before. Convertibles outsold the coupes by over seven to one. Jaguar called the XK8 a sports car, but with its 3867-lb curb weight and comfort-tuned suspension, it was really a posh grand tourer like its XJS predecessor. The XK8 was the first Jaguar to benefit from the manufacturing discipline and deep pockets of the Ford Motor Company, who bought Jaguar in 1990. It was powered by Jaguar's first V8 engine, an all-alloy, 32-valve, twincam 4.0 liter that emitted a wonderful silken snarl under throttle. The delightful V8's ample low-speed punch was enough to propel the the coupe to 60 mph in 6.5 seconds. The sole transmission was a 5-speed automatic from the German company ZF. Though billed as a 2+2, the rear seat was suitable only for small children, and front seating was extra-cozy as well. In 2000, Jaguar added the high-performance XKR model with a 370-bhp supercharged version of the 4.0-liter V8; eighteen-inch wheels improved the XKR's handling with little harm to the its absorbent ride. All XK8's offered refined performance in an elegant, luxurious package that would stand the test of time for visual appeal.

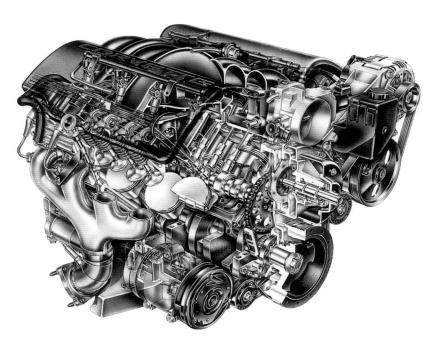

**Opposite top:** Journalists and buyers alike judged the fifth-generation (or C5) Corvette the first that could truly be called a "world beater." Only a hatchback coupe was offered for 1997. **Opposite middle:** A clean-sheet redesign of Chevy's classic small block, C5's new all-aluminum LS1 V8 was lighter yet more potent than the iron-block LT1/LT4 engines it replaced. **Opposite bottom:** Two suspension options were offered in '97: the autocross-ready (but tooth-rattling) Z51; and the high-tech F45 Selective Real Time Damping system that allowed driver-selectable "Tour," "Sport," and "Performance" modes. An optional $500 Active Handling System bowed for '98. It used the antilock-brake and traction-control sensors to brake individual wheels and thus minimize skidding—a boon for wet conditions. **Opposite right:** The C5 'Vette's styling managed to respect hidebound Corvette heritage while vastly improving ergonomics. Sculptured bodyside air scoops were largely decorative. Following standard Corvette practice, the time-honored crossed-flags emblem was redone for the new model. **Top:** The unloved digital dash display of the C4 'Vette was discarded in favor of attractive analog gauges. A four-speed automatic transmission was standard; the six speed manual was an $815 option. **Middle:** A six-speed-equipped LS1 could push the C5 to 60 mph in 4.7 seconds. Top speed was 172. On the skidpad, the C5's .93g was the best Corvette production number ever, while braking from 60 mph was a supercar-short 125 feet. **Bottom:** C5 was the first production 'Vette with a rear-mounted transmission linked to the engine via a stout aluminum tube. A performance rear axle ratio cost an additional $100.

**Above:** After a year off, the Corvette convertible returned for 1998 with the new C5 design and the first external trunklid on a 'Vette roadster in 36 years. Despite weighing slightly less than its C4 predecessor, the ragtop C5 was 4.5 times stiffer, sharing the coupe's strong new "hydroformed" chassis with frame rails measuring a stout six inches across. The new skeleton accommodated the convertible without a single structural reinforcement. **Left:** A passenger-side dashboard grab handle was a nod to sixties Stingrays; it could come in handy when the traction control was switched off via a console-mounted button. **Bottom:** The 1998 convertible was the fourth Corvette to pace the Indy 500. The bubbled tonneau cover/light bar identifies this 'Vette as the actual pace car, but Chevrolet sold 1163 nearly identical convertibles with a $5039 Pace Car Replica package.

**Above:** Introduced to America in early 1997, the SLK was Mercedes-Benz's answer to the BMW Z3 and Porsche Boxster. A novel retractable hardtop powered into the SLK's trunk at the push of a button, and under the hood lurked a supercharged 2.3 liter four-cylinder with 191 bhp. Initially, the only transmission was a five-speed automatic that electronically adjusted shifts to suit driving style, but a five-speed manual became standard for 1999. For the 2000 model year, Mercedes introduced factory-customized *designo* editions of almost all its models. The "Copper Edition" SLK shown featured copper-colored sport seats, center console, and roll bar trim.
**Below:** BMW enthusiasts appreciated the Z3's handling and quality, but, as ever, wanted more power. BMW obliged with a 189-bhp six-cylinder in 1997, then truly upped the ante in '98 with the M-Series roadster. The 1999 M coupe (shown) followed. Its unusual hatchback styling rankled some purists, but the closed body provided slightly more luggage capacity and extra chassis rigidity. Radically flared rear fenders covered nine-inch-wide tires. **Right:** M coupes and convertibles shared the same 240-bhp 3.2-liter inline six and mandatory five-speed manual transmission. M base prices started at $41,800 for the 1999 coupe, $42,700 for the convertible.

**Above:** The retro-style Boxster roadster hit showrooms in January 1997 as the first all-new Porsche in 19 years. Just as the BMW Z3 and Mercedes-Benz SLK reflected their makers' traditions, the mid-engined Boxster mirrored Porsche's unconventional spirit. It was the most serious performance sports car of the bunch, using its midship layout to create a track-ready feel. The styling was adventurous inside and out, and the designers encapsulated the liquid-cooled flat-six behind the two-seat cockpit. The 2.5-liter "boxer" engine produced 200 bhp. Base price: $39,980. **Below:** The hotter Boxster S debuted in 2000, packing a 250-bhp 3.2-liter six instead of base model's newly enlarged 217-bhp 2.7-liter. The S also gained a six-speed manual transmission in place of the base model's five-speed unit, 17-inch wheels instead of 16s, and a sport suspension. Optional 18-inch wheels were also available. Base price: $49,930.

**Above:** Starting around $40,000, Boxtster was briefly referred to as the "affordable" Porsche. However, with a tempting array of available high-ticket options including a $2600 navigation system, the "entry-level" Porsche could exceed $65,000 in S trim. **Left:** Until the Cayenne sport truck came online in 2003, all Porsche engines since the V8-powered 928 was discontinued were "flat." A design shared only with Subaru in America, the engine's horizontally-opposed cylinder layout was responsible for the Boxter's (and 911's) unique "blat-blat" exhaust note. All Boxters received a horsepower bump for 2003; base cars jumped 11 to 228, while S models went up 8, to 258. Performance was impressive given the modest engine sizes. According to *Road & Track,* base Boxters reached 60 mph in 6.0 seconds, versus 5.7 for S models. **Below:** There aren't many ads more effective than this one showing a Boxter carving up a twisty open road. The fine print above the photo reminds readers to obey traffic laws at all times.

You didn't think it got better than mile 8,453.
Then mile 8,454 comes along.

The top disappears in seconds. With a 258-hp mid-mounted flat six, so do you. And your memories of the last road instantly eclipsed by the joy that lies ahead. The Boxster S. There's even more fun waiting around the next corner. Porsche. There is no substitute.

The Boxster S

PORSCHE

**Above:** After 34 years of continuous honing, the legendary Porsche 911 was completely redesigned as an early 1999 model. The fourth-generation "996 series" 911 was about seven inches longer and one inch wider than its predecessor on a 3-inch longer wheelbase. Though clearly related to the Boxster up front, the 996 remained a true rear-engine car. **Right:** Previous-generation 911s were frequently lambasted for their dated interiors and poor ergonomics. Porsche designers responded with a thoroughly modern redesign more in keeping with the company's high-tech image. The sleek "tear drop" headlamp assemblies added to the new 911's aerodynamic look, but traditionalists bemoaned the passing of the old version's simpler round units. **Below:** Though longer and wider than the previous generation, the newest 911's silhouette was unmistakably Porsche. Visible through the wheel spokes, standard cross-drilled rotors cooled more quickly than less-expensive solid units.

**Top:** The 1999 Carrera 4's sophisticated all-wheel-drive system was based on a viscous multi-plate clutch arrangement. Under normal driving, the system sent five percent of the available torque to the front wheels. Traction loss at the rear wheels could send up to 40 percent of available power to the front wheels until normal traction resumed. **Left:** Per 911 tradition, the engine was a "flat" (horizontally-opposed) 6-cylinder mounted in the rear, but it switched from air to water cooling, single- to dual-overhead camshafts, and to four valves per cylinder versus two. The engine itself was basically the Boxster unit upsized to 3.4 liters, but with 14 more U.S. horsepower than the outgoing 3.6—296 in all. The standard transmission remained a 6-speed manual, while the optional automatic was Porsche's latest 5-speed "Tiptronic S" (ousting a 4-speed version) with full manual-shift capability. **Above and below left:** The Carrera Cabriolet's electronic soft top powered up or down in 20 seconds at the push of a button. In the event sensors detected an imminent rollover situation, safety bars popped up from behind the seats, which in combination with the windshield frame, protected occupants from injury. Prices began at $65,690 for the standard coupe, and topped out at $83,820 for the Carrera 4 convertible.

# Beyond 2000: A New Golden Age

It was really just the last year of the twentieth century, but the world rushed to welcome 2000 as the start of a new decade, a new century, a new millennium. The celebrations were large and lavish, spirits and hopes high. Hangovers clouded many a morning after, but most computers woke up just fine, their calendars clicking over to "Y2K" without the widespread digital calamities that had been feared. The parties over, life went on.

But on September 11, 2001, life shattered amid the death and destruction of the World Trade Center in New York City and a large portion of the Pentagon in Washington, D.C. The events of that day and the events still flowing from them require no comment here. Suffice it to say, as many already have, that America and the world have been changed in ways profound and fateful.

The automotive world had seen many changes already. Globalization, heralded as the new millennium's Big Thing in most industries, was old news here. But competition was now rougher than ever, the stakes enormous. Failures were not an option. Even the largest manufacturers could no longer afford to do an Edsel. Excess production capacity didn't help. Though India and China were emerging as huge new markets, the rest of the world found itself with too many factories able to make more cars than there were people to buy.

Manufacturers had been hedging bets by teaming up in various ways. Daimler-Benz made business history by "merging" with Chrysler Corporation in 1998 to form German-dominated DaimlerChrysler. Ford Motor Company had bought Jaguar and Aston Martin in the Eighties, then added Volvo and a controlling stake in Mazda, and finally Land Rover. General Motors, meanwhile, completed its purchase of Saab and forged partnerships with Subaru and Fiat to complement its holdings in Suzuki and Isuzu. Volkswagen/Audi rescued Lamborghini, snatched Bentley from Rolls-Royce, and retrieved the remains of a short-lived 1990s Bugatti revival. Even BMW got the urge to merge, acquiring Rolls and the Mini brand, the latter from its brief stewardship of Rover Group. Ferrari, which came under Fiat's wing in the late Sixties, had lately become a semi-autonomous enterprise that had prospered enough to take over Maserati. Thus, among major sports car powers, only Porsche remained independent, defiantly so despite its small size.

Happily, consolidation and globalization did not mean fewer or less-interesting sports cars in the new century. On the contrary, choices multiplied, and power and performance reached levels that would have seemed impossible even 10 years before. In addition, smaller producers like Aston and Lamborghini were making vast strides in engineering and quality, thanks to the financial might and greater production discipline of their big new owners. Because this book is being prepared in late 2003, we can only survey the field up to that point, but we already know that more great sports cars are just around the bend.

Let's start with the fantasy ranks, where an all-out war got underway. Ferrari, as usual, fired early salvos. The 360 Modena arrived in 2001 as a lovelier, faster, better-handling evolution of the midengine F355. A hotter front-V12 GT, the 575M, cruised in during '03. But even these paled next to the Enzo, a 2003 celebration of the legendary *Il Commendetore* and heir to the great tradition of the F40 and F50. Though no less a barely tamed Formula 1 car, the mid-V12 Enzo took everything to the next level—the fastest, most powerful road-going cavallino yet. It cost an Olympian $700,000, and only 399 would ever be built, but it deposed the 1994-98 McLaren F1 as the history's ultimate sports car. Nothing else around looked to come close.

Except, perhaps, the extraordinary Bugatti EB 16.4 Veyron. Though not quite reality at this writing, it's an all-wheel-drive wundercar backed by the very real engineering expertise and deep pockets of VW/Audi. An improbable W16 engine mounted amidships should deliver a mind-boggling 987 horsepower and a top speed of over 252 mph. Yet unlike the Enzo, the Veyron is furnished and equipped like a luxury sedan. Price? A mere $1.2 million. But get your order in fast. Only 50 or so will be built each year—in France, appropriately, just as Ettore did.

As noted, Lamborghini is also in the VW/Audi stable now. As such, it's enjoying a happy renaissance after limping through the Eighties and Nineties under three different masters. It began in 2002 with the mid-V12 Murcielago, as thrilling and charismatic as the Diablo it replaced, but infinitely more civilized and better built. Joining it in 2003 was the long-awaited "baby Lambo," the mid-V10 Gallardo, a 360 Modena/Porsche 911 Turbo rival that promises to further secure the marque's future.

Porsche's latest weapon for the supercar war is a sort of Boxster on steroids, with some 600 horses from the company's first production V10. As expected of Porsche, the Carrera GT is shot full of high technology, much of it lifted directly from the racetrack. It doesn't have a turbocharger, but no one would be surprised if Porsche bolted one on to get closer to the Enzo and Veyron. Crosstown rival Mercedes-Benz fires back with the SLR McLaren, a cooperative effort with the same British specialist that built the aforementioned BMW-powered F1. In name and character, the new supercharged V8 coupe recalls the seminal SLR racers of the early Fifties. It departs from other new-century überwagens with a traditional front-engine layout, but follows them with costly aluminum/carbon fiber construction. The Mac SLR is close to the Carrera GT in wallop and wallet-shrinking ability—to the tune of some $400,000—so the fight for bragging rights and sales supremacy should be fierce.

There was plenty of action in the popular-price ranks as well. The success of Mazda's Miata touched off a late-Nineties "retro roadster" craze that produced not only the Boxster but BMW's American-built Z3. The latter was redesigned for '03 to become the Z4, which earned plaudits for most everything except its postmodern styling. Audi, meantime, had weighed in with the TT, a cut-down VW Golf with shapely Bauhaus bodywork and available all-wheel drive. Honda joined in for 2000 with the ragtop S2000, a rear-drive cornering fool with a 9000-rpm redline. That same year, Toyota resurrected its MR2, this time as a convertible. But it was Nissan's all-new 350Z for 2003 that really got people talking. Here at last was the long-sought spiritual heir to the 1970 original. And it was a great drive besides.

Detroit was far from idle. Chevy delivered a "pure performance" Corvette, the Z06, for 2001, then gave it more power and stickier handling. Chrysler Corporation unleashed a slick new 500-bhp Dodge Viper for 2003, followed by the stylish Mercedes-based Chrysler Crossfire hatchback. And in a grand gesture to its historic 2003 centennial, Ford announced a fully road-legal replica of its fabled LeMans-winning GT40 racer, complete with a 500-bhp supercharged V8.

With these and other great new sports cars on the scene—and more on the way—we can't think of a happier ending for this book. Whatever the future may hold, we can be sure that sports cars will be a part of it. In many ways, we need them more than ever.

## newMILLENNIUM

**2000** DeTomaso launches new Mangusta targa coupe based on '96 Bigua concept • Jaguar hints at new sports car with F-Type concept • Panoz Esperante makes public debut • Porsche shows racy Carrera GT concept roadster with 560-hp midships V10 • Audi TT starts '01 early by adding Roadster models, 225-hp option • BMW Z3 roadsters sport beefier rear haunches • Dodge Viper GTS-R wins Daytona 24 Hours, takes third straight class win at LeMans • Honda uncorks S2000 "retro roadster" with revvy, high-tech 240-hp 4-cyl engine • Lamborghini adds 6.0-liter Diablo GT with 566 hp • Mazda Miata marks 10th birthday with limited-run 6-speed anniversary model • Porsche slots larger engine into base Boxster, adds even quicker Boxster S • Toyota revives midengine "Mister Two" as all-new MR2 Spyder convertible

**2001** DeTomaso Mangusta relaunched as Qvale Mangusta • Chrysler bows 2-seat Crossfire concept coupe, hints at showroom model • Briggs Cunningham III, ex-Chrysler boss Bob Lutz show new Cunningham C-7 V12 concept coupe, seek investors • Jaguar says F-Type is go for production • Porsche says it will build exotic Carrera GT roadster—1000 only • VW says Bugatti 18/4 Veyron will be built with incredible 1001 hp • Qvale sells Mangusta design, other assets to revived MG-Rover Group in UK • GM names Bob Lutz as "product czar" • MG shows X80 concept coupe based on Qvale Mangusta • Lamborghini unveils 570-hp Murcielago, Diablo's successor • Aston Martin replaces Virage/V8 line with all-new flagship, the burly V12 Vanquish

" **It** was my good fortune one October in Vermont to ride shotgun in an NSX-T. The driver was a sure hand. Flawless downshifts and rev-matching blips ushered in corners. Howling acceleration in the straights left a vortex of red leaves in our wake. It was serious speed beneath a canopy of trees speared by late-day sun. As we pulled into our destination, the driver explained the discomfort the strobe effect brought to eyes deep into their sixth decade. "Otherwise," said Denise McCluggage, who drove Ferraris and Maseratis and Jaguars at Sebring and Monte Carlo and Bridgehampton, who spoke casually of Sterling and Phil and Dan, "I think I would have been faster." "

– **Chuck Giametta**
Riverwoods, Illinois

**Top:** Hand assembled in the Buckinghamshire town of Newport Pagnell, Aston Martin's range-topping Vanquish sported V12 power and a lightweight frame of aluminum and carbon fiber. Made famous by its starring role in the James Bond thriller *Die Another Day*, the 460-bhp gentleman's sports car listed for just under $240,000 in 2002, its first year out. **Above:** Aging gracefully, Acura's aluminum-skinned NSX received a modest facelift in 2002. Gone were the dated pop-up headlamps, replaced by sleek-looking xenon-gas units. Though sporting one of the smallest engines in its class, *Road & Track* coaxed a freshened NSX to 60 mph in a competitive 5 seconds. A detriment to sales, NSX prices started at $89,000 in 2003, roughly double that of the similarly quick Corvette.

**Above:** A sculpture of arcs and circles, Audi's avant-garde TT drew more attention for its design than its performance. Capable on the road however, TT offered turbocharged 1.8-liter engines of either 180 or 225 bhp for its 2000 debut. A 250-horsepower V6 was added to the roster in 2004. **Right:** Circles dominated the TT's interior as well. Liberal doses of polished aluminum helped frame the otherwise stark expanses of matte black. **Below:** Bugatti's twenty-first-century renaissance began with Veyron and its promised 1001-horsepower V16. Federalized models actually delivered 987 horsepower, roughly double Viper's power output. Production began for 2005, and was limited to 50 vehicles annually. Now under Volkswagen control, the latest Bugatti revival was free of the financial limitations that killed a 1990's rebirth effort.

Improved engines spice up performance for BMW's Z3-series • Chevy Corvette hardtop becomes Z06 with 385 hp, special chassis and cosmetics • Dodge Vipers get standard antilock brakes at last • Ford revives 2-seat Thunderbird as all-new semisporting convertible for '02 • Lamborghini adopts 6.0 V12 for all Diablos • Another crisis forces Lotus to axe mid-V6 M250 designed largely for U.S. • Mercedes-Benz SLK adds standard 6-speed manual gearbox, first V6 model • First Panoz Esperante delivered • New "996" Porsche 911 Turbo bows with all-wheel drive, 415 hp, up to 189 mph • Volkswagen W12 prototype sets new 24-hour speed record **2002** Cadillac begins its centennial, previews production V12 with burly midengine Cien concept • Cadillac previews Evoq-inspired XLR convertible for 2004 • Chrysler confirms production Crossfire as '04 model • Dodge shows youthful Razor 2-seat coupe concept; production unlikely, though • Ford shows concept GT40 a la LeMans-winning '60s racer • Pontiac unveils 2-seat Solstice concepts, says it might build the low-price sports cars • Ford confirms GT40 for limited production in 2003-04 • MG okays production X80, hints at return to U.S. market • Jaguar F-Type canceled amid money troubles, executive changes • Ferrari unwraps wild "FX" successor to F50 • Maserati returns to U.S. with V8-powered 2-seat Spyder, 2+2 Coupe • Ferrari FX debuts at Paris; official name is Enzo • Chevy Corvette Z06 muscles up to 405 hp; chassis tweaked to match • Lotus rumored to be federalizing Elise for U.S. sale

**Above and Left:** Looking Like a traditional British roadster with sharpened edges, BMW's tautly drawn Z4 replaced the aged Z3 for 2003. Bigger and bolder than the outgoing two-seater, Z4 came with either a 184 or 225-horsepower inline six. An optional clutchless sequential manual transmission (SMT) was available with either engine. **Below:** Fast and rare, BMW's Z8 came on the scene in 2001 packing a 4.9-liter V8 with 394 bhp. A six-speed manual transmission was the only choice until 2003, when the automatic-only Alpina came online. Named for the legendary BMW aftermarket upfitter, Alpinas featured torquier engines better suited to use with the autoshift transmissions. The limited-production Z8 was pulled from the BMW lineup by 2004, after a run of 5000 units world wide. Prices stateside started at $125,000.

**Right:** Replacing the short-lived hardtop in the Corvette lineup, the Z06 became the ultimate expression of Chevrolet's long-lived sports car. Introduced in 2001, the Z06 featured the firmest suspension in the 'Vette stable and a breathed-on version of the standard 5.7-liter V8, good for 385 horsepower. Power jumped to 405 bhp for 2002. The bargain of the supercar crowd, the $53,000 Z06 was clocked reaching 60 mph in 4.5 seconds by *Road & Track,* on par with Ferrari's $170,000 Modena. Visible here are the red calipers of the Z06's enhanced brakes. With an all-new "C6" Corvette due for 2005, Chevrolet dropped the Z06 after 2004, planning to replace it with an even higher-performance version by 2006.

# DAVE HILL
## Goal: Attainable Joy

Summer, 1953. A Little League diamond in Pittsford, N.Y. Suddenly, "the whole game just stopped," remembered the kid behind the plate that day, "and everyone ran to see it."

Could Norman Rockwell—or Chevrolet's ad agency—have painted a warmer portrait? Here was a gleaming white 1953 Corvette, the first most anyone had seen, bringing to a standstill a game of Little League baseball.

And could Dave Hill, the kid catcher that afternoon, imagine that one day the Corvette and all it means to America would be entrusted to him? That fate was fulfilled in 1992, when Hill took the torch from Zora Arkus-Duntov and Dave McLellan as just the third chief engineer in the storied history of America's definitive sports car. The chief engineer has primary responsibility for the car's technology and performance.

Duntov preached horsepower and handling in the 1950s. McLellan boldly contemporized the car in the 1980s. Hill, whose first task was to organize existing design concepts into the 1997 C5, seemed by contrast low-key and methodical.

"In comparison to those two guys, I am fairly ordinary," Hill said. "I have tried to specialize in paying attention to detail, sweating the small stuff." As it turned out, there was little ordinary in that.

Born in Rochester, N.Y., in 1947, Hill's father sold commercial scales and put him at ease around things mechanical. Hill insisted "cars" was the first word he uttered, and "any machine that moved was fascinating to me as I was growing up. Those early English sports cars—the Austin-Healey 100, the Jaguar XK120—were vibrant, visual experiences." The first in his family to attend college, he earned degrees in mechanical engineering. He began his automotive career at Cadillac in 1965, advancing from engines and chassis to chief engineer for Allante and DeVille.

When McLellan retired, Hill applied for the 'Vette job. GM brass named him both chief engineer and Vehicle Line Executive, with the daunting task of coordinating Corvette manufacturing, design, and engineering. "I guess they saw I had the kind of vehicle integration and attention to detail that could benefit Corvette," Hill said.

Sounds unexciting. But to underestimate its significance is to misunderstand Corvette's modern-day mission. Its world-class performance, unmatched value, and ability to generate profit were secure. What it needed, as the C5 matured and the C6 dawned, was materials and assembly quality on par with the world's best sports cars. And that demanded disciplined, systematic, unglamorous toil.

It's revealing that Hill put Corvette's 2001 and 2002 ranking as Best Premium Sports Car in Initial Quality by J.D. Power and Associates among his top successes as chief engineer. But he also named the racing C5-R's 2001 and 2002 LeMans wins. Make no mistake, beneath all that structure, calculation, and focus was the giddy Little Leaguer who ran to see the '53.

Asked to sum up his engineering philosophy, Hill fell silent, answered other questions, addressed other points, circled back to the original question, and after more hesitation, was given the chance to pass on it. "No, no, let's see if I can do it," he said finally: "To create awesome, attainable cars that people care passionately about and give them great joy."

Mercedes' junior sports car adds hot SLK32 AMG version with supercharged V6 • Ferrari 550 becomes 575M with upsized V12, F1-style sequential manual gearbox • Porsche 911s get mild facelift, add 450-hp Turbo S and track-oriented GT2 models • Toyota MR2 adds 5-speed Sequential Manual Transmission option **2003** U.S. Automotive Hall of Fame inducts the late Max Hoffman • Death claims Italian sports-car magnate Alejandro DeTomaso • 2004 Chrysler Crossfire begins sale in U.S. and Europe • Aston Martin previews all-new "entry-level" '05 model with concept V8 Coupe • Chevrolet celebrates Corvette's 50th birthday, offers special anniversary option • Cadillac's Corvette-based 2004 XLR starts sale, earns instant press kudos • Redesigned Dodge Viper SRT-10 roadster barges in with 505 cubic inches, 500 hp • Long-rumored "baby" Lamborghini bows as slick Gallardo with midships V10

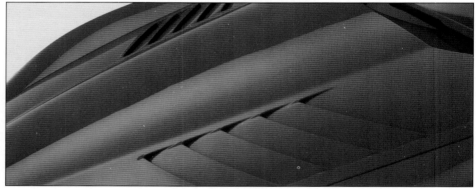

**Above:** Redone for 2003, Dodge's brutal Viper got a new body and an additional helping of power. Viper's 8.0-liter V10 grew to 8.3 liters, adding 50 bhp for an even 500. Performance was startling, with a 0-60 time of 4.1 seconds and a top speed approaching 180 mph. A single SRT-10 convertible model replaced the previous generation's RT/10 droptop and GTS coupe. Refinements for 2003 included a 100-pound weight reduction, a 2.3-inch longer wheelbase, and a return to the signiture side exhaust outlets that disappeared in 1996. A six-speed manual was the standard and only transmission available. Base price in 2003: $79,995.

**Above:** The new Viper enjoyed a true folding convertible top, a welcome improvement over the previous generation's awkward semi-weather-proof arrangement with snap-on side curtains. **Right:** Putting brawn before brains, Viper's enormous engine generated relatively little horsepower for its size, but produced a pavement-melting 525 pound-foot of torque. **Below:** Chrysler engineers dipped into the Mercedes parts bin to create the stylish two-seat Crossfire. Introduced for 2004, the rakish Crossfire shared its underpinnings and engine with the previous generation SLK roadster. The 3.2-liter V6 generated 215 horsepower.

**Left:** The latest in the company's line of midengined V8s, the 360 Modena replaced the F355 as Ferrari's "entry-level" offering. Introduced in 2001, the $160,000 coupe's 3.6-liter engine supplied a healthy 395 bhp. A convertible "Spider" was added to the line in 2001. **Above:** Carbon-ceramic brakes like these came standard on Ferrari's Challenge Stradale, a lightweight, race-ready version of the Modena. New in 2003, the Stradale listed for about $200,000. **Below:** The two-seat 575M Maranello became Ferrari's only front-engined V12 offering after the four-passenger 456 series was dropped in 2004. Previously the 550, Maranello was rebadged in 2003 to reflect a modest bump in engine size. Horsepower rose commensurately, from 478 to 515. Prices started at $230,000.

The crown jewel of the Ferrari lineup, the limited-production Enzo came and went in the blink of an eye. Applying the company's famous "demand minus one" formula, Ferrari built just 399 of the stunning coupes—all in 2003 and 2004. Extracting 660 horsepower from a 6.0-liter midship-mounted V12, and weighing less than 3000 pounds, performance was eye-popping. According to *Road & Track* magazine, the Enzo sprang from 0-60 mph in a scant 3.3 seconds, and topped out at nearly 220 mph. Equally breathtaking was the Enzo's price, about $650,000. The only available transmission was a 6-speed clutchless "sequential" manual unit with steering-wheel-mounted paddle shifters. Extensive use of exotic materials helped make Ferrari's lithe dancer the welterweight it was. Body panels were formed of a carbon fiber and Nomex "sandwich," while the chassis and tub were formed of carbon fiber. Named for the company's founder who died in August 1988, the car's official name was Ferrari Enzo Ferrari, but fans and the press quickly reduced it to simply Enzo. Color choices were limited to yellow, black, and Ferrari's trademark red. Guaranteeing the Enzo's rarity stateside, Ferrari shipped only 100 cars to America.

**Above:** Although plated as such, a breakdown in negotiations prevented Ford from licensing use of the GT40 moniker for its 2005 reinvention of the legendary LeMans racer. By production time, the all-new supercar was known simply as GT. Recalling its 1966 LeMans victory over Ferrari, Ford again set its sights on outperforming the Italian sports car builder, this time aiming to outgun its 360 Maranello. Power targets were impressive, 500 bhp and 500 pound-feet of torque from the GT's supercharged-5.4-liter V8. Intended to be a technological tour de force, the GT's credentials were impressive. Ultrastiff floor panels were formed of a lightweight mesh graphite and aluminum "sandwich." The rigid space frame and body panels were aluminum. **Left:** Applying a contemporary polished-aluminum treatment to the GT40's row-of-gauges layout, the GT's instrument panel was both retro and fresh. An aluminum "cue ball" capped the 6-speed manual transmission's shifter. An automatic was not available. **Below:** Though strikingly similar to the GT40, the GT was significantly larger. The new car's wheelbase spanned 107 inches, 12 more than the GT40. With pricing between $130,000 and $140,000, Ford's striking renaissance machine undercut its Ferrari target by a cool $30,000.

**Above:** Though a late-comer to the roadster renaissance, the S2000 arrived in typical Honda style. Like its NSX big brother, the S2000 made use of a relatively small, but high-output engine and lightweight construction. **Right:** An engineering marvel, the 2000's 2.0-liter four churned out an amazing 240 bhp; 120 per liter. Checking in at a lithe 2800 pounds, the frisky Honda held its own with pricier, larger-engined competitors. Clocked reaching 60 mph in 5.5 seconds by *Road & Track,* the S2000 kept pace with BMW's Z4 3.0i and Porsche's Boxster S. Honda trumped them all in price however, listing for just over $33,000. **Below:** Never a consistent player in the U.S. market, Maserati returned in 2003 with the 4200GT coupe, and added a convertible Spyder variant the following year. Now controlled by Ferrari, Maserati's latest offerings sported an enlarged, detuned version of the 360 Maranello's V8. Good for 390 bhp, the 4.2-liter engine propelled Maserati's shapely tourers to 60 mph in just 5.0 seconds. Cambiocorsa models replaced the standard 6-speed manual transmission with a clutchless steering-wheel-paddle-controlled sequential manual. Prices ranged from $83,000 for coupes to $103,000 for Cambiocorsa Spyders.

**Above:** Next in line to carry the Lamborghini's supercar torch, Murciélago took over where the Diablo left off. New for 2002, a roadster joined the line in 2004. Though Murciélago means "bat" in Spanish, the stealthy implications of the name were lost on green cars. **Left:** The beefy Lambo V12 returned for Murciélago duty, enlarged to 6.2 liters, up from the Diablo's 6.0. Producing a prodigious 575 bhp, the Italian sports car reached 60 mph in a scant 3.7 seconds, according to *Motor Trend*. Top speed was in excess of 200 mph. Rare among exotics, Murciélago put power to the ground through a full-time all-wheel-drive system. Murciélago prices started at $280,000.
**Below:** Flush with cash from its 1998 acquisition by Audi, Lamborghini pushed ahead with a long-rumored "baby Lambo" to sell alongside the large-scale Murciélago. Smaller and lighter than its big brother, Gallardo was also priced dramatically lower, stickering at "only" $160,000. Power came from a heavily modified version of Audi's 4.2-liter V8. Bored, stroked, and expanded by two cylinders, the Gallardo V10 produced a healthy 500 bhp and was reported to reach 60 mph from a standstill in 4.2 seconds, not far behind big-brother Murciélago. A 6-speed manual transmission was standard, but more relaxed cruising could be realized by ordering the paddle-shift controlled clutchless sequential manual. Like the Murciélago, Gallardo employed a full-time all-wheel-drive system. Applying technology used in its big A8 sedan, Audi helped develop the Gallardo's lightweight aluminum space frame and body panels. Weighing in at 3100 pounds, the bantamweight Gallardo was a cool quarter ton lighter than big brother Murciélago.

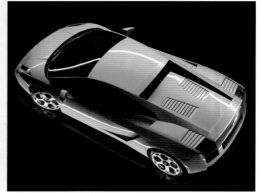

**Above:** Recalling the glory of Mercedes' 1950s racing success, the 2005 SLR McLaren probed the limits of front-engine performance. With a body and chassis codeveloped with McLaren Racing Development, and a heavily massaged version of Mercedes' already impressive supercharged V8, the SLR was granted instant supercar status. Weighing in at approximately 3000 pounds, and with more than 600 bhp on tap, performance was breathtaking. The SLR's flip-open doors recalled the "gullwing" arrangement of early SL coupes. High-tech features included a carbon-fiber chassis and ceramic brakes. Price: around $350,000. **Below:** A little more subtle and lot less expensive than the SLR, the SL55 was the ultimate expression of the Mercedes SL-Class. Having begun life as a normal SL roadster, the SL55 was worked over by AMG—Mercedes' in-house performance tuner—and given larger wheels and tires, unique trim, and an enlarged and supercharged version of the corporate 5.0-liter V8. Now measuring 5.4 liters, the enhanced powerplant cranked out 493 bhp. A 6-speed automatic transmission was standard. When pushed, the top-of-the-line SL reached 60 mph in just 4.5 seconds. SL55 prices started at $114,000.

**Above:** More a spiritual successor to the original 240Z than any subsequent Datsun/Nissan, the 350Z was a return to simple, affordable sportiness. New for 2003, the rear-drive 350 featured a 3.5-liter V6 good for 287 horsepower. Shifting was handled by either a 6-speed manual or 5-speed automatic transmission. Prices ranged from under $27,000 for base models, to just under $35,000 for Track models replete with 18-inch wheels, Brembo-brand brakes, and a rear spoiler. Quick for the price, *Road & Track* timed a Z to 60 mph in 5.5 seconds. **Below:** The Z line expanded in 2004 with the inclusion of a convertible body style. Officially named the Z Roadster, the topless 350Z shared its chassis and drivetrain with the standard car. Though a sports car first, the Roadster did not want for amenities. Convertibles started at $34,000, and came standard with power tops, limited-slip differentials, and xenon-gas headlamps.

**Above:** Bearing a name synonymous with sports cars, Porsche was not about to be left out of the supercar renaissance. The stunning Carrera GT arrived on the scene for 2004, and moved promptly to the head of the Porsche class. The GT boasted Porsche's largest-ever street-going engine, a 5.7-liter V10. With 605 bhp on tap, the midship-mounted-engine moved the 3000-pound GT to 60 mph in a factory-claimed 3.9 seconds. Top speed was reported to be in excess of 200 mph. To make the most of the car's limited storage space, Porsche included a matching five-piece luggage set with each car. Price: just under $400,000. **Below:** A veritable bargain by comparison, the 911 Turbo Cabriolet could be had for less than $130,000. Added to the 911 lineup for 2004, the Cabriolet was the first droptop turbo since 1989. Like its hardtop stablemate, the blown convertible was awesomely fast. Powered by the same turbocharged 3.6-liter flat 6, the Cabriolet boasted 415 bhp and a 4.0-second 0-60 mph time. For the truly power hungry, a factory-installed performance kit boosted horsepower to 450, and the price by $18,000. Like the standard Turbo, Cabriolets came with standard all-wheel drive.

**Above:** The product of one of America's smallest viable auto manufacturers, the Panoz Esperante boasted a Ford powertrain and an all-aluminum chassis. A version of the same engine found in some Mustangs, the 4.6-liter V8 produced 320 bhp. Esperantes were expensive and rare. Introduced in 2000 with an $80,000 price tag, fewer than 200 were produced annually. **Left:** Under hood stainless-steel plates bore the signatures of the craftsmen who hand assembled each car. **Below:** Brandishing the title of America's least-expensive midengine roadster, Toyota's MR2 offered buyers true sports car handling at Camry prices. Powered by a Corolla-sourced 1.8-liter four, straightline performance was more frisky than fast. The 138-bhp engine pushed the tiny two-seater to 60 mph in a middling 8 seconds. But with a near 50/50 front-to-rear weight distribution, the nimble MR2 garnered praise for its neutral handling characteristics and precise steering. MR2 also held the distinction of being the least-expensive car to offer a clutchless sequential manual transmission (SMT.) The 6-speed SMT allowed at-will gear changes without the use of a clutch. A 5-speed manual was the standard transmission. Base price: around $25,000.

**Above:** The 2003 introduction of Mazda's RX-8 marked the return of the rotary engine to America after a 12-year absence. With four doors and a rear seat, the RX-8 was not intended to replace the RX-7 but to be a practical alternative to other sports cars. Tweaked and updated since its departure in 1991, the 8's twin-rotor, 1.3-liter engine produced 247 bhp when coupled to the standard 6-speed manual transmission, 207 with an automatic. Mated with the manual shifter, the little rotary was capable of launching the RX-8 to 60 mph in under 6 seconds. **Right:** A nod to practicality, the RX-8's "suicide" front-opening rear doors made rear-seat entry a snap. RX-8 prices started at $26,000. **Bellow:** Best known for its aggressively modified Mustangs, Saleen Engineering entered the production sports car business in 2003 with the wildly extroverted S7. A true American supercar, the S7 boasted a massive 7.0-liter Ford-based V8 and a trim 2800 pound curb weight. Performance was predictably stunning—*Car and Driver* drove an S7 to 60 mph in 3.3 seconds. Price: $395,000.

# VINTAGE RACING
## Now with Rollbars and Radios

A Ferrari 250 GTO jousts with a 1966 Corvette roadster on a straightaway, straining V12 and V8 engines melding in an unholy roar. A Shelby Cobra growls as its driver downshifts for a sharp left-hander. Fat Goodyear Blue Streak tires moan in protest. A Ferrari 250 GT darts outside a Jaguar XK120 fixed head coupe, its twelve-cylinder song amplified for a split second by the overpass bridge. Spinning Borrani wire wheels sparkle wildly in the sunlight. The throaty blat of a lone Arnolt Bristol's inline six echoes through the trees. A pack of price-less Fifties legends...among them Porsche Spyder, a Jaguar D-Type, an Allard, a Testa Rossa...burble and cackle into a corner before erupting in a full-throttle cacophony of unmuf-fled exhaust. Scenes like these once existed only in dusty old photos and dusty old memories, but with the rise of vintage sports car racing, they are regularly experienced anew. Decades after their headlights were first taped-up, meticulous-ly restored sports cars are still being driven hard on tracks across the country.

The first Monterey Historics vintage racing event was held at Laguna Seca Raceway in 1974. Vintage racing organizations like the SVRA (Sportscar Vintage Racing Association) and the VSCDA (Vintage Sports Car Driver's Association) began forming in the late Seventies. Today, most road courses routinely host vintage racing events put on by a variety of sanctioning bodies. There are inevitable concessions to modern times, almost all in the name of safety: Drivers must wear full-face helmets, roll bars are more substantial, and modern fuel cells are usually required. All vehicles must also pass a thorough tech inspec-tion, but the overall focus is on keeping the cars as true to original as possible.

The on-track dueling isn't quite as furious as it was in the old days. Any kind of racing is an expensive hobby, and most par-ticipants are privateers who are highly cognizant of their cars' significant collector value. No matter—the experience is still an assault on the senses that is heightened by the historical cachet of the combatants. Vintage sports cars are widely recog-nized as classics and even art in some circles. Thankfully, many enthusiasts recognize that the best place to experience historic sports cars and racers is not in a stuffy museum or a gallery. It's on the track, with the cars doing what they were originally built to do...in all of their visceral glory.

# Index